Experience Northern Italy 2019

LEN RUTLEDGE

Experience Northern Italy

Len Rutledge

Copyright Len Rutledge 2012, 2013, 2014, 2015, 2016, 2017, 2018, 2019

Eighth edition – December 2018

Published by Northpress

17 Saltwater Drive, Toomulla Beach, Australia 4816

ISBN:
ISBN-13: 978-1792035128

CONTENTS

Introduction

Cover and most other pictures: Phensri Rutledge

51 photographs

34 maps

INTRODUCTION

Experience Travel Guides, the Guides the Travel Industry trust, are unique in that they are designed to be read in the same way as a novel. They are a valuable resource for those planning to visit a destination, a source of information for those just interested in finding out more about a country, and a pleasure for those armchair travelers who just enjoy a good read.

Experience Northern Italy 2019 highlights the more rewarding parts of the country so that those planning a visit can quickly and efficiently plan an itinerary. We locate and detail the best places to see and the top experiences to enjoy, and recommend accommodation options in all areas. All are based on the personal experience of the author.

We capture the personality and the underlying cultural and historical significance of the cities, regions, and holiday destinations. Each is put into context by chapters on **Essential Experiences in Northern Italy** and the country's **History**.

As more people travel to new destinations, guidebooks grow in importance. Hard-copy books, however, are often out of date before they are printed and users are frustrated by experiences contrary to what is described. This book has no such problem as it was thoroughly updated in December 2018 and it can be updated as often as necessary to keep it right up to date.

To make it easy to read, we have not filled the book with extensive specialist information which is of interest to only a few readers. Instead we have included appropriate websites for all destinations, facilities, and activities so that with one click you can obtain all the additional information you need for the places you are particularly interested in. This means the book is very useful both before you leave home and while traveling.

Please realize, however, that no guidebook can substitute for common sense. Northern Italy has a wide variety of topography and climate. The higher areas can be very cold in winter when snow covers everything and ski resorts do a roaring trade. In contrast, the Mediterranean coast can be very hot in summer. In both instances, you need appropriate clothing and you need to guard against sunburn and dehydration.

There are other precautions you need to take to ensure the safety of yourself and your possessions. Be aware of your surroundings, particularly after dark, and keep valuables close to you. Be aware that pick-pocketing and bag snatching can occur. These problems are probably no worse than they are at home but they can ruin a holiday if you are a victim.

We believe that every place in the world provides unique experiences which make a visit worthwhile. We encourage you to explore, meet the locals, and grab each new opportunity as it arises. Traveling is fun but do it with care and compassion. In that way, your northern Italy experience can provide lifetime memories.

1 NORTHERN ITALY

Italy's reputation has fluctuated wildly over the centuries but today it is generally considered to be cultured, fashionable, and sexy. For over 2000 years it has been one of the more interesting corners of the world even though for much of that time it didn't exist as a country at all.

Each time I visit, I find Italy to be a fascinating combination of the calming, rousing, romantic, and impractical. As a visitor from the New World, I marvel at how newness and antiquity mix so easily. I am blown away by the beauty that is everywhere; in the landscape, the art and architecture, and in human affection.

I watch lovers kiss enthusiastically on street corners while old men walk arm in arm down the street. I revel in the tropical atmosphere I find in summer on the Riviera and thrill to the excitement of ski resorts in winter.

I spend many hours on long lunches enjoying local cuisine and fine local wines. The sense of machismo, the self-conscious sexuality, and the fondness for showing off within a section of the population is at times frustrating and annoying but then there is amazement and delight in the friendliness and good manners you unexpectedly stumble across. These contradictions are what make Italy so enjoyable and so confusing.

For the purposes of this book, we have defined Northern Italy as comprising the regions of:

Liguria with Genoa as its capital;

Veneto with Venice as its capital;

Northern Tuscany with Florence as its capital;

Lombardy with Milan as its capital;

Piedmont with Turin as its capital;

Aosta Valley with Aosta as its capital;

Emilia-Romagna with Bologna as its capital;

Friuli-Venezia Giulia with Trieste as its capital; and

Trentino-Alto Adige with Trento as its capital.

The largest cities in this region are Milan, Turin, and Genoa while the major tourism cities are Florence, Venice, Bologna, and Verona. The north is home to the Italian Alps, the wonderful northern region of Tuscany, the beautiful Italian lakes, and the Riviera coast from the border with France to the Cinque Terre.

Although it can at times be crowded and frustrating, Northern Italy is packed with natural and built attractions, great art and history, and good food and wine.

The major airport for Northern Italy is Milan's Linate International Airport but there are other large airports in Venice and Genoa, so you can usually fly to an airport in the near vicinity of where you wish to go. Fast trains connect this region to France and Switzerland and within the region there are extensive intercity bus routes and excellent trains.

Cars are often a major problem in the big cities because of traffic jams and huge parking problems but if you are planning to travel extensively to the small towns and villages, you might find renting a car more practical than using trains. We have driven extensively through the region without troubles despite the reputation of Italian drivers and the sometimes-confusing road signs.

Northern Italy is packed with attractions. Outdoors enthusiasts might enjoy sailing or fishing at Lake Garda, skiing in the Alps, or hiking in the Dolomites. Religious visitors will marvel at the many mighty cathedrals and cute little churches and can venture to Turin and the Cattedrale di San Giovanni Battista, where the Shroud of Turin is kept.

The cities have fine modern hotels and luxury properties in old palaces while castles and villas converted to hotels throughout the region offer rural tourism. Great monuments, historic buildings, and works of art are found everywhere, such as Venice's St Mark's cathedral and Palazzo Ducale, Milan's Pinacoteca di Brera art gallery, and Verona's Roman arena.

A large portion of Northern Italy is occupied by the basin of the Po River between the Apennine Mountains and the Alps. The only part that is not in this basin is the area to the south of the Apennines which drains to the Liguria Sea, and the area in the east that drains directly to the Adriatic Sea.

Northern Italy is the most developed and productive area of the country, and it was the first part of Italy to be industrialized in the last half of the 19th- century. Much manufacturing is concentrated in the so-called *industrial triangle* formed by the cities of Milan, Turin, and Genoa. This is also an important agricultural area.

Of all the great things that Northern Italy has to offer, perhaps the best is its geographical diversity. There are times when you can ski the Alps in the morning and sunbathe on the Riviera in the afternoon. In between, you can stop and sample wonderful Mediterranean cuisine and some of the world's most enjoyable wines.

Elsewhere, you can visit Milan and revel in a fashionista's heaven on earth, get lost in the magic that is Venice, or become an art historian in Florence.

We marvel at the castles that outnumber towns in the Tirolean upper Adige and the Valle d'Aosta, where Italian is almost a foreign tongue.

We relax in luxury at Italy's majestic lakes and vaunted Dolomite resorts, and follow Shakespeare at the supposed home of Romeo and Juliet in Verona.

It is difficult not to be transfixed by a Renaissance masterpiece, and I strongly recommend that you eat and drink your way through the Po River valley.

Take full advantage of Northern Italy's fine food and explore dishes and matching local wines that are virtually unknown outside this region. Further south, there are the historic towns down the east coast, the wonderful hill towns and olive groves of Tuscany, and the fishing villages and chic resorts along the Ligurian Riviera. Truly this is a marvelous area.

This small and wealthy corner of the world lets us see a little of the Etruscans, slightly more of the Romans, and showcases medieval Italy in a seductive manner. To see it all you need to visit the grand old port cities of Genoa and Trieste, the graceful, art-rich cities of the Veneto, and the hill-towns of Tuscany.

But northern Italy also represents the sleek, modern Italy that is associated with names like Armani, Alfa Romeo, and Toscanini and a mastery of fashion, design, and music. It really is a complete vacation package.

2 ITAIAN RIVIERA – LIGURIA AND GENOA

Liguria (http://www.italia.it/en/discover-italy/liguria.html) has been a tourism destination for many years. It was once the province of choice for wealthy northern Europeans who wintered here in luxury to escape the cold but now it has opened up to mass tourism.

There are numerous coastal towns and villages that base their economy on tourism but most of the area has managed to retain some sanity and you can still find a quiet corner, except during peak times.

Portofina Harbor

I remember one evening dining under the blue-striped awning of a *trattoria* nestled on a cliff top high above the Mediterranean. It was one of those meals you wish would never end where the food, the company, the view, and the star-bright sky combined perfectly. That meal will never leave my mind and to me, it represents all that is wonderful about this region.

Liguria stretches east from the French border to La Spezia, along a coastline of around 340 kms. Its capital, Genoa, divides the coast into two parts: the Riviera di Ponente which lies between the city and the French border and the Riviera di Levante which stretches east towards Tuscany.

The two coasts are quite different but both are attractive. The Levante has mountains crowding the coast providing spectacular coves and cute villages in some spots. The Ponente has good beaches and cities like Savona, San Remo, and Bordighera. There is also a succession of pretty beach resorts, many of which contain important historical centers such as Albenga, medieval Cervo, Noli, and Alassio.

On one trip we had been visiting Monaco which is close to the France/Italy border and enter Liguria at **Ventimiglia** (http://ventimiglia.town/?template=home&page=home), the border city. Every Friday all year round, French residents and tourists from across the border flock to its popular street market along the seafront. There are several hundred stalls selling everything from clothes, shoes, pots and pans, to linens, and there are many food outlets.

The town is a good size for walking, with ample places to stop for coffee. There is an impressive range of boutiques to satisfy the fashion conscious. The *lungomare* (promenade) is a wonderful stretch of coast road with great views back towards France. There are many restaurants and bars along here with good friendly service, most serving Italian ice-cream. There's none of the glitz and glamour of its neighbors; instead it's an honest, understated, yet comfortable place to visit.

I must say we don't give this a fair go before moving on to palm-tree studded **Bordighera** (http://www.bordighera.it/international/english), which has been a favorite winter resort, especially for visitors from the United Kingdom. There was a period 120 years ago when English guests outnumbering the local population.

The majority of buildings of that period still survive today, helping to give modern Bordighera a prestigious cultural tradition, thanks also to the Bicknell Museum and the International Municipal Library. There is a beautiful little 4th-century chapel tucked away at the head of the promontory with medieval foundations visible through glass floor panels.

San Remo (http://sanremoguide.it/en/the-city-of-san-remo/) is in two parts; the traditional old city on the hill and the popular modern sterile-looking town on the water. The attractive old town has narrow lanes and small houses. The impressive Borea d'Olmo Palace was built in the late-fifteenth century while San Siro Cathedral was built in the twelfth century, in a Romanesque-Gothic style. The Torre della Ciapela in Piazza Erol is a significant building with one-meter-thick stone walls that was once part of the 16th-century town walls.

Piazza Eroi is in the town center and close to La Pigna – the medieval part of the town. The modern town has a palm-flanked ocean boulevard, a casino, a racetrack, stylish boutiques, and a rocky beach.

The town was founded by the Romans and has become a popular tourist destination. The celebrated annual San Remo Music Festival is a very popular song contest which inspired the Eurovision Song Contest. The city has a symphony orchestra, one of 12 in Italy.

Traveling further east along the coast, there is a succession of sea-side towns and cities. Some of the small ones are attractive while several of the larger ones have points of interest worth seeing. Inland, there is interest too with some pretty, small, villages high in the mountains. We drive inland. Some of the villages seem unchanged by time.

Many sit in the mountain valleys or on hilltops, like Bussana Vecchia, an abandoned town after an earthquake, which is now repopulated by artists. You reach it up a steep, narrow road but the effort is worthwhile as the cobblestone streets and crumbling stone structures are fascinating. As well as the cobbled streets with their many plants and flowers, you can see the original village church, now missing its roof. There is also a small garden with views across the area that is open to the public, and a couple of cafés in the village.

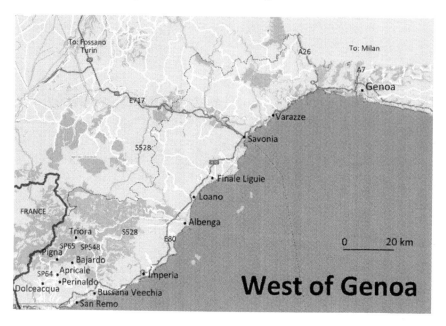

Dolceacqua is the most important medieval town in the Val Nervia. It is made up of two beautiful villages; the original ancient center, with its restored Doria Castle, and the other from the nineteenth century, which are connected by a spectacular medieval humpback stone bridge. The abandoned castle is approached by the narrow-cobbled lanes that meander up between the tall medieval houses, small courtyards, steep alleys, and vaulted passages. You can also see a 15th-century church which has an attractively decorated interior.

Another place worth seeing is spectacular **Apricale**, which is one of 7 villages in Italy with 'most beautiful' status. Apricale has a medieval castle, museum, several lovely churches, and an old town hall, all clinging to the steep sides of hills. The various parts of town are linked by tunnels, alleyways, bridges, and terraces.

Further up into the mountains are the hill towns of Perinaldo and Baiardo with their stunning views and Pigna, which is famous for its centuries-old architecture. In the steep mountain passes, herds of chamois goat-antelope graze among Italian military outposts dating from the Napoleonic era. This whole area can take days to explore properly.

Triora is the town of witches and watermills. In the heart of Triora, you will enjoy exploring the ancient alleys, arched passages, and steep pathways of what is claimed to be one of the oldest villages in Liguria. A famine in 1587 convinced the desperate residents that only the work of witches could bring such misfortune.

Thirty women were rounded up and tortured with the support of the church, and soon 18 broke down and confessed. Several (or perhaps all), were burnt at the stake. The Ethnographic Museum of Witchcraft has been set up to reconstruct the ancient rural life and the records of the famous trial of 1588.

Back on the coast, we take the old Roman Via Aurelia through Imperia and Alassio. **Savona** (http://www.savonaguide.it/eng/) is a good place to stop to visit the interesting castle and walk the waterfront. The towns' historical center with its characteristic narrow streets and sunny little piazzas has houses with façades of typical Mediterranean colors and unique architectural elements. The Cappella Sistina is located near the cathedral and was built in the 1480s. The chapel has a mausoleum that was built here by Pope Sixtus IV in honor of his parents.

The Palazzo Della Rovere is an old palace also located close to the cathedral and is still left unfinished. The church of Nostra Signiora de Castello is quite interesting not because of its architecture but because of its interior. At the entrance to the Old Dock, the fourteenth-century

Leon Pancaldo Tower is the remaining part of the old city walls facing the sea. There are some fine buildings in the center of town and we enjoy strolling and admiring the architecture.

Verazze (http://www.theitalianriviera.eu/varazze.asp), an ancient medieval village, is some 10 km along the coast and it is here that on one visit we spend a week or more with friends. The beachfront and marina are popular but we grow to love the pedestrian street which parallels the main road through town. Here there are small family-owned shops selling to the locals, and small restaurants and bakeries with food just asking to be enjoyed.

We quickly learn to enjoy the typically Ligurian focaccias and savory pies, particularly the focaccia filled with cheese. It is hard to resist the fragrance and aroma of this specialty. We are equally taken by the gelato and sit in the small town square on many afternoons enjoying the variety of flavors.

Genoa

This is the big city around here and we visit several times by train. The residential areas cling to the hills but it is foremost a port city. It was the boyhood home of Christopher Columbus and was for many years a powerful, wealthy, independent maritime republic. Today, there is almost a sense of aristocratic dilapidation about parts of the city

Like many Italian cities, Genoa (http://www.visitgenoa.it/en/app) has an old town and a modern city encircling it. While there are some narrow lanes and pedestrian streets there are also some boulevards, fine palaces, and marble churches in the old town.

Genoa sits in a steep, natural amphitheater. This means that land area is prized and over the years it has been carved into and built upon so that many streets are narrow, crooked, and rich with beauty. We start exploring at the lowest level in the **old harbor**. Most of the port activity has moved west from here and the present development is all new after World War II bombings destroyed the area.

The central attraction is the huge **aquarium** (http://www.acquariodigenova.it/en/), said to be Europe's second largest. Marine life from coral reefs to inland rivers is captured in an array of tanks that take hours to see. We enjoy our visit and watch younger visitors become excited as they help feed the animals at special feeding times.

In the same area, there is the fascinating *Il Galeone Neptune* a ship that was built as a prop for the film *Pirates*. Children love to explore this ship and find out about the life of a Genoese pirate in the 17th-century. Here too, is the large dome-shaped greenhouse called **Biosfera** (http://www.acquariodigenova.it/en/acquariovillage2/biosfera/) which is home to a tropical environment.

Then there is the *Galata Museo del Mare* (http://www.galatamuseodelmare.it/?lang=en) to the north, a huge maritime museum which opened in 2004 and tells of the interaction between man and the sea. You can step onboard the 17th century Genoa galley and the largest Italian submarine that can be visited still afloat.

Across the road and just south of the aquarium, is the handsome Palazzo San Giorgio built in 1260 by the uncle of Simone Boccanegra, the first Doge of Genoa. It is said that the material for the building came from the demolition of the Venetian embassy in Constantinople. After he was forced into exile, the palace was used for a period as a prison with Marco Polo being its most famous inmate.

Moving inland, the **Cattedrale di San Lorenzo** (http://www.visitgenoa.it/en/cattedrale-di-s-lorenzo) is outstanding, due to its distinctive black-and-white striped façade. Inside is the Cappella del San Giovanni Battista, a chapel that is dedicated to St. John the Baptist.

A shell landed on the cathedral during World War II, however, it failed to detonate and the building survives. There are 14th-century Byzantine style frescos, several sculptures, and some paintings by famous artists. The *Museum of the Treasury* under the cathedral has a collection of jewelry and silverware.

Another church worth seeing is the 16th-century Baroque **Chiesa del Gesù** (http://www.visitgenoa.it/en/chiesa-del-ges%C3%B9). Those interested in Rubens' work can see two paintings by the artist - one hangs over the altar, while the other is on display in a side chapel of the church.

Genoa is said to have Europe's biggest historical center and it is quite impressive. Parts of the Old City are a maze of seemingly unordered alleyways and cobbled streets. Other parts are quite formal. This area was built largely in the 16th century at the height of the Renaissance and it is home to some of the city's most interesting art museums and other cultural attractions.

We are getting tired so we find a small stone bench in a little courtyard and relax. The surrounding green plants provide a coolness and the sounds of the city are gone except for the sound of a small fountain spraying water. It is easy to recuperate.

The **Spianata Castelletto** (Belvedere Luigi Montaldo) is a good vantage point 80 meters above ground situated in the elegant Castelletto area. The best way to reach it is via the public lift in Piazza Portale or from the steps which start nearby.

From the top, the panorama over the old town is quite good. A better view is obtained, of course, from Monte Righi (302 m) which is served by a funicular railway some way to the west from here. The complete trip takes around 12 minutes for a total of 7 stations and there is a car every 15 minutes. There are pleasant walks on the surrounding hills and to the fortifications.

We take a stroll along **Via Garibaldi**, an elegant narrow street lined with grandeur. It is the cultural center of tourist Genoa. While Genoa has no principal museum, it has converted several of its palazzi to galleries. The town's best art collections can be visited in three palaces grouped together as the *Musei di Strada Nuova* (http://www.museidigenova.it/it/content/musei-di-strada-nuova).

Palazzo Bianco, Palazzo Rosso, and Palazzo Tursi have works by Rubens as well as many local artists. Paganini's famous Guarnieri violin is also here. Each building maintains its own specific features related to its history and collections. The 16th-century Strada Nuova (Via Garibaldi) has thus been turned into an authentic "museum-street" and is now part of the UNESCO World Heritage site. A combined ticket to the three buildings costs €9 (November 2018).

The area featured on the UNESCO list includes 42 palaces and also extends to the part of the historic center that runs through Via Lomellini, Piazza Fossatello, and Via San Luca to Piazza Banchi, the mercantile heart of the old town. The complete name of the site is "The New Streets and the system of the Rolli Palaces". A tour starts from the hall of Palazzo Rosso Museum (Via Garibaldi 18) on Saturdays at 3 p.m. for adults €14, senior and children 12-18 years old €12 (November 2018).

The *Galleria Nazionale di Palazzo Spinola* (http://www.visitgenoa.it/en/galleria-nazionale-di-palazzo-spinola) is nearby at Piazza Pellicceria. This under-rated museum was the former home of the Spinola family, so it contains some of the original furnishings and their extensive picture collection, including works by Antonello Messina, Rubens, Van Dyck, and others.

The third floor of the building is now home to the Galleria Nazionale di Liguria (National Gallery of Liguria). The furnished rooms give us a very good idea how the rich lived in 17th century Genoa. Each room has been lavishly frescoed and decorated.

Castello D'Albertis (Corso Dogali, 18) houses the *Museum of World Cultures* (http://www.visitgenoa.it/en/castello-dalbertis), a very interesting museum. It is the former home of sea captain Enrico Alberto d'Albertis who during his travels collected many amazing objects and brought them back here. Tickets are €6 adults and €4.50 for children and seniors. (November 2018)

From the city center, you reach it via what is claimed to be the only horizontal and vertical elevator in the world. Riding this is an experience just on its own. Below here is the main railway station (Stazione Porta Principe) and the monument to Christopher Columbus on Piazza Acquaverde.

Villa Durazzo Pallavinci is home to the *Museum of Ligurian Archaeology* and to the Botanical Garden established in 1794. This romantic park of the villa, located in western Genoa, is one of Europe's most important historical gardens. The park is also home to one of Italy's oldest collections of camellias, as well as important specimens of cork oaks, camphor laurels, Araucaria, Lebanon cedars, and many types of palm trees.

The **Monumental Cemetery of Staglieno** is considered one of the most beautiful and fascinating cemeteries in Europe. This veritable open-air museum was designed by the architect Carlo Barabino in 1835. Within the walls is the *Cappella dei Suffragi* (Chapel of Intercessions), also known as the Pantheon, which preserves the memory of Genoa's greats, while in the Boschetto Irregolare (irregular woods), you can admire the tombs of Mazzini and other heroes of the Risorgimento.

The **Palazzo Ducale** (http://www.visitgenoa.it/en/palazzo-ducale), the Doges' residence since 1339, is today a venue for important events and prestigious activities. Its construction began in 1298 when Genoa was asserting its economic power throughout the Mediterranean. The adjoining Palazzo Fieschi was incorporated into the new building during construction. Today, it is an arts complex containing bookshops, restaurants, bars, shops, and art galleries, and hosting regular photography and art exhibitions.

The **Teatro Carlo Felice** is Genoa's opera house. Designed and built in 1827 by the architect Carlo Barabino, it was completely rebuilt after WWII. The exterior is built in stone, plaster, and iron, while the interiors are adorned with marble and wood.

The **Palazzo Reale** (http://www.visitgenoa.it/en/palazzo-reale) was a noble residence built in the early 17th-century for the Balbi family. Later, it was sold to the Durazzo Family, who enlarged it. In 1823, the palace was sold to the Royal House of Savoy and from 1919 it has belonged to the state. The building is home to Liguria's Department for Artistic, Historic and Archaeological Heritage, and the *Galleria di Palazzo Reale Museum*.

Piazza San Matteo is a well-preserved example of an aristocratic neighborhood from the Middle Ages. It features the 14th-century church of San Matteo which is surrounded by palaces with characteristic bands of black and white stone. This was the center of power of the Doria family. The church was founded in 1125 by Martino Doria and later rebuilt in a Gothic style.

The **Lighthouse of Genoa** (La lantern), which was probably originally built in the 12th century and was rebuilt in 1543, is often regarded as the symbol of Genoa. It stands on a 40-meter-high rock and rises to a total height to 117 meters above sea level. The 172 stairs can be climbed up to the first observation terrace for superb views of the harbor and historic center. At the foot is a multimedia museum, with a variety of video material that would suit just about everyone.

Dialogue in the Dark exhibition (Dialogo nel Buio) (Calata De Mari) is a sensory journey on a ship in the total absence of light that transforms places and familiar gestures into an extraordinary experience. A small group is accompanied by visually impaired guides through the dark environments into authentic situations of everyday life for blind people who use the senses of touch, hearing, smell, and taste. This is a multi-sensory experience truly unique and unforgettable. Admission is €10 adults and €7 for children and seniors. (November 2018).

Genoa is home to an array of restaurants and bars. Many of these are in the historic part of town. The area around Piazza di Sarzano and Via San Lorenzo is populated with nightclubs and bars. We are told to head to Piazza delle Erbe, a small square hidden amid the labyrinthine alleys, so we do. There are locals patronizing wine cellars and tapas bars while enjoying the quiet ambiance.

The atmosphere on the weekends, however, is much more vibrant as the streets fill with people heading down to the numerous discos dotting this district. If bar hopping and clubbing is not for you then you might enjoy spending the evening at Teatro Carlo Felice (www.carlofelicegenova.it) which is Genoa's principal opera house where you can enjoy ballet, orchestral music, and recitals.

To the north of the city is the village of **Casella**. There are no world-shattering sights here but it makes a pleasant half-day trip. An interesting way to get here is to take the narrow-gauge railway, which operates from Piazza Manin in Genoa, and takes approximately an hour to reach Casella in the hills (https://rail.cc/en/train/genoa-to-casella). The first trip on weekdays is around 7.30 a.m.

There are several local beaches worth visiting. **Boccadasse** is the closest beach to the east, nestled between pastel houses and boats on the small pebble beach. It is about an hour's walk from central Genoa. With its old colored houses and small fishing harbor, Bocaddasse is a magical place that attracts many tourists. If the weather is nice, having an ice cream while sitting on the rocks is an attractive thing to do.

Then come Quarto and Quinto before you reach **Nervi** which is dominated by the enchanting seafront promenade providing a nice place to walk. There are some splendid views, especially in the direction of the Cinque Terre further east (see later). There is a lovely public park with many varieties of roses and some nice palm-lined streets. You can reach Nervi by bus or by train.

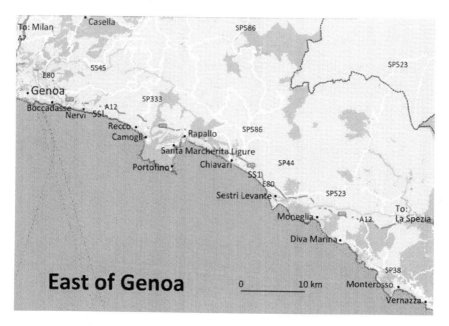

Pegli to the west of Genoa is the first part of the western Riviera. There are some hotels, restaurants, bars, and a sea promenade here that attract visitors but it is mainly a residential location. The Santa Maria Immaculate church with its pink dome, and the Villa Durazzo Pallavicini, are worth seeing. It is connected to Genoa by bus, water bus, and train.

Genoa Facts

Cristoforo Colombo Airport (http://www.genovaairport.com/) is located in Genoa's Sestri Ponente neighborhood, about seven kilometers west of the city center. It has recently been upgraded and is now a modern facility. The Hotel Sheraton is situated approximately 300m from the terminal building. A shuttle bus service called Volabus departs from the airport to both Brignole and Principe Train Stations (https://www.genovaairport.com/getting-to-genova-airport/genova-airport-buses.htm#/searchcars) .

The ticket costs €6 (December 2018) for a trip on Volabus plus a 60 minutes journey on the AMT network (buses, metro, public elevators and funicular railways) in the same day. Tickets are available on board the coach. Taxis are available outside the arrival concourse.

If you arrive in Genoa by train, there are two main railway stations. **Genova Piazza Principe** on Piazza Acquaverde 4 is the main departure/arrival point to and from the North and West, and **Genova Brignole** on Piazza Verdi 1 is the main departure/arrival point for connections to the East and South.

The city's **public transport** service is run by AMT and allows visitors to get around easily thanks to its extensive network of buses, an underground, funiculars, and lifts. Tickets can be purchased at newsstands, tobacconists, and many other shops and bars. Single tickets cost €1.50 (November 2018) and are valid for 100 minutes throughout the entire city network.

You should also consider a Tourist ticket sold at IAT (Informazione e Accoglienza Turistica) Tourist Offices. The most useful is a **Genova Pass**, which is valid for 24 hours. It costs €4.50 (November 2018) and allows the holder to travel throughout the entire city network with one ticket.

An open-top, double-decker **bus tour** of the city, with audio commentary available in 6 languages, operates from March to November. The hop-on, hop-off option allows visitors to enjoy the tour over 48 hours, hopping on and off as they please at 8 stops. The cost is Adults €15, children €8 (November 2018).

Another option is to discover all the charm of the old town of Genoa, every weekend on a **walking tour**. The Tour sets off from the IAT Tourist Office in the Old Port area and winds its way through Genoa's narrow alleyways and ancient squares. Participants are entitled to free admission for an independent visit to the Strada Nuova Museums, Genoa's main museum hub.

The adult cost is €14, children 12-18 years old and adults over 65 €12, and children under 12 years old are free (November 2018). It operates at 10 a.m. on Saturday and Sunday in Italian and English.

Portofino

For most international visitors, the best trip from the city is along the coast to Portofino (http://www.italia.it/en/travel-ideas/the-sea/portofino.html). This takes you into the heart of the Riviera di Levante and I defy you to be unimpressed by this charming tourist village. Portofino's minuscule bay is neatly packed with pricey yachts, polished pleasure craft, and a few small fishing boats.

The waterfront is lined with multicolored pastel buildings, canopied outdoor cafés, and a key just perfect for strolling around. Bougainvillea-garnished luxury villas decorate the surrounding hills.

Portofino is known as the resort of the rich and famous. The delightful seaside village has charming buildings lining the shore of the harbor now occupied by shops, restaurants, cafés, and luxury hotels. A castle overlooks the village from the top of a hill. It has been called the world's most charming port. The tiny town is almost too beautiful for its own good.

With its warm weather, luxury accommodation, and fine food, it is what we imagine as La Dolce Vita. The little port is cozily tucked into the side of a small wooded promontory and the best way to arrive is by boat - preferably your own. We didn't of course. Our transport was the local public bus.

In the 1930s, Portofino enjoyed a reputation with artists and then over the next few decades the town became known as a celebrity hideout.

Today, there is a feeling that you have gone back to the 1960's. That is when Portofino became popular with jet-setting celebrities such as Elizabeth Taylor, Frank Sinatra, and Brigitte Bardot.

They would arrive by yacht and lounge around the luxury hotels and private villas. It was a place to see and be seen. Hollywood stars and European royalty have since flocked to Portofino hotels for a little rest and plenty of relaxation.

Today it is a little different but there are still cameras around. Some rich and powerful people still occupy the private villas and crowds pour in during the high season drawn by the beautiful setting and the vague chance of seeing a celebrity.

After the mandatory jaw-dropping stares when we reach the small, central *piazzetta*, we find there is no better thing to do than to walk. The best walk is up the steps that lead from the port to the church of San Giorgio. From San Giorgio, there is a beautiful view of the harbor and bay.

Further up the hill is *Castello Brown*. The medieval castle is open for inspection and it has a nice garden. It became the residence of Yeats Brown, British consul to Genoa in the 1870s.

Continue up the path to the Portofino Lighthouse for an even better view. Returning from the climb we choose one of the small, expensive cafés around the harbor to enjoy an espresso and glass of wine while watching the passing parade of people and boats.

Portofino belongs on anyone's list of places to see in Italy. To stay here can be a little pricey, however, for many of us. Portofino just doesn't have enough hotels, and because of the high demand for rooms, they're all extremely expensive.

Best is the *Hotel Splendido* (http://www.belmond.com/hotel-splendido-portofino/), a spectacular property originally built during the Middle Ages as a monastery. Rates here start at around $750 a night.

Fortunately, there are a number of nearby towns with nice hotels along the coast where you can stay and make Portofino a day trip.

We choose **Santa Margherita** (http://www.comune.santa-margherita-ligure.ge.it/Default.aspx?pageid=page204&lang=en) which is a pretty town in its own right with more hotel options than Portofino. From Santa Margherita, you can hike to Portofino, take the bus, or ride a boat. Buses to Portofino leave about every 30 minutes from well-marked bus stops. Ferries run at regular intervals during the day. It is worth checking out Villa Durazzo which is in a shady hillside park where there is a church and coffee shop.

Ferries also operate to Portofino from **Camogli** (http://www.theitalianriviera.eu/camogli.asp), a lovely fishing village a few kilometers west of here which has pastel houses crowding the steep shoreline, and a pebbly beach. Both towns are easily reached from Genoa by train, at very reasonable cost.

The best way to explore around here is on foot. Heading south from Camogli, I suggest you take the stone path that briefly follows a shaded creek and then climbs a series of stairs, leading you past olive and citrus trees, and stands of palm. After half an hour walking nearly all uphill, you arrive in San Rocco. Here you can take in the spectacular view of the surrounding countryside and enjoy a snack or meal.

If you're looking for an energetic hike to work off those Italian meals, I recommend you spend some time in the Portofino Regional Park (http://www.aboutliguria.com/regional-park-of-ligurian-portofino.html). Its 50 km of hiking trails offer scenic landscapes featuring lush chestnut and olive groves. Many provide spectacular views.

The northern part of the park is wooded while in the southern part you will find more wildflowers and grasslands. Olive trees are cultivated in many places and close to the villages you may see orchards and gardens.

Most of the sea along the coast from Santa Margherita around to Camogli is a protected area. There are 20 dive sites and diving can be arranged through local dive agencies. Swimming is allowed only in certain areas and boating is restricted near some of the shoreline.

On the other side of the peninsula, reached from Portofino by a 2-hour walk or by boat, is the Abbazia di San Fruttuoso. The abbey, built in the 11th-century, is surrounded by pine and olive trees. Near San Fruttuoso is a huge under-water bronze statue of Christ, *Cristo degli Abissi*, protector of sailors and divers.

Cinque Terre

The coast gets more rugged as you go east from here. There are a few more towns but the undoubted highlight is the Cinque Terre (The Five Lands) (http://www.cinque-terre-tourism.com/en/tourist-information-offices-in-cinque-terre.html). Four small villages and one larger town make up this small region.

The westernmost town, Monterosso is the tourist hub but it lacks the picture-perfect aspect of the smaller villages. This gorgeous UNESCO World Heritage-listed landscape has been worked for a thousand years but has a history of floods, sieges, and destruction.

People don't come here for museums and art, for grand hotels, or for soft sand beaches. They come for the spectacular scenery and because, until recently, life here has remained much the same for centuries. Fishermen still haul up their boats to the quay, farmers climb to vineyards perched precariously behind retaining walls, and housewives hang laundry to flap in the wind at open windows.

If we ignore the television antennas on every house, we could be back a century or more. The rural villages, in olive and chestnut groves on steep rock terrain overlooking the blue Mediterranean Sea, seem unchanged for centuries. Mountains trap the region between rock and sea, creating an island-like solitude until the tourists arrive.

We have taken a train to Riomaggiore with the intention of walking through the national park to the other villages. This has been stymied, however, by landslides which have closed the track in several locations.

Riomaggiore
(http://www.cinqueterreriomaggiore.com/en/guides/riomaggiore) dates from the early thirteenth century and, is known for its historic character and its wine. Located on a steep hillside leading down to the rocky shoreline, this little town has a magic all its own. There are many reasons to love Riomaggiore but for photographers, it is the ability to get stunning photographs, particular on dusk when you can savor it on the cool, seaside rocks with the fishermen.

A tunnel leads from the train station to the Piazza del Vignaloto and from here the street heads steeply uphill past bars, restaurants and a few hotels to the parish church of San Giovanni Battista, built in the 1340s, and a castle built in 1260 which provides a quiet retreat and spectacular views.

A staircase leads down to the marina which is home to colorful boats, several seafood restaurants, and the ferry terminal. It has a small beach and a tiny wharf hemmed in by sheer rock walls and by a jumble of tower houses painted in traditional colors. A nice garden and bird watching center sits on a rocky promontory up the hill from the beach.

There is almost a complete lack of English even in the information center so people are milling around trying to determine what options there are. Finally, we line up to buy a park entry card and head off towards Manarola.

The **Via dell'Amore** (Way of Love) (http://www.cinqueterreriomaggiore.com/en/guides/lovers-street) between Riomaggiore and tiny Manarola is flat and paved, and nearly anyone could manage this 20-minute hike. There are great views of the sea, cliffs, and vineyards.

The walk is spectacular as the path skirts the cliffs and offers wonderful views along the Cinque Terre coastline. There are also many people on the path. Too many for us, explained perhaps by the fact that this is the only section of the coastal trail that is open today.

Manarola (http://www.aboutliguria.com/cinque-terre/manarola.html) spills down a ravine to the wild and rugged coastline. A tunnel leads from the train station to the central plaza. From here you can go right past the church, a hostel, and some restaurants, or left down to the water.

The tiny harbor features a boat ramp, picturesque buildings, and the town's swimming hole. There is no beach but this is one of the best places to swim in the Cinque Terre. Punta Bonfiglio, a short uphill hike on the path to Corniglia, has fabulous views, a playground, ruins of an old chapel, and a bar.

We wander around, take photographs, and try to pack the beauty into our memory. Locals go about their business, their faces as weathered and rugged as the landscape. The Trattoria dal Billy (Via Rollandi 122) is probably the best restaurant. It is up the hill past the church plaza but the food and the views from the various tables outside are beautiful.

On some summer nights, the town provides entertainment for visitors and locals in the form of a DJ in the main plaza and movies down by the harbor. If this is not on, head for the La Cantina dello Zio Bramante (Via Birolli 110) where there will be guitar music, drinking, and fun.

All the towns in the Cinque Terre have railway stations so it is relatively easy to move about by train. Trains and station platforms seem always crowded in Italy. I was told that it is because of the Italian horror of solitude.

Perhaps a more likely explanation is the lack of an adequate train service. It's only a four-minute ride to Corniglia but the train service is patchy. Finally, a train arrives and we travel almost all the way in a tunnel.

Corniglia

(http://www.cinqueterre.com/eng/information/cinque_terre/villages/corniglia.php) is different from the other towns because it is perched high above the sea. It is surrounded on three sides by many picturesque vineyards and terraces, while the fourth side falls steeply down to the waters below.

A road from the train station takes us to the village. It is a long, steep climb but the alternative of 400 steps in 33 flights of stairs doesn't appeal. Part of the charm of Corniglia is that it isn't as frequented by tourists as much as the small fishing villages.

There are four-story houses painted in cheerful shades of yellow and orange, narrow lanes, and a delightful square with its Oratory Santa Caterina which dates back to the 14th century.

We buy a coffee and relax under the large trees then walk through the village to the marvelous viewpoint called Terrazzo Panoramico Santa Maria. The best food in town is had at the Cantina di Mananan (Via Fieschi 117) and the setting is charming and old-fashioned.

While it is perhaps less spectacular than the other villages, Corniglia is very likable, but now it is time to move on. It's down the stairs and off by train to Vernazza. We could walk if the trail was open (it takes about 75 minutes) and this is one of the less difficult sections of the coastal walk, but today there seems little alternative to the train.

Vernazza (https://www.incinqueterre.com/en/vernazza) is similar to the other towns in having no vehicle traffic within the heart of the village and this helps it remain one the truest "fishing villages" on the coast.

There is a small beach within the protected harbor and some nice restaurants overlooking the scene. Piazza Marconi with its sea-facing amphitheater of pastel houses is a delight A steep road leads down to the shore then there is a climb to Doria Castle which was built in the 15th-century to protect the village from pirates.

This is perhaps the most sophisticated of the towns with nice accommodation and good restaurants. It tends to be slightly more expensive than the others. The town was devastated in the 2011 Cinque Terre flood but it has now recovered. You can see the devastation in a large photograph near the railway station.

Our camera works overtime as there are spectacular views in all directions. The tiny port was once the place from where most of the Italian Riviera's wine was shipped. There is a castle on the hill reached by lots of steps and it is sometimes closed when you get there, but the view is just great.

Our last visit is to the Church of Santa Margherita d'Antiochia which was begun in 1318. Evenings are well-spent sitting on a bench and enjoying the scene, either with a gelato or a glass of local white wine.

Batti Batti Friggitoria (Via Visconti 21) provides anchovies, calamari, and codfish on fried bread at cheap prices while Gambero Rosso (Plaza Marconi 7) serves serious food at serious prices on scenic outdoor tables.

The hike from Vernazza to Monterosso is the most challenging of the inter-town walks but it provides breathtaking vistas of the towns and the sea. In parts you climb through lavender-scented vineyards and on hot summer days the occasional drink stall is very welcome.

Monterosso (https://www.incinqueterre.com/en/monterosso) is the largest and busiest center. The town is divided into two parts with one-half having a crowded sandy beach and restaurants, bars, and hotels and the other having narrow streets and historic buildings. There are more tourist shops, gelato stands, and bathing suits than anywhere else on this coast.

In the new town, the beautiful seaside pedestrian promenade is a good place to stroll although it gets very crowded in summer. At certain times you can get plump anchovies served right off the boat in the marina. Piazza Garibaldi is a shaded square that remains cool on hot days thanks to a number of large trees and its proximity to the sea.

The medieval Torre Aurora or Dawn Tower separates the two parts of town and they are connected by a tunnel. High above the old part of town is the San Francesco Church with its art works and impressive views, and it is great just wandering the streets seeing the varying sights and a number of shops selling quality souvenirs.

There is a good range of hotels from 4-star to simple B&B properties and rented rooms, some with lovely views. The town also has some lively restaurants which give an opportunity to taste local seafood, edible mushrooms, olives, pine nuts, and leeks. Local wineries produce *sciacchetra*, a somewhat rare sweet wine variety.

You can sample this and buy a bottle at Cantina du Sciacchetra (Via Roma 7), or dine in a World War II bunker built into the cliff while gorging on Ligurian specialties at L'Ancora della Tortuga (Salita Cappuccini 4). I recommend the homemade *trofie alla Genovese* (Ligurian-style trofie pasta).

Fast Bar (Via Roma 13) is a favorite spot for tourists and for the locals as well. During the day, it has a large selection of sandwiches and salads, and after 9 p.m. it transforms into a busy, lively pub.

While we have stuck to the land, an alternative way to travel between the villages is by excursion boat. A consortium owns a fleet of 16 boats which transport tourist passengers from the ports of **La Spezia**, Lerici, and Portovenere to the villages of the Cinque Terre.

An alternative is a four-hour lunch trip from Monterosso with Angelo's Boat Tour. We spoke to some American people who had just done the tour and they raved about it. It would depend very much on the weather as far as I am concerned.

3 FLORENCE

Florence was the birthplace of the Renaissance. The Renaissance changed the world. Now Florence successfully lives off its past like few cities in the world. Every visitor to Italy has this city on their 'must-see' list and these visitors make the city rich. Some of the locals complain about the crowds in summer which cause them some inconvenience but they happily accept the prosperity tourism brings.

For many centuries, Florence was the canvas on which successive generations of artists and aristocrats tried to outdo each other. This has left the city stuffed with treasures which demand your time and attention.

Visitors come to Florence primarily for the art. UNESCO has stated that Italy is home to up to 60 per cent of the world's most important works of art. Florence claims over half of Italy's total. The city was home to a great number of fine artists such as Leonardo da Vinci, Michelangelo, and Botticelli.

The city has some of Italy's best museums, beautiful cathedrals, and churches, but we are equally impressed by the interesting streets and squares with elegant buildings and shops. Note that many museums are closed on Mondays.

Michelangelo has long been associated with the city of Florence, and we find many of his masterpieces here. There is the sculpture of *David*, which is one of the great icons of Renaissance art, as well as numerous other sculptures, architectural projects, and a painting from the Italian artist.

Unfortunately, there are far fewer works by Leonardo. Only a few of his paintings were finished because he was impatient but you can see some of his numerous drawings. A visit to the museum named in his honor is a 'must'.

Many visitors are surprised to find that Florence is great for shopping. On our first visit here many years ago, we concluded that Florence has some of the finest shopping in Europe and we haven't changed our opinion since.

You'll find leather goods, paper goods, and jewelry as well as nice souvenirs, and art reproductions. Not all are in high-priced stores. The city has a number of open-air markets selling food, clothing, and antiques. The most famous is around **Piazza San Lorenzo**.

A car can be a hassle in Florence so we arrive by train. Trains are a great way to meet locals. Particularly if you travel in an old-style compartment carriage you will be engaged in conversation before you leave the station. Italians have this impulse to courteously interrogate a stranger.

On the train to Florence, it started off with a question about our destination, moved on to ask about our opinion of Italy then branched into all sorts of other discussions about life. Soon the whole compartment was involved and the free-for-all soon surpassed our ability to follow the rapid Italian.

I don't think anyone noticed our exit from the conversation, and certainly the loveliness of the passing countryside was completely lost on everyone else as they explored each other's lives.

Santa Maria Novella rail station is close to the city center and there are many hotels nearby. Some of these are not particularly good (and the area can be problematic at night) but some of the best hotels in the city are within walking distance. We choose one, settle in then go walking.

Florence is a city designed for walking. Most of the sights are within a compact area and much of the central city is a traffic-free area. If you use the dome of the Duomo (cathedral) and the River Arno as reference points it's hard to get lost.

To help find your way around there are large maps in many squares and other places but I still recommend you carry a paper map or one on your tablet or phone.

If you are not into walking, it is possible to rent a bicycle. There is a council scheme with hire points at railway stations and other places. Bikes can be rented by the hour or day and if you have a rail pass the cost reduces considerably. There are also private companies renting bicycles and mopeds. You will need a credit card, cash for a deposit, and ID. Small electric buses cover the center of the city.

For those who want a guided tour, many companies offer English-language options. Most are walking tours but some include some bus transport. Several bicycle tour companies exist so check the web for these options. Some offer e-bikes.

The large modern-style rail station (amazingly from the early 1930s) is on **Piazza della Stazione** which runs into Piazza dell'Unita Italiana and in turn into the huge, frantic **Piazza Santa Maria Novella**.

Here is the **Santa Maria Novella Basilica** (http://www.chiesasantamarianovella.it/en), one of Florence's most distinguished churches, which was established in the 13th century. The geometric façade, with bands of white and green marble, is from the 15th century.

Most visitors see many churches and museums in Florence and we are no different. The façade is the oldest of all the churches in Florence but it is also the only church with its original, planned façade still in place today. The church contains some memorable paintings and the Gondi Chapel and Strozzi Chapel are two of the areas not to be missed.

The Strozzi Chapel, to the right of the main altar, is dedicated to St. John the Evangelist and scenes of his life are portrayed in the beautiful frescoes by Filippino Lippi. The Gondi chapel to the left of the main altar contains a wooden 'Crucifix' by Brunelleschi from 1410-15.

A little to the east, is the Basilica di San Lorenzo. One of the highlights here is the **Medici Chapels** (http://www.museumsinflorence.com/musei/Medici_chapels.html) which form part of a complex developed in close connection with the adjoining church. The chapels are entered from Piazza Madonna degli Aldobrandini and are divided into three distinct parts: the crypt, the Cappella dei Principi (Chapel of the Princes), and the New Sacristy (Nuova Sacres).

The Nuova Sacres is Michelangelo's gloomy mausoleum for the Medici family who lived in the neighboring palace on Via Larga. It strikes many that it is somewhat ironic that Michelangelo's best works are reserved for obscure members of the family while Lorenzo the Magnificent, one of the greatest of the family members, has a simple monument.

Michelangelo began work on the New Sacristy in 1520. After completing the architectural works in 1524, he worked until 1533 on the sculptures and the sarcophagi that were to be featured on the chapel walls but only a few were completed.

Many visitors are drawn to Michelangelo's powerful *Night and Day*. Two figures are seated on top of the sarcophagus of Giuliano de' Medici. *Day* is a powerful man in his prime with his reclining muscular body in an energetic pose. *Night* is a pensive woman showing some grief. Michelangelo has successfully shown a conflict here which can be easily seen.

The Chapel of the Princes has a huge dome which was begun in 1604 but not completed until the 20th century. Its sumptuous octagonal interior is completely covered with semi-precious stones or marble. Six grand dukes are buried here. The sarcophagi of the Grand Dukes are contained in niches and complemented by bronze statues. The crypt is the part where minor members of the dynasty were unceremoniously laid to rest.

The adjacent **Basilica di San Lorenzo** (http://www.visitflorence.com/florence-churches/san-lorenzo.html) is one of the oldest churches in Florence with origins that can be traced back to the late Roman era. It acted as the city's cathedral for several hundred years then later it became the parish church of the Medici Family.

The present church, originally designed in the 15th century, is an excellent early example of ecclesiastical Renaissance architecture with its rough front façade still incomplete. Michelangelo apparently created a marble design for the façade but it was never built.

The Renaissance style interior, in contrast, is elegant with its columned arcades and two bronze pulpits. Don't miss the old sacristy, designed by

Brunelleschi and built in the 1420s. Donatello decorated it with beautiful colored stucco and reliefs. The cloister has a formal garden planted with many hedges.

From here you enter the **Medici Library** (http://www.bml.firenze.sbn.it/index_ing.htm). Michelangelo designed and supervised the construction and it survives to this day without modification. He started working in 1524, but he did not finish it. It was finished by some of his students. It opens Monday to Saturday from 9 a.m. to 1 p.m.

The collections of books, which are mainly ancient priceless codices, were amassed by Cosimo the Elder. His son, grandson, and others enlarged the collection. It is considered the most important library in the whole of Italy. The sweeping stairway in the vestibule is a classic construction.

Across the square from the basilica is the **Palazzo Medici-Riccardi** (http://www.palazzo-medici.it/eng/home.htm), the first Renaissance building erected in the city. This building was designed to be the symbol of the economic power of the Medicis and they continued to live here even after they became Dukes of Florence. It was later purchased by the very wealthy Riccardi marquises who enlarged and partially refurbished it.

The beautiful courtyard is decorated in the Baroque style while the Great Hall has a ceiling covered in frescoes dating from 1682 by the famous Neapolitan painter Luca Giordano. The lovely Madonna and Child by Filippo Lippi is a highlight. The exhibition area of the palace has temporary exhibitions.

The heart of Florence is just a few blocks to the south along one of the cobbled streets. We catch a glimpse of the bright façade of the cathedral from a crook in the cobbled street. We also notice that we are increasingly besieged by battalions of tourists controlled by flag-waving guides.

Santa Maria del Fiore (http://www.museumflorence.com/) is the third and current cathedral of Florence. The different styles on display testify to the varying tastes over the long period of time between its founding and completion. The cathedral complex, located in Piazza del Duomo, includes the Baptistery and Campanile and these three buildings are part of the UNESCO World Heritage Site covering the historic center of the city.

It was started in 1296 around the existing Santa Reparata church. The distinctive octagonal cupola was built in the 1420s. The cathedral was, however, only completed during the 1800s. The simplicity of the Latin cross interior divided into a nave and two aisles by pillars enhances the church's impressive dimensions. There are often long lines to get in here but they tend to move quite quickly.

Some visitors are disappointed with the interior of the Duomo, but in fact, there is much to see. The highlight is the huge 90 m-high dome which is quite breathtaking and is one of the largest frescoed areas in the world. The remains of the original church are another highlight and, in the crypt, you can see remains of Roman shops and houses.

There are 463 or so steps to reach the top of the Cupola. The last two or three flights are particularly taxing, but the rewards are great. On the way up, you get great views of the frescos then at the top, the view is stunning. Access is available from 8.30 a.m. and it pays to be early as the staircases are narrow and it's much better if you don't have to pass too many people on the way up or down.

Giotto's slender **Bell Tower** (Campanile) clad in polychrome marble, rises 85 meters to the right of the cathedral. Giotto first began work on it in 1334. By the time the artist died, he had completed only the lower section, with its distinctive reliefs set in hexagonal panels.

Work continued under the supervision of Andrea Pisano and was completed under Francesco Talenti who was responsible for the top three floors. We walk the 414 steps to the top, stopping at several observation decks where we catch our breath and take our photographs.

The octagonal **Battistero San Giovanni** (Baptistery of St John) is located directly across the street from the main entrance of the cathedral. It is one of the oldest buildings in the city. The architecture is in Florentine Romanesque style.

The Baptistery has three sets of magnificent bronze doors. The first set (south side) was built in 1336, the north set in 1400, and the east doors (Gates of Paradise) which took 27 years to make were the last. The interior is rather dark but look up and you will see a magnificent mosaic ceiling.

The final attraction in this area is the *Museo dell'Opera del Duomo* which must be considered one of the most important church museums in Italy. Since the end of the 1800s, various works of art have been removed from their outdoor locations and placed here.

We see the originals of the statues by Arnolfo di Cambio for the first partial façade of the Cathedral, Ghiberti's now restored original panels for the door of the Baptistery, the famous Reliquary of St. Paul's Book, and the second of the three *Pietas* by Michelangelo. Of particular interest are the tools and machinery used to build the cathedral and wooden models of the structure.

The day has gone and we have only touched the surface of all the things there are to be seen in Florence. On the way back to the hotel, we stop at Trattoria Antellesi near the Medici Chapels for some local Tuscan food. This is an authentic, unpretentious, friendly, and comfortable place with good food and good prices. They have a fixed-price menu and friendly service.

Another day

Tickets to some of Florence's best museums can be difficult to come by. We have pre-arranged tickets for the Uffizi Gallery and the Palazzo Pitti and are heading for both places today. *The Uffizi* (http://www.uffizi.com/) is probably Italy's most crowded museum so it's a good idea to buy tickets ahead to avoid long ticket lines. As we approach we see the gallery is slowly devouring a long queue.

The building was damaged by a car bomb in 1993 and while this was a disaster, it has allowed the gallery to expand and improve facilities. The displays are now grouped into periods and this helps me understand the development of Italian art. The audio tour also helped.

It takes a long time to see the whole collection and most visitors aim to see only the most important works. No doubt you will find your own favorites amongst the many galleries but we are taken with Giotto's *Ognissanti Maesta*, Lippi's *Coronation of the Virgin*, and Botticelli's supreme *Birth of Venus*.

The highlight to me, however, is Leonardo da Vinci's unfinished *Adoration of the Magi*, but Mantegna's *Ascension* is also up there. It is best to start your viewing from the top floor and realize that you will be constantly fighting with other people for good viewpoints.

There are works also by Giotto, Fabriano, Bronzino, Titan, and many others. The most beautiful room in the gallery has a dome of pearl shells and a copy of the Greek *Venus of the Medici* at its center. There is also a Michelangelo panel painting called *Holy Family*.

The Uffizi is normally open Tuesday through Sunday, 8:15 a.m. – 6:50 p.m. During summer it stays open until 10.p.m. on Tuesdays. There are 3 types of tickets: full, reduced, and free but in practice, most adults pay the full price, and under 18 is free. Every first Sunday of the month, the museum follows normal opening hours and entrance is free for everyone. A tour is conducted in English which lasts 1 hour and 30 minutes and is offered every Tuesday, Thursday, and Saturday at 12.30 p.m.

We need some lunch after a full morning at the Uffizi and find a small place with limited selection. Across the Ponte Vecchio is the huge **Pitti**

Palace (http://www.florenceartmuseums.com/pitti-palace/) on the south side of the river. This is a treasure trove of museums, paintings, and other major art works. The *Galleria Palatina,* where there is an abundance of works by Titian, Rubens, and Raphael, is a good starting point.

We enjoy several of Titian's paintings including the masterpiece called *Man with Gray Eyes* and his gold *Mary Magdalene*. Other rooms contain well-known works by Rubens such as *The Four Philosophers* and his *Consequences of War* and two famous Raphael's, *La Velata* and *Madonna of the Choir.*

There are many more famous works but we are 'galleried out' by now so we leave the Galleria Palatina, decide to miss the Modern Art Gallery and the Gallery of Costume and go straight to the *Museum of Silver*, and the Boboli Gardens.

The *Silver Museum*, in 25 rooms of the palace, contains a collection of priceless silver, cameos, and works in semi-precious gemstones. There is also a collection of ancient vases and a fine collection of German gold and silver artifacts.

The core of the collection is of Medici origin but this is supplemented by some extraordinary works collected by Ferdinando III of Lorraine, and donations to the museum. These include jewels from the 17th to the 20th-century, articles in the 18th-century floral style, 19th-century neoclassic pieces, and the spectacular amethyst and diamond-studded Cartier Diadem from 1900.

The large park and gardens at the rear of the palazzo, which is meticulously maintained and latticed by trees, is the **Boboli Gardens** (http://www.museumsinflorence.com/musei/boboli_garden.html). For four centuries it has been the garden of the residence of the Grand Duke of Tuscany and for a short period of the kings of Italy. It is a true open-air museum, decorated with ancient and Renaissance statues and adorned with large fountains and grottos.

On one side of the Gardens is the bizarre grotto designed by Bernardo Buontalenti. The first chamber has copies of Michelangelo's four unfinished *Slaves*. A short passage leads to a small second chamber and to a third which has a central fountain with Giambologna's *Bathing Venus* in the center of the basin.

Elsewhere, this verdant place is punctuated by pools and fountains. Don't miss the delightful Isolotto, a small island with a fountain in the center. The *Porcelain Museum* is housed in the Casino del Cavaliere in the Gardens. The imposing 16th-century star-shaped Forte di Belvedere provides excellent panoramic views of the city

This local area south of the river, has some other things of interest. A few streets to the west is Piazza Santo Spirito where a morning market is held six days a week. In summer, this is a lively place with bars, restaurants, and events. The beautifully proportioned Santa Spirito church (http://www.museumsinflorence.com/musei/museum_of_santo_spirito .html), which fronts the square, was designed by Brunelleschi but never finished, however, it is well worth seeing.

The area between here and the Pitti Palace comprises grand Via Maggio, a maze of small lanes, and a mix of medieval towers and clothes shops along Borgo San Jacopo which follows the river. You are now away from the tourist crowds and find couples lingering over lunch, locals walking their dogs, and the elderly sitting at tables and benches enjoying conversations. It is an area that I enjoy.

Just past Ponte Vecchio, there are some pretty lanes meandering uphill. One of these, Costa San Giorgio, leads to the very attractive **Bardini Garden** (http://www.aboutflorence.com/parks-in-Florence.html). This has an extraordinary view of the Florence skyline, a rich array of foliage in woods and gardens, a delightful walk through the tunnel of wisteria, the Baroque stairs, six fountains with mosaic treatments, and Villa Bardini.

The hill is crowned by a pair of baroque statues and the Belvedere Terrace, where there's a pleasant café. The villa at the top of the park goes back to the 14th century and contains two small galleries. A wonderful collection of antiques is displayed in the *Bardini Museum* in the square below.

We had rushed across the **Ponte Vecchio** (http://www.turismo.intoscana.it/allthingstuscany/tuscanyarts/bridges-of-florence/) earlier but now we return for a closer look. The bridge was built in 1220 but may have been reconstructed in the 14th century.

It is the last of the medieval bridges spanning the river because the Germans blew up the rest towards the end of World War II. The bridge was once home to butchers but today it houses goldsmiths and jewelers and is closed to vehicular traffic.

It is fantastic from a distance but somewhat disappointing up close. The yellow Arno River meanders today, but there are reminders that it is not always like this. The day is clear and bright with a touch of yellowness in the air which is part of that indefinable color which Florence seems to have as you gaze at it from its bridges.

This seems to be an appropriate point to mention the Corridoio Vasariano. This 1 km-long covered passageway connects the Palazzo Vecchio with the Uffizi Gallery and then crosses the Arno River above the shops on the Ponte Vecchio to Palazzo Pitti. It was designed by Vasari in 1565 to allow the Medicis to wander between their two palaces in privacy and comfort.

In the 17th century, the Medicis strung it with hundreds of artworks, including self-portraits of Andrea del Sarto, Rubens, Rembrandt, and Canova. The corridor is open to a privileged few by guided tour which does not operate all the time, so check the internet for current details (http://www.uffizi.com/online-ticket-booking-vasari-corridor-uffizi-gallery.asp).

Next day

Last night we ate and slept well so today we are ready for more of Florence. There are plenty more galleries to visit and there are still some special pieces of art we want to see so we concentrate on these.

Top of our list is Michelangelo's *David* so we hurry to the *Galleria dell'Accademia*   (Via   Ricasoli) (http://www.accademia.org/?gclid=Cj0KEQiA1NWnBRDchObfnYrbo78B EiQA-2jqBbSU1V1lEeP6_jZuKo-ZPcRR-cP6UsPgliWh-pCEfWkaAk2E8P8HAQ) straight after breakfast. Unfortunately, by the time we get there, the line to get in is long.

This masterpiece originally stood in Piazza della Signoria and we briefly consider the idea of going there to see the copy which is now in the square rather than waiting here. Reason kicks in so we wait.

There are several other Michelangelo sculptures in the museum including *St. Matthew* and the quartet of *Slaves* still struggling to escape from their marble blocks, but nothing compares with *David*. It is very impressive.

As you look, the marble almost becomes flesh and you can see cords of sinew emerge from the statue's neck and a bulging vein which runs down its right wrist. It would be worth visiting the city for this alone. The rest of the collection is less inspiring but the Grand Ducal collection of forty musical instruments, the plaster model for the stunning marble sculpture of Giambologna's *Rape of the Sabine Women*, and gold backed altarpieces by Giotto and his followers, are all interesting.

You might spend more time in line waiting to get in than in the museum itself. The museum is open from 8:15 a.m. to 6:50 p.m. Tuesdays through Sunday.

In fact, *David* is so impressive that we walk across town to the *Bargello Museum* (Via del Proconsolo 4) (http://www.visitflorence.com/florence-museums/bargello.html) for the chance to see three more *Davids*. The first is by Michelangelo but was carved some 25 years after the more famous version in the *Accademia*. It is not nearly as impressive. The second is Donatello's bronze *David*, a remarkable piece that has him like a transvestite.

The third is by Andrea del Verrocchio, one of the best 15th-century sculptors. The museum has several other Donatello works worth seeing including his *John the Baptist* and his *St. George*, Michelangelo's *Drunken Bacchus*, and Giambologna's *Mercury*.

The **Piazza della Signoria**, one of Florence's most beautiful squares, is nearby. It is a huge sculpture gallery which commands our attention. Here too is the controversial but not particularly attractive *Fountain of Neptune* designed in the 16th century by Bartolomeo Ammannati.

It was designed to illustrate Florentine dominion over the sea and is symbolized by the chained sea monsters around and between the legs of the god. The fountain was finished in 1575 and filled with water from an ingenious aqueduct.

For centuries, Michelangelo's *David* was in this square but what you see today is a copy. It does, however, offer great insight into the Renaissance ideals and the realism depicted in facial expressions and muscular definition. *David* represents the Biblical hero who defeated a much stronger enemy and came to represent the defense of civil liberties against the threats from more powerful rival states.

Bandinelli's *Heracles* is an original but critics say it is far inferior to a Michelangelo. The horse in the bronze statue by Giambologna was considered a major achievement in its time because it was cast in one piece. The square is lined with restaurants and cafés, many of which are tourist traps. I suggest you eat elsewhere.

The **Palazzo** **Vecchio** ((http://www.museumsinflorence.com/musei/Palazzo_vecchio.html) which fronts the square is an imposing place which was built at the start of the 14th century as the seat of the Signoria, the ruling body of the city. The building was home to the Italian government's House of Deputies for six years when Florence was the first capital of Italy in the mid-19th century. The 94-meter-high tower was an engineering feat at that time and 416 steps will take you to the very top to enjoy a breathtaking view of Florence. You pass through passages that offer lovely views of the city and entire valley.

Inside, the Hall of the 500 contains Michelangelo's *Genius of Victory* and there are some significant frescoes. There are various other rooms and art pieces that make this building quite special. Of note are the over-the-top Sala d'Udienza, the subtle Sala dei Gigli, and Donatello's *Judith and Holofernes*.

Don't miss the Map Room which has a large 16th–century globe and numerous maps. The 14th-century Loggia della Signoria off to the side houses a copy of Cellini's renowned *Perseus*. I adore the secret routes which exist within the palace, and these are perfectly suitable for visits by families with kids, and curious visitors.

From here we wander through the city, to the Piazza Santa Croce and its **Basilica di Santa Croce** (http://www.santacroceopera.it/en/default.aspx). This church contains the tombs of many of the most famous Florentine people including Michelangelo, Dante, Galileo, and Machiavelli. A more recent guest is Marconi, inventor of the radio. The building was rebuilt for the Franciscan order in 1294 and the exterior was covered with a polychrome marble façade added in 1863.

The basilica is famous for its frescoes (1380) by Gaddi, and beautiful frescoes by Giotto which show scenes from the life of St. Francis and St. John the Evangelist. The memorial to the 19th-century playwright Giovanni Battista Niccolini is said to have been the inspiration for the *Statue of Liberty*.

Continuing to walk north, we pass by the Santa Maria Maddalena dei Pazzi church and eventually get back to the lovely Piazza Della Santissima Annunziata where we had started our day.

Near here the *Archaeology Museum* (Piazza SS. Annunziata 9/b) (http://www.museumsinflorence.com/musei/Museum_of_archaeology. html) has one of Europe's most outstanding Egyptian and Etruscan collections. It is housed in a palace which itself is worth seeing.

It opens Monday 2 p.m. - 7 p.m.; Tuesday and Thursday 8.30 a.m. - 7 p.m.; Wednesday, Friday, and Saturday 8.30 a.m. - 2 p.m. Despite our initial reluctance to spend the day in galleries we have done just that and, in fact, we have enjoyed it. Florence has that effect on us.

Sitting with *Spritz* in hand watching the light drain from a darkening blue sky is an experience hard to forget. Walking home after dark along streets softly lit by lanterns is a delight. Through sagging shutters, we see light from dazzling chandeliers and wonder what stories these ancient buildings could tell.

Shopping

Today my wife wants to do some shopping, so we are advised to go to impressive Via Tornabuoni with its Renaissance palaces and Italian fashion houses. At its northern end is Palazzo Antinori (1461–69) and opposite, huge stone steps lead up to 17th-century Chiesa di San Gaetano.

Nearby, is the smaller Via della Vigna Nuova. Walking down these streets introduces us to Florence fashion, style, high quality, and beauty. There are boutiques such as Dolce & Gabbana, Roberto Cavalli, Christian Dior, Yves Saint Laurent, Hermes, and so on.

At the other end of the price scale is the Mercato di San Lorenzo sprawling along streets to the north of San Lorenzo basilica. Here we find leather and clothes bargains but you need to be careful with quality. Most visitors to Florence make a stop here.

The vendors we encounter are not overly-aggressive and all appear to speak some English. There are all kinds of leather goods - coats, wallets, belts, etc., as well as souvenirs, hats, ties, t-shirts, jewelry, and more.

At Mercato Centrale (http://www.mercatocentrale.it/en/), we find a food stall and grab a quick lunch. The market has every kind of food, drink, and vegetable that you want and we select some for a picnic lunch tomorrow. My wife is still not finished so we wander down Via dei Calzaiuoli, a 600-year-old pedestrian boulevard originally renowned simply for shoe production, but now one of the city's very best shopping streets.

Our final visit is to La Rinascente (https://www.rinascente.it/rinascente/en/store/80/florence/), a department store housed in an historic palazzo right beside the Piazza della Repubblica. Over six floors, it sells a wide range of designer fashion and accessories along with perfumes, jewelry, home furnishings, and even food.

Florence Facts

Florence is well-connected with the rest of Italy and with Europe and is easy to get to by air or land. In the last few years, there has been a significant increase in traffic in and out of Florence's **Vespucci Airport** (http://www.aeroporto.firenze.it/en/), and the infrastructure and facilities are constantly being upgraded.

The center of the city can be reached from here in about 15 minutes by **taxi** (€20 plus baggage supplements), and in about 20 minutes with the Busitalia SITA Nord "Vola in Bus" **bus shuttle** operating between the airport and the central railway station of Santa Maria Novella. A one-way ticket costs €6 while a round-trip ticket costs €10 (November 2018). One-way tickets can be purchased directly on board from the driver.

Florence is also a key node on the Italian **railway** network. It has good connections with the main cities in the north, and Rome is only about an hour and a half away. From Florence to Bologna is about 100 km and the train travel time is just over 30 minutes. There are approximately 50 trains per day.

Make sure to ask for a map of Florence at one of the five tourist information offices. The main historic center is relatively small so that it is easy to move around on foot. Using a car around Florence is not ideal, as there is little parking, many streets are pedestrian only, and streets are often one-way. A fleet of small electric buses also provide links between main key areas in the center.

In the historical center, getting around by bicycle is very practical as many areas are closed off to motor traffic. There aren't any bike paths in this area so you'll have to go along the main streets along with everyone else. "Mille e una bici" is a program run by the Florence City Council to encourage the use of bicycles. These can be rented at the central railway station and at about another three locations. Tourist rates are 1 hour - €3; 5 hours - €7; 1 day - €9. Electric bikes are available at twice these prices.

Public transportation is widely used outside the central area. Tickets for the city buses (ordinary single use 90-minute ticket, and four 90-minute rides on one single ticket) can be purchased from coffee shops, tobacconists, newsagents, anyone with "ATAF" stickers on their shop windows, and from the ATAF booth within the SMN train station. Tickets also work on the city trams.

The weather in Florence and Tuscany is generally pretty mild. The warmest months are July and August, while June and September are my favorite times to visit. Keep in mind that in August many Italians escape the city so outside of the historical center, a large number of businesses including shops and restaurants close down for two to four weeks. The coolest months are December and January while November is the month with the most precipitation.

Another day

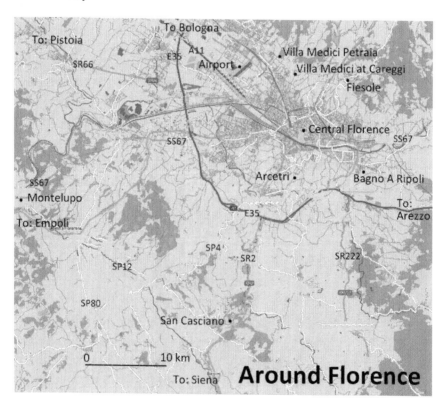

There are several places close to Florence worth visiting while you are here. **Fiesole** (http://www.fiesole.com/) is one of the easiest to get to because the city buses go here. The town spreads over a cluster of hills about 8 km north-east of central Florence and provides a nice grandstand view of the city.

Fiesole is actually older than Florence as it was first settled in the Bronze Age. Later, it was occupied by the Etruscans then the Romans and finally in the 12th century by the Florentines. This later occupation destroyed most of the city but early 11th century Duomo di San Romolo was spared.

Christianity was introduced to Fiesole by St. Romulus, a disciple of St. Peter, hence the name. The cathedral contains the shrine of St. Romulus and also the shrine of St. Donatus a monk from Ireland who was bishop of Fiesole from 826.

The other interesting site is the 3000-seat Roman theater. This is within the Etruscan-Roman Archaeological area and there is also a small museum here. After visiting the outdoor area and museum, head down the street that runs behind here to see remnants of the massive, ancient Etruscan walls that have survived.

There are several small bars as well as trattoria on the main square. A few restaurants are located on the street heading up to the monastery of San Francesco located at the very crest of the hill.

The Vincigliata Castle is of medieval origin but it was reconstructed in neo-Gothic style in the middle of the last century. The castle is used today for weddings and events.

Some readers will be interested in visiting some of the **Medici villas** that were built in the 16th and 17th centuries. Two good examples are just to the north-west of the city. The *Medici Villa of Petraia* (Via della Petraia, 40) is an interesting museum with excellent furnishings, an Italian-style garden, and a glorious park that surrounds it. It has been adapted from a medieval castle. It opens daily from 8.15 a.m. and closes from 4.30 p.m. to 7.30 p.m. depending on the time of the year.

The nearby Villa Medicea di Castello is not open to the public but the gardens with their sculptures, fountains, and man-made cave are a delight.

Arcetri is a small hilly area just a couple of kilometers south of the center of Florence. There are many historic buildings, such as the house in which Galileo Galilei lived and died. Other important buildings are the church of San Leonardo in Arcetri, the convent of San Matteo, and the villa where Francesco Guicciardini died. A bus departs from Piazza Sauro in Florence every 5 minutes or so during the day on one of routes 11, 36, or 37.

Bagno a Ripoli is a town of Etruscan origin that assumed importance as a trading center in Roman times. There are many castles, Renaissance villas, and tower-houses in the town. It is located about 7 kilometers southeast of Florence. The impressive Oratory of Santa Caterina, built in 1354, seems so simple from the outside but inside there are stunning, bright frescoes recalling the tale of Saint Catherine of Alexandria. You can reach Bano a Ripoli from Florence with either bus 8 or bus 31 from Piazza San Marco, or bus 32 from Piazza San Marco.

San Casciano in Val di Pesa is a town located 25 kilometers south of Florence. It is famous for the production of extra-virgin olive oil, and wine. You can visit the observatory of Torre Luciana, an Etruscan tomb from the seventh century BC, the *Museum of San Casciano* with its works of sacred art, and the Quattro Pievi (four ancient religious buildings of artistic and architectural importance).

Other interesting things are the walls of San Casciano, and many beautiful castles. The village has some good restaurants, pubs, bars, and pizzerias. There is a regular bus service from the Florence coach terminal in Via Santa Caterina da Siena.

Montelupo Fiorentino, a town surrounded by walls, green hills, and lush forests, is situated about 30 kilometers southwest of Florence and there are many prehistoric sites in the area. Places worth seeing are the

Villa Medicea dell'Ambrogiana, the parish church of San Giovanni Evangelista, the *Archaeological Museum* (via S. Lucia) which opens from Tuesday to Sunday 10 a.m.-6 p.m., and the impressive *Museum of Ceramics* (via Vittorio Veneto 8-10) which also opens from Tuesday to Sunday 10 a.m.-6 p.m.

Eating and drinking in Florence

After all the museums, churches, and artwork you might be looking for something else and Florence can deliver. You can sip Chianti at the many cafés and bars and enjoy traditional Tuscan cuisine in *trattorias* and restaurants. Thinly sliced T-bone steak prepared on chestnut wood and served with salt, pepper, and a drizzle of olive oil is a Florentine specialty.

Enoteca Pinchiorri (Via Ghibellina, 87) (055 242 777) is a three-Michelin-star restaurant with a renowned wine cellar. It has character and charm with mosaics, parquet floors, a pink marble chimney, and antique furniture, but it is the restaurant's cuisine rather than its décor that is the attraction. One popular dish on a single plate is crawfish filled with zucchini and thyme, fried in batter and stewed with onions and bacon. It opens for dinner Tuesday to Saturday.

Cibrèo (Via del Verrocchio 8r) (055 234 1100) is a renowned meeting place for writers, musicians, and intellectuals but you will be welcome too. The restaurant creates elegant dishes from ancient recipes, including roasted pigeon stuffed with fruit mustard, and calamari and spinach stew. The waiting staff are multilingual and will describe the daily specials for you. Apart from the restaurant there are also the nearby Cibrèo Trattoria, Caffè Cibrèo, and the recently opened Ciblèo.

Borgo San Jacopo (Borgo San Jacopo 14) (055 281 661) produces dishes with distinct flavors to a consistently high standard as indicated by its Michelin star. There is also an excellent wine list of over 600 labels. In summer, treat yourself to dinner on the delightful small terrace overlooking the Arno River.

There are many cheaper options which the locals have discovered. Sit down at the table of an ancient *trattoria*, find a seat at a *fiaschetteria* (wine bar) or just stand up at a traditional *trippaio* (tripe stand), and you can have a meal that hasn't changed in centuries.

Trattoria Mario (Via Rosina 2r) (055 218 550) is one of these. There will be more locals than tourists here and you are likely to share a table with one of them. Try the classic *ribollita* vegetable soup or the daily specials.

Gusta Panino (Via dei Michelozzi 13r) is a sandwich place on the south side of the river that makes your focaccia or wrap to order and you can see the ingredients prepared in front of you. A favorite is the turkey, pesto, tomato, and mozzarella combination. The dinner pastas are also very good.

For a completely different experience, try Il Teatro del Sale (via de'Macci 18) (055 200 1492). You need to pay a small membership to join this artistic club, open from Tuesday to Saturday for breakfast, lunch, and dinner, with a live show at night.

A tempting buffet is laid out, then the chef shouts out dishes from his open kitchen and guests line up (or crowd in) to sample the wonderful creations. The meal spreads over 10 dishes, with wine and coffee included in the price. Live entertainment is also included in the price of dinner.

Grom (Via del Campanile on the corner of Via delle Oche) (055 216 158) is the city's most famous *gelateria*. It is more expensive than most, and perhaps more popular with tourists than locals. No trip to Florence is complete without a scoop of mouth-watering Italian gelato so it might as well be here.

You don't even have to eat in a restaurant to enjoy a good meal. Food markets are great for classic Tuscan prosciutto and cheese picnics which you can eat in a square, park, or down by the river.

4 NORTHERN TUSCANY

One of the delights of northern Italy is to drive through Tuscany with no clear itinerary. The landscape of rolling plains, cypress trees, olive groves, walled hill towns, and fabled vineyards is fascinating.

You are almost guaranteed to stumble across a place that has special appeal and there are charming places to eat and to stay, everywhere.

On this trip, however, we are time limited so we have an itinerary that includes some of the best towns in the region and finishes with some wine tastings and exploring.

We leave Florence on a bright morning and head out west for about 20 km to **Prato**, a surprisingly large city of about 200,000 with a strong link to the textile industry. Like Florence, Prato became rich during the early Renaissance on banking and trading. The Duomo of Prato has some important works of art including frescoes in the high chapel, by Filippo Lippi (1465).

The *Textile Museum* (via Puccetti 3) (www.museodeltessuto.it) has textiles from as early as the third century, from Italy, Europe, India, China, and the Americas. The *Pecci Center* (www.centropecci.it) is the first museum in Tuscany dedicated exclusively to contemporary art.

Palazzo Pretorio (www.palazzopretorio.prato.it), the old town hall, is now the *Palazzo Pretorio Museum*. Prato has a very Asian Chinatown, on via Pistoiese, a bustling street lined with Chinese stores restaurants and shops selling imported goods and foods from China.

From here, we head south to Empoli, an interesting mid-sized Tuscan town about 35 kilometers south-west of Florence. It sits in a plain just a little south of the Arno River. We start our exploration in the Piazza Farinata degli Uberti, where we find the Collegiata di Sant'Andrea from the 11th century, the Palazza Ghibellino, built by the Guidi counts at a similar time, and the Pallazo Pretorio, which up until modern times served as Empoli's town hall.

The Palazzo Ghibellino now houses an auditorium and the *Museo Paleontologico* (Paleontology Museum) and the *Archivo Storico* (historical archives). Not far from the Piazza is the Chiesa di Santo Stefano, dating from the late 14th century. Adjacent to the church is a 16th-century convent, the Convento degli Agostiniani.

Cerreto Guidi (http://www.discovertuscany.com/cerreto-guidi/) is a few kilometers to the west. Situated on a hill and surrounded by vineyards and olive trees, this is a typical Renaissance village where we leave the car and walk. The small, circular center is dominated by the magnificent 16th century *Villa Medicea*.

This is now a museum where there are many portraits and antique furniture of the Medici family. The brickwork and stone façade of the Villa is austere, but it is balanced by the stone staircases leading to the square in front of the villa.

Outdoor types will be in paradise following the wine route called "Strada del Vino e dell'olio del Montalbano". It is an extraordinary journey through the vineyards and olive trees from Cerreto to Vinci or from Cerreto to Padule di Fucecchio.

Vinci (http://www.discovertuscany.com/what-to-see-in-tuscany/birthplace-of-leonardo-da-vinci/) is close by, so we visit to explore Leonardo da Vinci's origins. The town itself is on a hill but the farmhouse where Leonardo was born is about two kilometers away in the village of Anchiano. There are some reproductions of his drawings at the house and a life-sized hologram of an old da Vinci who entertains visitors by directly recounting his life story, sharing information on his land, and some details of his quite mysterious private life.

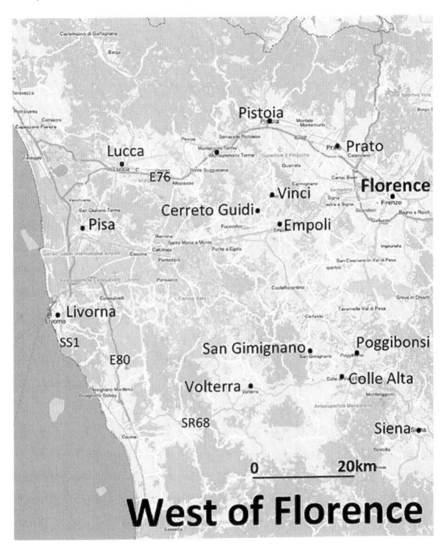

Vinci has a *Museo Leonardiano* (http://www.museoleonardiano.it/eng) spread over two buildings which has some statues and monuments based on Leonardo drawings. The museum covers the history of the master both as architect and scientist. A new section on "Leonardo and Anatomy" opened in 2016 detailing Leonardo's interest in the human body. Your entrance ticket (€11 adult €7 children and seniors)

(November 2018) covers both sections of the museum. It takes a couple of minutes and some very steep steps to get from Palazzina degli Uzielli, in Piazza Guidi, to the Conti Guidi Castle, which overlooks the town from its highest point.

It's now time to go north to **Pistoia** (http://www.italia.it/en/discover-italy/tuscany/pistoia.html) with its well-preserved medieval town center. As we approach the town, we see the garden nurseries for which the area is famous. The town has three splendid Romanesque churches worth seeing.

The cathedral, with its tiled arcades and striped black and white marble, is in the vast Piazza del Duomo. Also here, is a campanile, the Baptistery, and a large civic building with a museum. The bell tower of the Duomo is 67 meters-high and there are two hundred stairs which you can climb to obtain panorama views if you get a ticket from the tourist office. The octagonal Baptistery of San Giovanni in Corte, an elegant example of 14th-century gothic architecture, faces the cathedral.

The majestic San Giovanni Fuorcivitas, which was founded in the 8th century, is in the main shopping street while just to the south is the 13th-century church of San Domenico looking smart after its rebuild in the 1970s.

To the west lies civilized **Montecatini Terme** (http://www.italia.it/en/discover-italy/tuscany/pistoia.html). This is considered to be Italy's top spa resort and from April to November it is a very popular spot. Many visitors here are serious tourists, determined to drink and bathe in the thermal waters with their supposed magical powers.

We visit the grand 19th-century Tettuccio spa with its beautiful gardens and walk through the Parco dei Terme with its neoclassical temples. There are several other spas here and something like 200 hotels, so you are spoiled for choice.

An historic funicular railway, more than 100 years old, runs from Montecatini Terme up the hill to the picturesque hill town of Montecatini Alto. Here, there's a small castle, three churches, a large square with restaurants and outdoor cafés, and a few tourist shops. It is an enjoyable area but we don't linger long. The spa treatments and mud baths will have to wait for next time. So too will the expensive boutiques that cater to the rich and famous.

Lucca

The dour looking medieval city of Lucca (http://www.discovertuscany.com/lucca/) is our next port of call. The Romans were responsible for the rectangular grid of its historical center, and the Piazza San Michele occupies the site of the ancient forum. Fortunately, many of the streets are pedestrianized so walking is pleasant.

Here we rediscover the problems you can have with a car in Italian cities. The town had been described to us as sleepy but it appears the local cars are content to sleep in all the available parking spaces. We finally give up and park outside the walls. The walls are actually one of the prime reasons for visiting here.

The town has existed for more than two millennia and the third and final set of city walls was erected in the 17th-century. They are now the best-preserved Renaissance ramparts in Europe. The walls, which are up to 12 meters high, are surrounded by a tree-filled park. You enter at one of the bastions and can walk the four-kilometer circuit. The mulberry trees remind us of the city's Middle Ages silk trade.

Inside the old town, there are several delights. The Cathedral di San Martino (http://www.sacred-destinations.com/italy/lucca-cathedral-san-martino) is the town's main monument and the exterior is exceptional although somewhat unbalanced. This impression is caused by the bell tower which was erected before the church. The dim interior contains some sculptured tombs, some paintings, and a carved crucifix called *Volto Santo*.

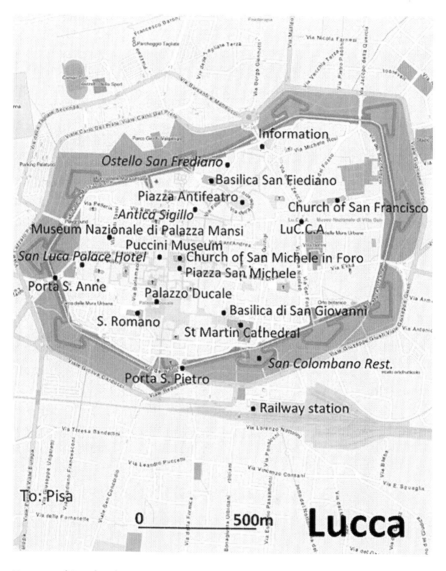

You need to check out two other churches – the imposing San Michele in Foro (http://www.sacred-destinations.com/italy/lucca-san-michele-in-foro) started in the 11th century with its exquisite façade and less elaborate interior, and the Romanesque San Frediano (http://www.welcometuscany.it/tuscany/lucca/santa_zita_lucca.htm)

with its unique mosaic façade and a delicate interior with some fine treasures.

On the west side of town, is the Villa Guinigi National Museum an art museum featuring works by local and visiting artists (http://www.luccamuseinazionali.it/) in a 17th-century building which has some outstanding interior decoration. Also part of the National Museum is Palazzo Mansi, an original house-museum in the center of the city.

Lucca was the birthplace of Puccini, one of Italy's greatest operatic composers. It's easy to see his unpretentious house which now operates as a museum (€7 adults and €5 for children and seniors) and contains some original artifacts but more difficult to catch a performance of one of his operas. To be certain of seeing an opera you need to visit in September during the Festival of Santa Croce.

For something second best, visit the lovely little Oratorio di San Giovanni (http://www.puccinielasualucca.com/) which has a one-hour nightly concert. This is a perfect introductory crash course for anyone who has never been thrilled by opera.

If you have the time, check out the *Duomo Museum* (http://www.toscanatoscana.it/eng/lucca.htm) but the lovely weather does not encourage us to spend much time indoors. There are also contemporary art galleries of some repute including the cleverly named Lu.C.C.A (Via della Fratta 36) (http://www.luccamuseum.com/en) the Lucca Center of Contemporary Art.

Many of the city's loveliest dining spots are in alleys and hidden courtyards but you will find them after dark by the lines of candles that they display. Antico Sigillo (Via degli Angeli 13) is one of these with a few alley seats, delicious fresh bread, and some local specialties. San Colombana (Baluardo di San Colombano) is housed in part of the wall and is open every day until around 1 a.m.

Pisa

The great weather continues to Pisa (http://www.italia.it/en/discover-italy/tuscany/pisa.html) where the tower is one of the most recognized buildings in the world. While Pisa has other sights, the Tower, the Cathedral, and the Baptistery in the Campo dei Miracoli (Field of Miracles) together form something outstanding. There is nowhere else in Italy where the key religious buildings are so in harmony. The site is at the edge of the old medieval town.

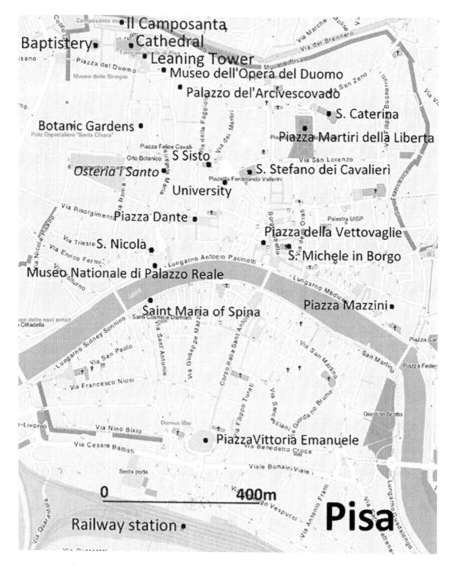

The **cathedral** (http://www.sacred-destinations.com/italy/pisa-cathedral), which is built on the remains of the old Etruscan and Roman temples, was designed in 1063 but the façade was erected in the 13th century. A fire in 1595 destroyed much of the interior but some features remain or have been rebuilt in the original style. One of these is the 1310 polygonal pulpit and there is a 13th-century mosaic.

Note the huge bronze doors with some figures particularly polished because people have been touching them for centuries in search of good luck, health, and fertility. Also, see the indications of Moorish architecture in the buildings vaulted arcades.

The **Leaning Tower of Pisa** (http://www.leaningtowerofpisa.net/history-tower-of-pisa.html) was intended as a free-standing bell tower for the cathedral. Construction started on the eight-story tower in 1174 but by the time it had reached the third level, it had started to tilt. Construction was halted for a century and the tower wasn't finished until the late 14th-century.

Unfortunately, it continued to slowly lean and by 1990 it had to be closed because of safety reasons. A mammoth engineering exercise has now rescued the tower and it now sits firmly with a lean of about four meters. It is once more possible to climb its 293 steps but only with a guide.

Several people had told us that they thought the baptistery was the most interesting building and we tend to agree. The 1153 building has a beautiful exterior with arches and columns and the interior is noteworthy because of the hexagonal pulpit supported by columns resting on the backs of marble lions.

The **Camposanto** (cemetery) (http://www.aboutpisa.info/piazza-dei-miracoli-pisa.html#cemetery), which takes the form of a giant cloister, is also interesting although it was hit by a bomb in 1944 which destroyed many of its famous frescos. Fortunately, a few were preserved and you can now see them in one of the restored rooms.

Finally, there is the *Duomo Museum* which is south of the tower and contains works of art removed from the other buildings. I recommend this as the best museum in the city. Do not miss a walk in the square at night. It is a totally different place and is really impressive.

Just a few steps away from the Campo dei Miracoli is the impressive Palazzo Arcivescovado, home to the Archbishop of Pisa. For those into little markets and ethnic crafts, exit the square on the west side and you will find a real ethnic market to your right.

Tickets for the leaning tower, the monuments, and museums at the Piazza del Duomo can be bought on line (http://boxoffice.opapisa.it/Turisti/) or from a ticket office in the square. The cost of a leaning tower ticket is €18 (November 2018). A cathedral ticket is free with any other ticket and a ticket to any one of the Baptistery or Monumental Cemetery or Opera Museum is €5. Children under 8 years old cannot climb up the Leaning Tower of Pisa.

After spending some hours in the square, we are now intent on finding somewhere to stay.

The town center on the river is remarkably un-touristy. Piazza dei Cavalieri is a delightful square with many of its facing building designed by Giorgio Vasari. It is also home to the prestigious Scuola Normale Superiore, a university established by Napoleon.

Elsewhere, the *Museo Nazionale di Palazzo Reale* (Lungarno Pacinotti 46), which displays tapestries, paintings, porcelain, and weaponry; the Orto Botanico (university garden) with its ponds, gardens, and exotic trees is one of the oldest in Europe; and the lovely Santa Maria della Spina on the south bank of the Arno River, are all worth seeing.

Walking tours of Pisa are popular and, naturally, they include many of the city's most interesting landmarks. They help you to understand Pisa's impressive history. Tours are available daily.

This port city is big on seafood so that is a good bet in many restaurants. There are several reasonable pizzerias along Via Santa Maria between the leaning tower and the river. Here too is Osteria i Santo (Via Santa Maria 71) which offers nice outdoor seating and affordable lasagna and spaghetti. Close by, is Dolce Pisa (Via Santa Maria 83), a café with excellent pastas and salads.

Caffe dell'Ussuro first opened in 1794 so it must be doing something right. It's located in a 15th-century palazzo at Lungamo Pacinotti 27. You'll find traditional food at Al Ristoro dei Vecchi Macelli, (Via Volturno 49) and this is recommended by the Touring Club of Italy.

Pisa has many bars and pubs with cheap drinks and a fun atmosphere. Piazza della Vettogaglie is lined with small pubs, picnic tables, and late-night food while Borgo Stretto which runs north from the river beside the church has more up-market offerings.

Pisa has an international airport, named Galileo Galilei. From the Pisa airport, you can take a train or a bus to the city. The bus runs four times an hour, and a ticket to the Field of Miracles costs €2. The automated train runs every five minutes or so, and a ticket costs €1.50.

North of Pisa is **Viareggio** where there are 10 km of sandy beaches. La Passeggiata, a wide road running parallel to the beach, is decorated with gelato stores, cafés, and park benches. This is the place to stroll for good restaurants, sandy beaches, and local shopping. Tower Matilde, dating back to the 16th century, was built to protect the city from sea incursions and pirates. It is located just in front of the first little harbor built in the 1820s, and today it is home to many art and cultural exhibitions.

One of the best-known festivals in Italy, the Carnival in Viareggio, started at the end of the 19th century. The parades draw thousands of visitors of all ages, who come to see the spectacular floats and parade, and to participate in the festive air. It takes place in the four weeks that precede Lent (which is the forty-day period before Easter). There are 5 days of processions each year.

Going South

Pisa is enjoyable but there is so much more to see in Tuscany that we now head south - slowly. After a while, we stop beside a bridge and admire a small stream curving through a sun-dappled valley dotted with olive orchards and farm houses. The scene is picture-perfect so it becomes a lunch stop.

Livorno (http://www.livornonow.com/) is a worthwhile stop and there are few tourists here. This was developed as a port after the Arno River silted up and it has been a cosmopolitan place for centuries. It has boat connections with Sardinia and Corsica to this day and is Italy's second largest port.

The city was badly bombed during WWII so few historic monuments remain but the Quattro Mori monument from 1623 and the portico of the 16th–century Duomo are worth seeing. It was no surprise to find some good fish restaurants and the local spicy fish soup is excellent. The Terrazza Mascagni, a great chessboard-style terrace made of many white and black tiles, is located along Viale Italia.

La Venezia, a Venice-style quarter with canals (dating back to the Medici era), small bridges, and boats, is one of the most enchanting quarters of the city. In early August, this holds one of the most important summer events of the region, the Effetto Venezia when the area comes alive until late into the night as it hosts music, theater, and entertainment for all ages.

There are resorts and villages on the Costa degli Etruschi (Etruscan coast) south of here but none are outstanding. Many of the beaches are pebbly and all are covered with beach huts. You can pay to use the Quercetano beach or go further south to Castiglioncello where there are long stretches of sand. From here we go inland towards the famous hill towns.

Volterra

This is a walled town with medieval and Renaissance buildings, a 1st-century B.C. Roman theater, and Etruscan sites. There are remains of Roman baths dating from the 4th century A.D. and also remains of the Roman forum. At first sight, it looks rather bleak but we find the cobbled medieval center of Volterra (http://www.volterra.net/) quite interesting.

The cathedral, which was constructed on the site of a previous church, dates from 1120. It has a Romanesque façade and an entrance added in the 13th-century. The octagonal Baptistery dates from the 13th-century although parts of it may be older. Its façade is decorated with green and white marble stripes.

The *Guarnacci Etruscan Museum* (via Don Minzoni 15) (http://www.volterra.net/guarnacci_museum.htm#.VPaPy_mUfCk), founded in 1761, was one of Europe's first public museums. The large collection of artifacts makes this one of Italy's major archaeological museums and the finds from the 4th to the 1st centuries BC are impressive.

The 13th century Palazzo dei Priori which still acts as the town hall is worth a visit. Climbing the tower gives great views and you can see the council chamber which has been used since 1257.

The Etruscan acropolis with panoramic views of the surrounding countryside is on the highest point in Volterra. The archaeological site is part of a park where there are foundations of two Etruscan temples, some dwellings, a system of cisterns, and medieval tower ruins. The town has one of the finest collections of Etruscan art in Italy.

Driving now is through rolling countryside and tiny villages. Everywhere we see yards full of laundry and sometimes it is festooned in the street. Personal cleanliness obviously has considerable significance here.

We remember that in Milan we had remarked that every T-shirt, skirt, or trousers worn by the locals was ironed and pressed in a flawless manner. It seems to be the same in these tiny communities. Washing and ironing must be of paramount importance to the whole region.

San Gimignano

This has to be one of the highlights of Tuscany. This area has known considerable conflict over centuries and the walled towns are much like fortresses. It's best to park outside the town wall and admire the 13 towers which are still preserved.

Few Italian towns handle the crush of summer visitors more gracefully than San Gimignano. The packaged tourists arrive mid-morning and shuffle through the streets until almost dusk, when they are herded once more into their air-conditioned coaches and whisked back to their hotels in Siena or Florence.

Walking into San Gimignano (http://www.sangimignano.com/en/) is fascinating and we head for Piazza del Duomo via Piazza della Cisterna, the most beautiful square in the town, where we are transported back to the 13th century.

In the middle, there is an octagonal travertine well that gives the name to the square. Ancient buildings and towers alternate in perfect harmony all around the square. The red brick pavement with irregular triangular patterns leads us to Via del Castello.

Entering Piazza del Duomo, on the left you can see the Palazzo Comunale which stands next to the staircase leading to the entrance of the Duomo. The Palazzo Chigi-Useppi and the former governor's palace, Palazzo Vecchio del Podestà, with its Torre Rognosa that was once used as a prison, are on the right. The church, palaces, and towers are probably almost unchanged from when they were built. No wonder this is a UNESCO World Heritage Site.

The town is well preserved and quite monumental and it is surrounded by some of the loveliest countryside in Tuscany. It has only one problem – too many day-trippers from Easter to October. Buses pour in bringing sometimes rowdy tourists who disturb the peace and bring litter with them. In this period, it is best to stay the night here so you can enjoy the place in the late afternoon and evening.

On first look, the church seems a bit plain and severe but inside our opinion rapidly changes. There are striped arches, gold stars, and some memorable paintings. Frescos are everywhere: The stunning frescos in one of the chapels were done by Michelangelo's fresco teacher. Bartolo's *Last Judgement* is mandatory viewing. Surprisingly, San Gimignano is also a center for contemporary art and there are several galleries worth a visit.

The entrance to one of the fascinating towers is through the *Civic Museum* (http://www.sangimignano.com/en/art-and-culture/town-museums/town-hall-picture-gallery.asp) which is upstairs in the town hall. We pay our fee and are rewarded with a wonderful bird's-eye view of the town. This is definitely worthwhile. The museum itself has a couple of interesting paintings and a room dedicated to Dante which contains the *Virgin and Child* by Lippo Memmi.

In another tower, there is a bizarre place known as the *Museo della Tortura (Torture Museum)*. There are devices to suit all persuasions. Not quite so bizarre is *San Gimignano 1300* (via San Giovanni), a museum that offers a beautiful, large, and super detailed miniature reconstruction of medieval San Gimignano in 1300.

There is also a model reconstruction of the convent of San Francesco which was completely destroyed in the 16th century by Florentine forces, and scenes of daily medieval life.

From Piazza del Duomo, crossing Piazza delle Erbe on the right side of the church, you can climb towards Rocca di Montestaffoli. This was originally a castle of the Lombard Astolfo, built by the Florentines in 1353, which later became a Dominican Convent.

The Piazza Sant'Agostino in the northern part of the town is one of the most interesting squares of the town. The small Church of San Pietro is located next to the large building which is the Convento di Sant'Agostino. This contains some good paintings, an impressive altar, and several large fresco cycles. The 17-panel *Life of St. Augustine* around the high altar provides a good record of life in Renaissance Italy.

It is possible to walk along the perimeter (2,176 m) of the second circle of the city walls (13th century) that delimit the historical center of San Gimignano. This walking tour, has different access points, and provides lovely views of the scenic surrounding hills and the Elsa valley beyond.

There are literally scores of walled villages in this area. Some seem almost unchanged for centuries. **Colle Val d' Elsa** or more specifically

Colle Alta (http://www.italythisway.com/places/colle-di-val-d-elsa.php) is one of these. This is the walled upper town situated above the much less interesting Colle Bassa. A lift will take you from Colle Bassa to a terrace where you can enjoy a breathtaking view of the lower part of the city, the Tuscan hills, and countryside.

Via del Castello is the main street and along here we see the small 12th-century Romanesque church of Santa Maria in Canonica and the Duomo. There is a marble pulpit, a bronze lectern, an impressive bronze crucifix, and what is supposedly a nail from the Cross.

Monteriggioni (http://www.monteriggioni.info/) is another interesting town to the east. The 14 towers and preserved original walls are from the early 13th century. Its perfectly circular perimeter was created by just following the curves in the natural ground. The town is immortalized in Dante's *Inferno* and the scene today is little different.

As you turn off the main road to enter Monteriggioni, you'll find a parking lot at the bottom of the hill. It's best to leave your car here and walk the short climb to enter the small village through the Franca or Roma Gate. Inside there is almost no traffic and the buildings are for the most part original and attractive. The main piazza, the Piazza Roma, is dominated by a Romanesque church with a simple, plain façade.

The "Festa Medievale" of Monteriggioni takes place on the first weekend of July. This is one of the most famous medieval pageants in Italy. Local people dressed in medieval costume display ancient arts and crafts while magicians, ballad singers, jesters, jugglers, and acrobats entertain. Medieval dishes and drinks are available. Unfortunately, at this time (and most days from April to October) the town is crowded with day trippers.

This immediate region is one for self-exploring. Each of the villages has its own charm and wandering around is the best way to see them. Allow plenty of time as there is much to see.

Siena

Approaching Siena (http://www.discovertuscany.com/siena/), it is clear that this is the largest town we have seen since leaving Florence. It spreads over three hills and in the center of the medieval city there is something special about it. The locals like to claim that theirs is the most perfect medieval city in the world, and they may be right. It is a center of art and music and provides a taste of unspoiled Italy.

The Piazza del Campo is the heart of Siena and where the Roman Forum used to be. It is stunning and we linger longer than we intended. Siena had the wisdom to keep cars out of here so it retains its timeless feel. Each piazza we see in northern Italy reminds us of a theater or a living room where life is portrayed in the raw and this is very much the case here.

It is where the young and old, rich and poor, energetic and sick come together then dissipate without trouble or strife. During the day and early evening, a piazza can be bright and lively then at night the tables, chairs, and potted plants of the cafés stand silent and untroubled.

The Piazza del Campo is surrounded by several old palaces of which the Palazzo Pubblico is the most interesting. This palace, built between 1297 and 1310, still houses the city's municipal offices much like Palazzo Vecchio in Florence. Its internal courtyard has entrances to the Torre del Mangia and to the *Civic Museum* (http://www.aboutsiena.com/museums-in-Siena.html), and within is some of the most fascinating frescos (from the 1330s) we have seen.

The Sala del Mappamondo and the Sale della Pace hold the palaces' highlights: Simone Martini's huge *Maestà* and *Equestrian Portrait of Guidoriccio da Fogliano*, and Ambrogio Lorenzetti's murals *Allegories of Good and Bad Government*, once considered the most important cycle of secular paintings of the Middle Ages. The murals cover three of the four walls of the Council Room.

The museum gives access to the Torre del Mangia (https://www.discovertuscany.com/siena/tower-of-mangia.html) which even today dominates Siena's skyline. There are over 400 steps to reach the top of the 80-meter tower and to see the city and the surrounding countryside spread out around us.

We are impressed. The tower was obviously not built with tourists in mind, so the narrow stairways with irregular heights can be a bit of a challenge.

The view shows us that Siena has several other attractions so we head for nearby Piazza San Giovanni where the **cathedral** (http://www.operaduomo.siena.it/eng/index.htm) dominates proceedings. The building is an original from the 12th and 13th-centuries and it is dramatic and stunning. It has been called an architectural fantasy and it's easy to see why.

Its colored bands of marble combined with lacy pinnacles, sculptures, and pointy arches make this a unique building. The striped interior, art covered floor, and octagonal pulpit all impress. It is quite a while since a building has made this impact on us. We pay to visit the richly adorned cathedral library and admire some well-preserved frescos.

The adjacent Baptistery is renowned for its lavish and intricate frescos and the baptismal font which is sometimes called the greatest in Italy.

Even better in our mind is the *Museo dell'Opera Metropolitan* which houses paintings and sculptures originally created for the cathedral and surrounds.

We see Duccio's *La Maesta* from 1310 which is considered to be one of Europe's greatest late-medieval paintings. There are several other museums but as the day is now well gone it's time to find a hotel room and stay the night.

Located in front of the Duomo, **Santa Maria della Scala** (http://www.santamariadellascala.com/w2d3/v3/view/sms2/complesso --24/index_en.html) was built in the 9th century. It was one of the first hospitals in Europe, taking care of pilgrims, and poor and sick people.

Today, it is being restored as a museum hosting a wonderful collection of artworks, frescoes, decorated chapels, temporary exhibitions, and underground tunnels. Work is still in progress but it is worth dropping by to see what is on display.

There are several other churches to see and three or four worthwhile museums. One is near the town walls on the west called the Basilica of San Doménico (http://www.basilicacateriniana.com/index_en.htm). It is a severe brick building in Cistercian Gothic style. Originally built in 1226, it was subsequently much altered and enlarged. The church has an aisle-less nave with an enclosed rectangular choir and a surprisingly high and spacious transept.

Another is *Pinacoteca Nationale* (Palazzo Buonsignori, via San Pietro 29) (http://www.discovertuscany.com/siena/what-to-do/pinacoteca-siena.html) in a lovely building containing some masterpieces by Sienese masters.

Fortezza Medicea is a fort built in the northern part of the city between 1561 and 1563. The fortress is a substantial structure with an entrance on the north-east side. The wide walls are topped with broad paths, lined with trees and benches. A permanent theater-shaped structure has been created within the walls and this is used for concerts and other events.

One of the reasons for staying is to visit the *Enoteca Italica Permanente* inside the Fortezza Medicea, a place which showcases Italian wines in a dramatic architectural setting. Much of the structure was built in the 1560s but today it is a thoroughly up-to-date tasting setting. During the day there are several terraces for wine tasting and in the evening, there is a wonderful stand-up bar with wine for sale by the bottle or glass. There is also a restaurant and wine school.

Siena is well known for its **Palio** horse race which is held in the Piazza Dei Campo twice a year on July 2 and August 16. This is probably the most exciting festival in Italy and it draws tens of thousands of visitors to the town. Days of preparation, pageantry, and excitement precede the actual race. On the day, there is a parade of drummers and flag carriers in bright costumes then the horses race around the square three times.

Securing a hotel room in Siena can be a problem during the peak tourist season so booking ahead is advised (see recommended hotels in chapter 13). The city is not particularly known for its restaurants but La Taverna di San Giuseppe (Via Giovanni Dupre 132), Antica Osteria da Divo (Via Franciosa 25-29) near the cathedral, and Antica Salumeria Salvini (SS 73 Ponente, 46) near Piazza del Campo have all passed the taste test in the past.

Via Camollia is a charming street located a bit away from the crowded streets around Piazza del Campo, but still within walking distance of it. Here you will find several recommended restaurants, all serving local dishes. In the summer, they have tables outside and prices are very reasonable; for around €25 you can eat two dishes, and drink some wine and water.

You might like to try beef from the special *Chianina* breed of cattle, *pici* which is pasta with toasted breadcrumbs, *fagioli all'uccelletto* a bean and sausage stew, and *pasta e fagioli* a meatless pasta with beans. The city is noted for its cakes and biscuits such as *panforte* a delicious wedge of nuts, fruit and honey; *ricciarelli* which are rich almond biscuits; and *cantucci* which is somewhat similar.

This is about as far south as we will go, so we make off to the east towards Cortona and Arezzo. Rather than go straight there we wander through the claylands to the south-east.

Ignore the industrial suburbs as you approach the old walled town of **Buonconvento** (http://www.turismo.intoscana.it/allthingstuscany/aroundtuscany/buo nconvento-one-of-the-most-beautiful-villages-of-italy/) with its excellent *Museo d'Arte Sacra* as it makes a good first stop. The museum contains a collection of works of art removed from local churches.

The heart of the historical center is Via Soccini, where most restaurants, cafés, the church, the town hall, and the *Religious Art Museum* are located. Though partially destroyed in WWII, the little town is almost completely surrounded by walls built from 1371. Amongst the other sights worth seeing are a large number of fine Liberty-style noble houses.

Buonconvento is just 25 kilometers south-east of Siena and is easily reached by train. The trip takes around 25 minutes and trains leave approximately every hour from the station in Siena. From the train station in Buonconvento, you can walk to the historical center in just 5 minutes.

Then it's off through oak and pine forests to the abbey of **Monte Oliveto Maggiore** (http://www.monte-oliveto.com/). This was founded in the early 14th-century and you can still see the marvelous fresco cycle in the cloister and visit the famous library. An imposing square tower with a drawbridge stands at the entrance and the courtyard opens onto a broad avenue of cypresses. This leads to the impressively austere, late-gothic church.

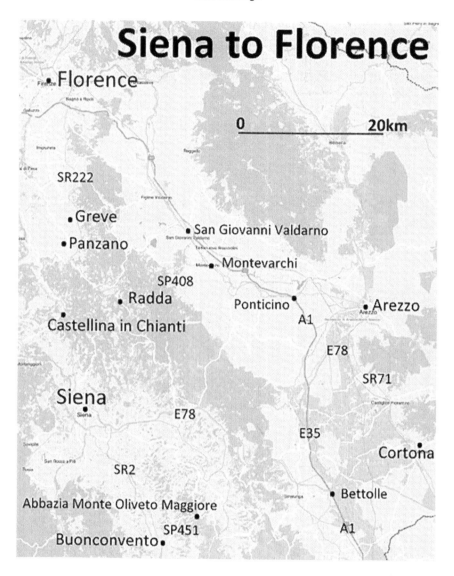

The rectangular Chiostro Grande is the most impressive of the abbey's cloisters, constructed between 1426 and 1443. It is made up of two passages, one above the other, supported by columns.

The country to the east is flat and not particularly attractive but it does allow the hill towns to really stand out. This is certainly the case with

Cortina which is approached by a winding road through vines terraces and olive trees.

Cortona

Charming Cortona (http://www.cortona.com/), enclosed by stone walls, became very popular because of the book and film "*Under the Tuscan Sun*". Now in summer, Cortona can be a town overflowing with camera-toting tourists achieving a tourist per square meter concentration equal to Florence. At other times it is a quiet and meditative hillside gem.

The Etruscan tombs on the flatland below the town are our first stop. I must confess that my knowledge of these people, until my first trip to northern Italy, was limited to the fact that they preceded the Romans. Now I at least know that this civilization endured from about 800 B.C. until its assimilation into the Roman Republic in the 1st-century B.C. The origins of the Etruscans are murky but it is likely that they were indigenous people from this Tuscany region.

We climb the hill, gently at first, then in a series of switchbacks. Rather than trying to take your car into the center of town, I strongly recommend that you leave it in one of the parking areas just outside the old city walls.

The center is built around the main square of Piazza della Repubblica (http://www.discovertuscany.com/cortona/) which is overlooked by the Palazzo Comunale with its 24 broad stone steps. The steps serve as ringside seats for watching life on the piazza. The town seems to have a jumble of uneven buildings which somehow add to its charm. The absence of cars amazingly restores human importance and multiculturalism is alive and well here.

The *Diocesan Museum* (http://www.cortonaweb.net/en/museums/diocesan-museum) which displays a beautiful *Annunciation of Cortona* by Beato Angelico is a 'must-see', and so too is the *Museum of the Etruscan Academy* (Palazzo Casali, Piazza Signorelli)

(http://www.cortonaweb.net/en/museums/cortona-maec-museum-01)
that holds important Etruscan and Roman findings. The museum is laid
out over 4 floors of the palace including two below ground that were
once used as prisons.

The collections of the Accademia Etrusca are housed in the upper floors.
There are numerous books, manuscripts, ancient finds, art, and
handicraft objects which make up the collection. Among the highlights is
a magnificent Etruscan bronze chandelier.

Cortona Cathedral was built over the remains of an ancient Roman
temple and it existed in the 11th century. It was the seat of the Bishops
of Cortona from 1507 to 1986. Santa Maria Nuova, built in 1554, is a
domed church with a centralized Greek cross layout. The church is in
poor condition, and the interior is not open to visitors.

Many tourists never get to the higher neighborhoods in Cortona
although they are some of the best places to explore. Following the
path that follows the city walls, you can also enjoy a beautiful view over
the surrounding countryside. Don't miss the church of Santa Margherita
(http://www.en.cortonaguide.com/chiesa_di_santa_margherita.html),
where you can see the body of the saint in a glass case. The stone fort
up above the church is the Medici Fortezza, one of the many Medici
fortresses that were built in the Middle Ages.

Cortona has a large ex-pat British community so there is more English
spoken here than other places in rural Tuscany and we meet a few of
them in a local wine bar. Great red wines are made in the area and we
taste some made from the local *sangiovese* grape. Cortona is also home
to the Tuscan dessert wine *vin santo*.

There are some nice restaurants in town. Trattoria Tacconi (Via Dardano
46) is a true family-run trattoria with about six tables which opens for
lunch from Tuesday to Sunday. La Bucaccia (Via Ghibellina 17) with its
tasteful interior and good food is great for dinner and the owner speaks
excellent English. Trattoria La Grotta (Piazza Baldelli, 3) is one of the

best restaurants in Cortona with homemade pastas, and other great food. It opens for lunch and dinner.

Cooking classes, wine tours and tastings, and food tours are all available here. An excellent range of vacation accommodations is available, ranging from rental villas, through agritourism, to fine hotels, and Bed & Breakfasts.

The **Tuscan Sun Festival**, held in Cortona every year usually during August, has classical music concerts, art exhibitions, etc. The **Cortonantiquaria** is one of the most important antique furniture fairs in Europe. The exhibition is housed in the 17 C Palazzo Vagnotti, located in the old town center and is held in the last week of August and the first week of September.

Five kilometers from the town is the Franciscan hermitage of Le Celle, the first monastery built by Saint Francis of Assisi in 1211. A small community of friars still lives here today. Saint Francis's small cell has been conserved in its original state and can be visited.

Back towards Florence

Arezzo (http://www.italia.it/en/discover-italy/tuscany/arezzo.html) to the north was established by the Etruscans, maintained its pre-eminence under the Roman, expanded during the Middle Ages but was then taken over by Florence in 1348 and it has never been the same since. It has not been helped by the bombing which occurred during World War II.

The old inner core looks somewhat run-down but Piazza Grande is still impressive with its palaces and towers. Arezzo is one of the wealthiest cities in Tuscany and my wife is tempted by the antique and gold shops.

Walking through gardens to the nearby cathedral (http://www.visitarezzo.com/visit-churches-cathedral-arezzo-domenico-cimabue-san-francesco-annunziata-maria-gradi), which is in

Gothic style, is charming. It was started in the 13th-century but was still being worked on in the early 20th-century.

Like all the churches in these parts, it contains paintings and other treasures considered masterpieces by experts. Off to the north-west, the Church of San Domenico has a wooden Crucifix by Cimabue and some gorgeous early 14th century frescoes.

The highlight of Arezzo, however, is another church, Basilica San Francesca (http://goitaly.about.com/od/arezzo/qt/piero-della-francesca-frescoes-arezzo.htm). This was finished in the 14th century and it contains a restored fresco cycle by Piero della Francesca. Unfortunately, we don't get to see this because it has become so popular that you have to make reservations to get in. Each group of 20 is allowed 30 minutes to enjoy the experience.

You should then head uphill to the Medicean Fortress then back down to the remains of the elliptic sandstone and marble Roman Amphitheatre where the 16th-century Monastery of S. Bernardo and the *Archaeological Museum* were built on the remains of the southern semi-circle.

We are now heading back to Florence through the **Chianti region**. This region has green hills covered by vineyards and olive groves, ancient walled villages, and panoramic roads curving into the distance. **Radda** (http://www.chianti.com/radda-in-chianti/) with its ancient walls and its maze-like streets preserves its original medieval look.

The Palazzo del Podestà and the Romanesque Church of S. Niccolò overlook the main square. There is much history here as the Palazzo was the headquarters of the League of Chianti for over four centuries. The ancient Franciscan Cloister of S. Maria in Prato is another building worth seeing.

Radda is a great place for wandering the medieval streets and stopping for a glass of wine but you can see how middle-class tourism is having an influence on the town in both facilities and prices.

There are many wineries and farms that produce good Chianti wine in this region and you see the vineyard-covered hills surrounding the town. We particular enjoy Chianti's intense color and pronounced taste at some of the small estates that only supply within Italy. Most wineries offer local products and wine tastings.

Further west, **Castellina** (http://www.chianti.com/castellina-in-chianti/) is an ancient town. Its position in the middle of the Chianti region between Florence and Siena made it a strategic center in the past. A massive castle dominates the town offering panoramic views, and a fascinating complex of subterranean Etruscan burial chambers is a short walk from the town center.

Walking through the small town we notice many historical buildings. A highlight is the *Archaeological Museum of Chianti Senese* (http://www.castellina-in-chianti.net/what-to-see-and-do/) with its archaeological finds from the Chianti region and Etruscan findings from Montecalvario. Before leaving, we do a wine tasting in a wine bar accompanied by the unforgettable taste of fresh and aged salami and cold cuts. Yum!

Panzano (http://www.panzano-in-chianti.info/) has played an important defensive role for Florence since the 12th-century and it is now the most populous town in Chianti. The Castle of Panzano was fundamental to this and although the castle is now in private hands the courtyard and the surroundings can be visited. The houses along the downhill road have a medieval character.

The Church of Santa Maria, which stands next to the castle, was completely rebuilt in the 19th-century on the site of an ancient church, but it possesses a small 14th-century Senese *Madonna and Child* attributed to Botticini.

Several wine bars and restaurants in Panzano offer wine tasting and we recommend this as the local wines are excellent. You should also visit the Antica Macelleria Cecchini, a butcher shop famous for its Florentine steak where the owner entertains customers by reciting passages from Dante's *Divine Comedy*.

Dario Cecchini has opened a restaurant, named Ristorante Solociccia ("Only Meat") across the road from his butcher shop. It has a fixed price menu and most customers sit at communal tables. It has been so successful that he has since opened others nearby.

Only two kilometers from Panzano, the Panzanello Estate has been producing wine since 1427 and we can confirm it still produces excellent Chianti that can be tasted along with delicious appetizers after the tour of the wine cellars.

Greve (http://www.chianti.com/greve-in-chianti/) is a lively town famous for its triangle-shaped square that has been a market place for the surrounding castles and walled villages since the Middle Ages. The attractive square with porticos along three sides has a bronze statue of Giovanni da Verrazzano, the explorer that discovered the Bay of New York. Every Saturday morning the weekly market still takes place here.

The Church of S. Croce, originally a medieval church, has been remodeled in Renaissance Revival architectural style. The *Wine Museum* within the Le Cantine di Greve wine shop makes a good visit and you can learn more about the history of wine in this region while enjoying a tasting.

Just three kilometers from Greve stands the ancient Castello di Vicchiomaggio (http://www.vicchiomaggio.it/eng/index.html), a castle surrounded by 130 hectares of picturesque vineyards. The Castello offers custom-made wine tasting tours upon request.

5 VENICE AND AROUND

Put simply, **Venice** is perhaps the world's most enchanting city. This place that shouldn't even exist delights millions of visitors each year with a magic that can be found nowhere else on earth. In some respects, however, it is a place where fantasy looms larger than reality. Venice's great landmarks are for many people the stuff of dreams and romance.

Grand Canal

I admit I was seduced by Venice even before I arrived here for the first time and that visit is still firmly in my memory. Subsequent visits have generally been good and the city's appeal grows as I learn more about its hidden quarters.

The city was built here out of a need for security. It was protected by the lagoon and this also gave it political stability which led to riches, trade, and conservatism.

It is not just the architecture, the palaces, the bridges, and the general splendor that make Venice special. It is a combination of these with water, light, and color added that impresses just about everyone who visits.

But all is not necessarily rosy when you visit Venice. In the height of summer, hordes of tourists overwhelm the squares and crowd the streets making walking at times quite difficult. If you take to the water you will find yourself on overcrowded ferries or paying a fortune for a private motorboat or a gondola.

In winter, the rain, mist, cold winds, and high seas can make everything dank and depressed, turning every bridge into a bridge of sighs and making seeing the city a nightmare at times. It is all the times in between that make this one of my favorite places in all of Europe.

Venice lies four kilometers from the Italian mainland and is connected to it by the Ponte della Liberta. When arriving by train or car you cross this causeway/bridge but then you can't go any further. Here are the parking garages and this is where the railway station (Stazione di Santa Lucia) is located. While many people think of Venice as being an island, the city actually occupies an archipelago of 118 islands.

Venice has more than 150 canals which act as water streets. These are spanned by 400 bridges. The Grand Canal, which snakes through the city, is the main street. This cuts the main town into two and there are only four bridges linking the two halves.

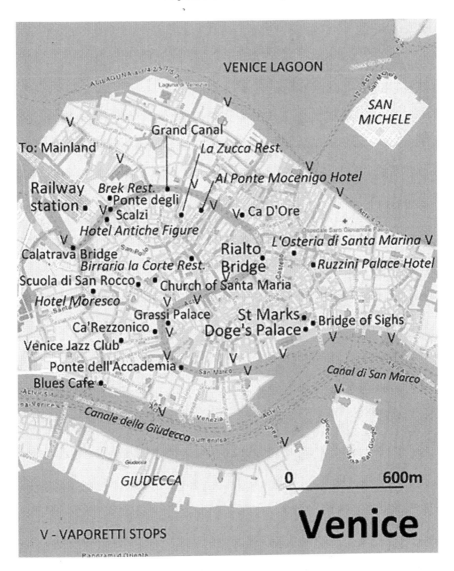

None of this is important at first to most visitors because they just want to reach Piazza San Marco. You can do this by water buses or on foot. **St.** **Mark's** **Square** (http://www.italyguides.it/us/venice_italy/st_mark_s_square/piazza_sa n_marco/st_mark_s_square.htm) is the center of Venice. It was the heart of the city in its seafaring days and today it draws tourists like no other place. This area is so interesting that you can spend a whole day here.

The piazza is dominated by St. Mark's Basilica, one of the world's greatest churches. Just outside is the reconstructed bell tower, the tallest structure in Venice, built after the original collapsed in 1902. Around the corner is the Doge's Palace with its famous Bridge of Sighs.

The square has many expensive cafés with their competing orchestras. By day, it's great for people-watching and pigeon-chasing. By night, under lantern light, it becomes a different world.

We find it difficult to know where to start when we first reach here. We arrive from Merceria, a main pathway that leads through shopping streets from the Rialto, the commercial and financial center. We pass the clock tower, completed in 1499, above a high archway.

Two bronze "Moors" stand at the top of the Clock Tower and each hour they swing their giant clappers. The elaborate clock dial shows the 24 hours, the signs of the zodiac, and the phases of the moon.

Now the square is before us. There is a long arcade along the north, west, and part of the south side of the Piazza with shops and restaurants at ground level. On the west, behind the shops, a ceremonial staircase forms the entrance to the *Museo Correr* (http://correr.visitmuve.it/en/home/), the Civic Museum of Venice.

This museum seems almost ignored by visitors but there is an immense collection and some interesting art. It is also the main entrance to the *Archaeological Museum*. This has coins and statues from the 4th and 5th-centuries BC, Greek and Roman sculpture, and Latin epigraphs. There are also impressive displays of finds from the Egyptian and Assyrian civilizations.

Continuing anti-clockwise, the building around the corner is the Bibliotheca Marciana or National Library, started in 1537 and designed to hold a collection of classical texts which had been given to the city. The arcade continues to the end of the building with cafés and shops and here is the entrance to the library, which occupies the floors above.

It is worth visiting the main hall where paintings cover the walls and ceiling. The anteroom has been restored to its 16th century glory and Titian's *Allegory of Wisdom* is on the center panel of the ceiling. At the end of the library building there are two large granite columns which are thought to have been erected in the 13th century.

St. Marks Basilica (http://www.basilicasanmarco.it/eng/index.bsm) is stunning with a façade that is rich and dramatic. There are round, Roman-style arches over the doorways, golden Byzantine mosaics, a roofline ringed with pointed pinnacles, and five Middle Eastern onion domes.

It is probably the most lavishly decorated church in the world. The interior and the multiple domes are encrusted with gold-backed mosaics crafted between the 12th and 17th centuries.

The baptistery alcove with its famous font and the presbytery with its *Pala d'Oro,* a gem-studded golden trophy altar from Constantinople, are both superb. Above the church proper is the *Marciano Museum* and this gets you up onto a balcony and affords you a close-up look at some of the mosaics.

It also houses the original *Triumphal Quadriga* of four horses which came from the Hippodrome in Constantinople, replicas of which now stride across the façade of the church. These life-size bronze equines are one of Venice's treasures.

The cathedral gets extremely crowded during the height of the tourist season and the authorities will try to shuffle you through as fast as possible. If you attend the Sunday 6:45 p.m. mass you will have more time to see the awesome sight of all those mosaics. We spend as long as allowed in the basilica before going next door to the Palazzo Ducale.

You enter through the impressive 15th century Porta della Carta into the splendid courtyard. No books, movies, paintings, or fantasizing had prepared me for what I have just seen and that feeling continues in the palace.

The **Palazzo Ducale**, or **Doge's Palace** (http://palazzoducale.visitmuve.it/en/home/), was the government building and the home of the Doge (the elected ruler of Venice) for centuries but it also contained the law courts, the civil administration and bureaucracy, and the city jail.

We walk up the Giants Stairway in anticipation of seeing some of the palace's greatest paintings. Here is the *Museo dell'Opera*, and the Scala d'Oro, or golden staircase.

This leads us to a succession of rooms from the 16th century. These contain masterpieces by Veronese, Titian, and Tintoretto. Most impressive is Tintoretto's massive *Paradise* in the Hall of the Grand Council which is said to be the largest oil painting in the world. While here we marvel at the marble floor and the frieze of paintings of 75 of the first 76 doges.

The 1602 Ponte dei Sospiri (**Bridge of Sighs**), leads to the city's 'new' prison. Casanova was one of the famous prisoners to cross this bridge in an earlier time. The prison cells are located in the basement of the building, and the feeling here is gloomy and cold. There is a café within the palace if you need a drink or some lunch.

The 'Secret Itinerary Tour' is rated as excellent by most people. This gets you past the long line outside, and more than that gives you access to the secret chambers of the bureaucracy where you hear of their vast spy network.

You'll see the lead-lined cells where Casanova was held and from which he famously escaped, the torture chamber, the Chancellery Hall, and Inquisitor's Room. You then have free access to the rest of the palace.

Elsewhere in the city, there are some other magical places. There are four 'must see' sights across the Grand Canal and we now head there by a round-about route through the back alleys of San Marco. We pretty much retrace our steps to the **Church of San Salvador** (http://www.chiesasansalvador.it/eng/presentazione.php).

This was consecrated in 1177 but the present façade is from the 17th century and the interior from the 16th century. The church contains two pieces by Titian and many of the paintings are dedicated to saints.

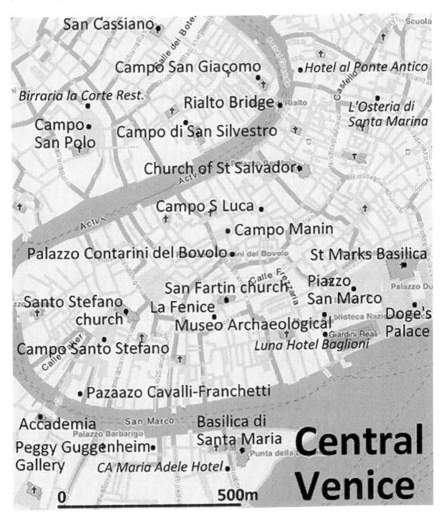

By walking south-west past the front of the church you come to Campo San Luca. This popular social center has several fast-food outlets but there is little to hold us here and we walk on to Campo Manin. The attraction here is the **Palazzo Contarini del Bovolo** (http://www.comune.venezia.it/flex/cm/pages/ServeBLOB.php/L/EN/ID Pagina/175) but we are having difficulty finding it. We are eventually pointed in the right direction and find the flamboyant external staircase as interesting as expected.

It takes us some navigating to reach nearby Campo San Fantin with its graceful church of San Fantin. The square is dominated, however, by **La Fenice** (http://www.teatrolafenice.it/site/index.php?&lingua=eng), Venice's oldest and largest theater. It may be old but what you see today is actually a new version along the lines of the original from 1792 and the rebuilt version from 1836.

It appears to me that the designers and builders have succeeded in recreating the ambiance of the old theater and have constructed one of the most elaborate and beautiful theaters in the world.

There are several ways to reach the bridge to the Accademia and we decide to just wander and walk down alleys and through several squares until finally reaching Campo Santo Stefano. This is a large space closed at one end by the Church of Santo Stefano.

At the other end, the square is closed off by **Palazzo Franchetti-Cavalli**, now home to the Instituto Veneto di Scienze and past this is the bridge to take us across the Grand Canal to the Dorsoduro area.

Many of Venice's greatest paintings are still in their original buildings but the most important art gallery, the **Accademia** (www.gallerieaccademia.it/en), is still worth a visit. Tickets cost €15 if you are over 18 (November 2018).

Be aware, however, that this is a very popular spot and admissions are restricted. In summer, you need to book ahead by email or telephone. The gallery is in the former church of Santa Maria della Carita and the adjoining school.

Every reader will find their own favorites but the small paintings in rooms 4 and 5 are acknowledged as some of the finest in the collection. Giorgione's *Tempesta*, depicting a naked mother and child sheltering by the ruins of an ancient city is fascinating but resists our interpretation.

The larger canvases by Titian, Tintoretto, and Veronese in room 10 should not be missed either. Veronese's *Feast in the House of Levi,* which was originally painted as *The Last Supper* is outstanding.

I am fascinated to discover the beautiful San Giobbe altarpiece where a statuesque Madonna sits with a child above a collection of saints and angels beneath a coffered ceiling with columns and a half dome. This was produced by Giovanni Bellini, the teacher of both Giorbione and Titian. Bellini revolutionized Venetian painting by creating rich tints, and detailed shadings in his work while still using classical composition.

While in this area, don't fail to see the **Peggy Guggenheim collection** (http://www.guggenheim-venice.it/inglese/default.html) of modern art, probably the most distinguished in Italy. The wealthy American heiress and generous benefactor built up her collection mainly in the 1940s.

She bought the Palazzo Venier dei Leoni in 1948 and lived there surrounded by the paintings until her death in 1979. On passing, she left her estate to the Solomon Guggenheim Foundation.

The collection is wide-ranging, with works by artists such as Pollock, Picasso, Kandinsky, and Dalí. The sculpture garden with its lovely views over the Grand Canal is particularly enjoyable. Admission is €15 adults, €13 seniors and €9 children (November 2018).

It is quite a walk from here north-west to the 1330s glorious Gothic **Church of Santa Maria Gloriosa dei Frari** (http://www.sacred-destinations.com/italy/venice-santa-maria-gloriosa-dei-frari), where Titian, one of Venice's most famous painters, is buried. One of his best works is the huge altar piece, *The Assumption of the Virgin*, painted in 1518.

Later, he painted the *Madonna di Ca' Pesaro*, another masterpiece which also hangs here. Apart from these, there are various other works by Donatello, Bellini, Vittoria, and others.

Close by, the **School of St Roch** (http://www.scuolagrandesanrocco.org/home-en/) is famous for a series of canvases by Tintoretto. The school was founded in 1478, and Tintoretto won a commission to decorate the entire Scuola in 1564. He spent the next 23 years doing so.

Large paintings with scenes from the life of Christ are on the ground floor together with his *Flight into Egypt* which is superb. In the Sala dell'Albergo we are confronted with the stunning wall-wrapping expanse of the *Crucifixion*, one of the world's great works of art. There are more Tintoretto paintings in the neighboring church of San Rocco.

The **Grand Canal** is an ancient waterway 3,800 meters long that ranges from 30 to 90 meters wide. It is lined with buildings that were mostly built from the 13th to the 18th-centuries. Most were constructed by wealthy Venetian families. The canal is justifiably one of the greatest visitor attractions in Venice and you need to travel its length to fully appreciate its majesty.

Many tourists time their visit to correspond to when the glorious past of Venice returns once a year to the Grand Canal during the historic Regata

Storica on the first Sunday of September. The first of these regattas was held here in the 14th century. The races are preceded by a spectacular boat parade.

Three famous bridges cross the canal: the **Rialto Bridge** (http://www.italyguides.it/us/venice_italy/rialto_bridge_venice.htm), the Ponte Degli Scalzi, and the Ponte dell'Accademia while The Calatrava, a modern bridge, has been added not far from the Scalzi Bridge. Venice was originally located on Rialto Island. In the 10th-century, a market developed on an adjacent island and eventually the first wooden bridge linking the two islands was built.

This collapsed in 1444. It was replaced in 1588, by Antonio da Ponte's stone arched bridge we see today. It is lined with tiny tourist-related shops. Until 1854, this was the only bridge across the Grand Canal.

In 1420, Venice's most magnificent palazzo, originally known as the Palazzo Santa Sofia but now commonly known as the **Ca' d'Oro** (House of Gold) (http://www.cadoro.org/?lang=en), was built. The principal façade faces the Grand Canal and is one of the most photographed buildings along the waterway. Ca' d'Oro is open to the public as a gallery.

It houses an extensive art collection, which features works by Venetian artists as well as a number of non-Venetian artists such as van Eyck and van Dyck. Interestingly, contemporary works are exhibited alongside Renaissance classics. Entry for those over 18 is €8.50 (November 2018).

Another palazzo fronting the Grand Canal is the marble **Ca' Rezzonico** (http://carezzonico.visitmuve.it/en/home/). This has been turned into a museum of the 18th-century, the age of Casanova and costume balls. The city has outfitted this gracious palace as an actual house from the era using pieces culled from across the city. In addition to collections of antique furniture, there is also a fine collection of Venetian glass. Entry is €10 adults and €7.50 for children and seniors (November 2018).

Palazzo Grassi (Campo San Samuele 3231) (http://www.palazzograssi.it/en/) was the last palace built on the Grand Canal before the collapse of the Republic of Venice in 1797. It presents major temporary modern art exhibitions, some of which are based in whole or in part on the Pinault Collection.

The walk here from the Accademia Bridge is one of the most pleasant in Venice as you quickly leave the tourist path and zigzag through a wonderful antique district. These water-lapped palaces are just as you see them in the brochures.

Venice is a relatively expensive city to visit but most of the sights of the main city can be seen by walking. We particularly enjoy walking at night when the streets are almost empty. One evening, we twist and turn through the labyrinth of laneways catching glimpses of secret canals, seeing small treasures in the street lights that we would miss in the day time, and glimpsing home life through rare un-shuttered windows.

We are transfixed as street lamps throw strange shadows across alley walls and we watch our wavering reflection in a small canal below a narrow footbridge. Time and place become blurred.

The original Venice Card is no longer available. It has been replaced by the **Venezia Unica** (https://www.veneziaunica.it/en/e-commerce/services) , an all-in-one pass to use for public transportation, admission to tourist attractions, and cultural events in the city. There are a range of options starting with a card to give access to Museums and Churches of Venice from €21.90. It can be a good buy if you plan on extensive sightseeing. You can buy your Venezia Unica City Pass online or at one of the many Points of Sale and Collection in the city. There is no price difference.

There are also **Tourist Travel Cards** that are good for all for most all normal ACTV vaporetto (water bus) services around the Venetian lagoon, including out to Murano, Burano, Torcello, Guidecca, and the Lido, and ACTV urban bus services in Mestre, and on the Lido. The cost of these depends on the length of time; €20 for a 1-day travelcard, €30 for 2 days, €40 for 3 days, and €60 for 7 days (November 2018).

The **Lido** (http://www.venicelido.it/) is a 12 km long sand island a 20-minute aqaubus ride from the city itself. There are impressive views of the city from across the lagoon The Lido, unlike the main area of Venice, has cars. Much of the Adriatic Sea side of the island has a sandy beach but some of this belongs to the various hotels.

The heart of the island is the Gran Viale Santa Maria Elisabetta, a wide street that leads from the lagoon on one side to the sea on the other. It is flanked by hotels, shops, and tourist-centric restaurants. At the seaside end, you can follow the sea promenade north to the public beach or south to Alberoni Oasis, following the Murazzi path.

The impressive looking Tempio Votivo Church next to the Vaporetto station is a war memorial. It was built between 1925 and 1935 and was designed to show the gratitude of the Venetians that the city escaped the First World War without major damage

There are hundreds of hotels and resorts on the Lido. Some are very expensive but many of them are quite reasonable in cost compared to Venice itself. This quiet island is full of family run restaurants and stores and we actually see locals walking down the streets and sitting in the cafés. Trattoria Andri, (Via Lepanto 21) is a popular seafood restaurant where you can dine on the terrace.

I suggest that you rent a bike from one of the numerous shops at the Gran Viale and explore the island. Alternatively, just stroll along the quiet, shaded streets, people watch, and window shop. You can partake in golf and tennis, as Lido is more about relaxed leisure than frantic tourist activities. The Oasis of Alberoni is a protected natural reserve, located on the south end of The Lido island. This consists of a pine forest and a complex dune system.

Malamocco is a picturesque village located at the southern part of Lido. It is an island on its own, connected to Lido by a series of bridges. The most prominent landmarks include the Church of Santa Maria Assunta, Ponte Borgo (the oldest bridge in the village), and Palazzo del Podestà, where the mayors of Malamocco lived until 1339.

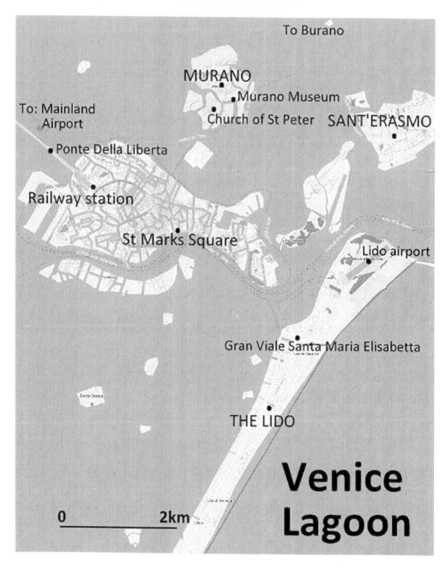

Thousands of people come to the Lido on the first week in September for the Venice Film Festival. The festival was started in 1932 and is the oldest of its kind. Venice, Cannes, and Berlin, are now the big three film festivals around the world. Palazzo del Cinema is the main screening theater of the event.

Murano is a small island situated north-east of Venice city, about 15-20 minutes away by water bus. It was a commercial port as far back as the 7th century, and by the 10th century it had grown into a prosperous trading center with its own coins. Then the Venetian Republic ordered glassmakers to move their foundries to Murano because the glassworks represented a fire danger in Venice.

Murano glass became famous and the glass-blowing industry profited. Murano is still an exporter of traditional products like mirrors and glassware but there's a growing emphasis on art glass and the souvenir trade. There are a few places that give free glass blowing demonstrations.

If you are keen on glassware, you should visit *Museo Vetrario*, where you can do a tour of Venetian glassmaking over the centuries. The city-owned museum is located in the Palazzo Giustinian near the island's center. It has samples of glass from Egyptian times through to the present day.

We have lunch on Murano in the courtyard of the Chiesa di San Pietro Martire, on the Campiello Michieli, and for the first time in Venice, we feel we are with locals. The church was first built in 1437, reconstructed in 1509 after a fire, and decorated with paintings by artists such as Veronese, Giovanni Bellini, and Bartolomeo Letterini.

We now move on to **Burano**, the most picturesque of the lagoon islands. The island can be recognized from a distance by the tall, tilted tower of its San Martino church. Walking through the brightly painted fishing village and around the waterways, you see lots of little fishing boats. Piazza Galuppi is where the San Martino Bishop's Church is located. In the same square, there is the *Museo del Merletto* (Lace Museum), the Town Hall, and a well.

Burano is famous for its lace. In the 16th century, Burano's lace was the most sought after in Europe. These days it's hard to find genuine hand-made pieces. Even if you're not interested in lacework, you'll enjoy exploring this island.

Burano is well known for its fish dishes, the most famous of which is the risotto de gò: the broth in which the rice is cooked and creamed is extracted from the Go fish which is found in the Venice lagoon.

Eating and drinking

It is easy to find an over-priced restaurant with mediocre food in Venice. Just look around San Marco or along the main tourist streets. It is, however, possible to find good restaurants if you know where to look. Here are a few suggestions:

Osteria Santa Marina (Castello 5911, Campo Santa Marina) (041 528 5239) is on a pretty square just north of the Rialto. The cuisine might be described as "Creative Venetian" with an edge of refinement. Try the sea bass ravioli in mussel and clam broth; it's delicious. The outside tables are lovely, but there is also an air-conditioned option.

Il Ridotto (Castello 4509, Campi Santi Filippo e Giacomo) (041 520 8280) is a small gourmet restaurant not far from Piazza San Marco. It can seat around 18 diners in two rooms with exposed brick walls and basic furniture. Meals are not cheap but the quality is excellent. They have a lunch menu and two five-course tasting menus in the evening.

La Zucca (Santa Croce 1762, Ponte del Megio) (041 524 1570), with its interior slanted oak paneling, is a good-value, alternative trattoria in San Polo that has been going for years. Unusually for Venice, the menu features as much meat and game as fish. In summer, there are three or four tables outside on a lane.

Birraria La Corte (San Polo 2168) (041 275 0570) is a large pizzeria popular with local families and young groups, as well as tourists. In the summer it has lots of tables outside on Campo San Polo. The pizzas are excellent, the salads are good too, and there is also a selection of pasta dishes. Cheap house wine includes sparkling *Prosecco*. Desserts are also rich and filling.

The Dorsoduro area has the best nightlife in the city. This is where you find the excellent Venice Jazz Club (Dorsoduro 3102, Ponte dei Pugni) (http://venicejazzclub.weebly.com/) where you can grab dinner then spend the evenings with a drink listening to the best jazz in Venice.

Osteria ai Pugni is a buzzing student bar by the 'bridge of the fists' (Ponte dei Pugni), where the average age can't be more than around 28, is a lively, friendly place to stop off for a drink if you're in the area, and prices are low. Occasional DJ sets and live rock and jazz sessions keep things loud, but even without them the joint is usually hopping.

Venice facts

The Marco Polo airport (http://www.veniceairport.it/en/) is 12 kilometers from Venice by road and 10 kilometers by boat across the lagoon. Transport from the airport is by bus, taxi or boat. The bus will drop you at Piazzale Roma, the bus station located in the northern part of the city. The **regular ATCV bus** stops at many places between the airport and the city. The **airport shuttle** is non-stop and takes about 20 minutes. A 15 minutes trip by **taxi** costs around €35.

You can also take a **boat** which takes about an hour and costs 20€ from the airport. These operate about every hour. Alternatively, you can arrive in 30 minutes via the *motoscafo*, or the **boat taxi** for approximately €100.

Several **car rental** companies are present in Venice, at Piazzale Roma and also at Marco Polo airport. A car is useful for visiting the area around the city. **Tourist information offices** are located at the airport, railway station, St. Mark's Square, and The Lido.

Walking is the best way to get around the central area. Note that roller skates, skateboards, scooters, and bicycles are banned here. You can rent a bike in the Lido and there is also a Town Car Sharing service there.

In Venice, the **Vaporetto** is effectively the bus. All boats are managed by a single company, the ACTV Company, which simplifies the problem of the purchase of tickets. One single trip ticket is €7.50. For 24 hours the rate is €20 and there is a 2-day ticket for €30.

Gondolas have a tradition dating back centuries and are one of the strongest symbols of Venice. Their history is as beautiful as Venice, being guardians of the secrets of the ladies. Most visitors expect to ride a gondola in Venice but when the price is revealed, many decide the romantic notion is not for them.

Prices start at €80 base price for 40 minutes and €40 for each additional 20 minutes. At night the rate increases to €100 for 40 minutes and €50 for each additional 20 minutes. The rate for a singer is additional and must be negotiated.

A **Traghetto** is used for crossing the Grand Canal at certain locations. A feature of the traghetto is that locals stand on this long gondola and that you have two gondoliers, one at the front and one at the back. It will cost you €0.40 per person.

If you don't like public transport, you can always take a **water taxi**. They are quite pleasant if you choose to spend the money but you need to pay attention during the negotiation of rates. In general, the prices which are given to you are in effect prices per person.

Out of town

Venice is clearly the most interesting place in this region but there are other places to see. The **Brenta Canal** running from Fusina to Padua functioned as a mainland extension of Venice during the Renaissance.

The 17 km length from Malcontenta to Stra is renowned for its gracious villas even today. Fourteen of these villas were designed by a local architect named Palladio in a style that was square, perfectly proportioned, and functionally elegant.

The villas can be visited by road or river. Several are open for tours and each is well worth seeing. We take a boat from Venice, lunch at Oriag, tour several villas, and make a quick tour of Padua before returning to Venice by bus.

The Villa Foscari (http://www.lamalcontenta.com/index.php/en/) is closest to Venice. It was constructed by Palladio in 1560. The magnificent Greek temple-front design of the villa is impressive but the building is actually just a simple cube, under a hip. It is open to the public on Tuesday and Saturday mornings from May to October for € 10 per person.

Right at the entrance to Mira, the main town on the Riviera del Brenta, lies the Villa Widmann Rezzonico Foscari. It was built in the 18th-century for the Serimann Persian noble family. Fifty years later, it was bought by the Widmann family and completely redesigned in French rococo style.

If you want to stay in this area, the 17th-century Villa Margherita could be the answer. The Hotel Villa Margherita (http://www.villa-margherita.com/) offers the opportunity to experience an authentic villa.

The Villa Pisani (http://www.villapisani.beniculturali.it/?lng=en) is probably the most famous villa. This impressive building from the 18th century looks almost like a palace and has 114 rooms. It was built for the wealthy bankers, the Pisani family. The building has a striking façade and some rooms are decorated in sumptuous rococo style. The two-story high magnificent ballroom is certainly one of the highlights.

The gardens are not particularly well kept but the maze will appeal to children. The villa is a national museum and is not occupied, and many rooms are empty or partially furnished. Interestingly, the Villa Pisani was bought by Napoleon when he invaded Italy, and Hitler and

Mussolini met each other for the first time here in 1934. It opens Tuesday to Sunday. Admission to the villa and garden is €10.

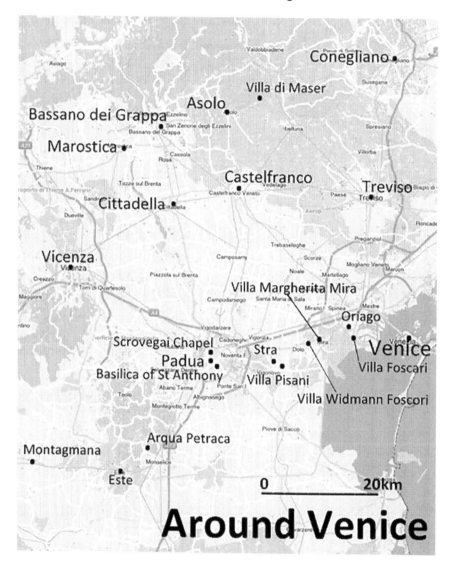

Around Venice

Padua

The town has some appeal and it has a university which is the third oldest in Europe. Galileo lectured here at one time, as did Copernicus.

The students preserved Galileo's desk, a pulpit they built specially for him so he would be heard by everyone in the Great Hall.

Medicine was always important. The original dissection hall is well preserved. Gabriele Falloppio taught anatomy here in the 16th century. The first female graduate in Europe (1678), Elena Cornaro Piscopia, is immortalized in a graceful statue. You can see the buildings on an organized tour.

The highlights of the city, however, are the Chapel of the Scrovegni (http://www.cappelladegliscrovegni.it/index.php/en/) and the Basilica di Sant'Antonio (http://www.basilicadelsanto.org/ing/home.asp). The modest chapel contains remarkable Giotto frescos from the early 14th century depicting biblical scenes.

These are considered to be key works in the development of European art. One depicts Judas kissing Christ, another Lazarus being raised from the dead, and a third is called the *Last Judgement*. The chapel is breathtaking, however, the number of visitors is strictly limited so at peak periods you won't get in unless you pre-book tickets. You should visit the multimedia room before going into the chapel.

It is a half kilometer walk from here to the basilica with its Romanesque and Gothic features and its minarets and bell towers. On the way, we pass the main university building and then go a few blocks to the left to come to two squares with some attractive buildings.

Separating the squares is the Palazzo della Regione. It was once one of the largest halls in the world and was decorated by Giotto, but much was destroyed in a 15th century fire. Despite this, the grandiose assembly hall still has richly frescoed walls, a huge astrological calendar, and contains a 15th century wooden horse.

The Basilica di Sant'Antonio is quite a sight with its towers and domes. The interior is richly frescoed and the marble tomb in the Saint's Chapel is a masterpiece. A constant stream of people files past the saint's tomb to press their palms against it. They leave flowers, small gifts, pictures, and written prayers asking him to help them find something in life.

We see Donatello bronzes at the main altar and a fresco cycle by Menabuoi in one of the chapels. Donatello restored the art of the equestrian statue and there is a great example in front of the basilica. There are dozens of small rooms to explore and you will stumble upon altars, tombs, and capellas, each with their own style.

We need to relax after visiting all these buildings so we spend some time in the Orto Botanico, the oldest botanic gardens in Europe. It was originally the university's collection of medicinal herbs and is not very exciting except for the age of many of the trees.

To the south

It's now south to a group of spa towns in the Euganean Hills. The scattered villages, little churches, attractive villas, and vineyards are picturesque but we are disappointed with the spas towns which are overwhelmed by modern hotels serving the spa trade.

More to our liking is **Arqua Petrarca** (http://www.arquapetrarca.com/index.php?lang=en) where we visit the 14th century farm of poet Francesco Petrarca. His desk and chair and some remnants of the house's interior decoration can still be seen.

Driving west, we arrive at **Montagnana** (http://www.bestsmalltownsitaly.com/town/montagnana-veneto-north/) and are amazed by its medieval walls. There are 24 towers along a two-kilometer length and we later discover that these are considered among the finest medieval fortifications in Italy.

North of Venice

Thirty kilometers north of Venice is prosperous **Treviso** (http://www.italia.it/en/discover-italy/veneto/treviso.html). The suburbs we drive through are not particularly appealing but once we reach the center inside the city walls, it changes dramatically. While Treviso can't compete with its neighbor, it is a pleasant enough town with several attractions.

The town center is a delight with arcaded walkways lining a rambling maze of streets. There are still a few fragments of the painted frescoes which once decorated Treviso's houses. The town's defensive walls, moat, and imposing gateways are impressive sights as are the willow-lined canals which carry water around the town.

Piazza dei Signori in the center of town is a pleasant square with some cafés with outdoor tables and the historic town hall, the Palazzo dei Trecento.

The *Museo di Santa Caterina* is in a former church and convent which houses the *Civic Museum*, the town's art gallery, and archaeological collection. The day is gone but we finish with a pleasant stroll on the shady gravel walkway along part of the city ramparts, which are dotted with benches.

Montagnana was impressive yesterday and now we are equally impressed by **Castelfranco Veneto** (https://www.venetoinside.com/discover-veneto/venice-art-cities/treviso/surroundings/castelfranco-veneto/), a town 30 km west of Treviso. The great brick walls were erected around 1200 and five of the battlements still stand.

The walled part of town is very small, containing just a few streets but it is large enough to contain the town's cathedral, which sits grandly behind a row of statues opposite the town hall.

Castelfranco Veneto was the birthplace of the painter Giorgione, and his *Madonna with St Francis* is in the cathedral. Next door to the cathedral is the so-called Casa del Giorgione which is open to the public, but we decided that we would prefer to wander around the little arcaded streets so typical of the Veneto.

Walled towns continue to attract us so when we hear about **Cittadella** (http://turismo.comune.cittadella.pd.it/en/visitare-cittadella/) we can't resist. It is a pleasant 15 km west to this small town. On the way, we pass through fields with yellow mustard and centuries-old farmhouses.

The center of town is enclosed within a tall circular wall, studded with towers and ringed by a moat which was constructed in 1220. There is an admission charge to walk the high town wall which is a kilometer and a half in circumference. There are great views down onto the medieval town center where the cathedral presides over a very pleasant open square.

It's now north to Bassano del Grappa then west to **Marostica** (http://www.veneto-explorer.com/medieval-towns-and-villages_marostica.html). There are more walls and the town has two castles, one at the top of the hill above town, the other in the main square. The town is most well-known because every two years a medieval-themed festival is held here when a giant chess game is enacted with human chess pieces.

We see the chessboard laid out in paving stones, and admire the view up to the upper castle. The castle proves too tempting so we climb the hill by the zigzagging main path. It is fairly steep but there are benches en route. The view from the top is excellent.

Back east of Bassano dei Grappa, we reach **Asolo** (http://www.visitsitaly.com/veneto/asolo/index.htm) an interesting medieval hill town which immediately wins us over with its 15th century charm. On the main square, the frescoed Loggia del Capitano houses a small museum, and the cathedral, rebuilt in the 18th century, contains several artistic treasures.

We are happiest, however, just strolling its streets and taking in the views. There's an antiques market on the second Sunday of each month which draws thousands.

The top attraction around here is the Villa Barbaro (http://www.villadimaser.it/en), one of Palladio's most celebrated houses. It lies down in the valley, east of Asolo outside the hamlet of Maser. We have seen several of the villas between Venice and Padua but none impress us more than here. The villa is privately owned and we are sensibly required to don slippers to do our inspection.

Trieste

While it is more than 100 kilometers from Venice, Trieste (http://www.italia.it/en/discover-italy/friuli-venezia-giulia/trieste.html) fits in this chapter better than anywhere else. The city has many neoclassical buildings, a fascinating history, and an important harbor.

By 177 B.C., it was a colony of the Roman Republic. Over the next centuries, the region passed through the hands of the Goths, the Lombards, the Byzantines, and the French.

In the Middle Ages, Trieste grew into an important port and trade hub and in 1382 a relationship was created between Trieste and the Hapsburgs which lasted until 1918.

The city was occupied by French troops three times during the Napoleonic wars and was later annexed by Napoleon. After the Napoleonic Wars, Trieste continued to prosper as a free city under Austrian rule. In the aftermath of the Second World War, Trieste was invaded by Yugoslavian troops. It was not until 1954 that the city returned to Italy. The consequence of all that is a glorious jumble of architectural and ethnic influences.

The Trieste - Friuli Venezia Giulia Airport (http://www.aeroporto.fvg.it) is located some 40km north of the city. Frequent buses connect it with Trieste. Trieste's central train station (https://www.italiarail.com/pages/train-stations/trieste) has been renovated and expanded and now includes a bar/restaurant, bookshop, pharmacy, and other shops. There are frequent direct links to most major Italian cities.

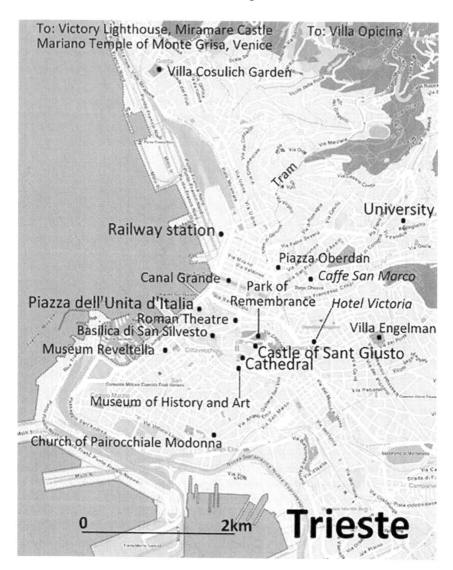

The **Piazza dell'Unità d'Italia**'s (http://www.promotrieste.it/en/visiting-trieste/squares-and-streets/piazza-unita-d-italia/) central position in Trieste makes this our first port of call. This vast square is home to an array of grand buildings and palaces, including the Town Hall. A short distance away is an archway which is said to date back to 33 B.C. This ornate monument is, in fact, the only surviving gateway in the Roman city walls.

The **Piazza dell Borsa** is right next door and is almost as interesting. It is a great place to take in the local life and enjoy a meal. In the middle is a decorative statue of the sea god Neptune. Markets and small fairs are sometimes held here.

As you walk along the **Canale Grande**, it is obvious that this is a city of great diversity with leanings towards the east. You pass a 19th century version of a Venetian palazzo, a blue dome Serbian Orthodox church, and a square lined with brightly colored houses reminiscent of the Czech Republic or Slovenia.

The *Museo Revoltella* (Via Diaz 27) (http://www.museorevoltella.it/museo.php?sub=7&ID=39) is both an attractive mansion and a modern art gallery. There are some interesting marble sculptures, wood paneling, and other features over three floors in the mansion such as the fountain at the foot of the grand staircase and the library.

Several of the rooms, including the original private residence, have been preserved with their original furnishings and make up part of the impressive collection. The adjacent art gallery with its excellent modern art spaces contains an eclectic collection from the 20th century.

Some of Trieste's top tourist attractions can be found on the hill which dominates the city, and also around the medieval quarter below. It is certainly worth climbing the narrow, paved streets of the Old Town, lined with tall, shuttered, sorbet-colored buildings. Trieste's distinctive **cathedral** was built in the 14th century and is dedicated to St Just. The cathedral's interior has a chapel, which is said to date back to the 13th century as well as Byzantine mosaics.

The *Museum of History and Art* (Piazza della Cattedrale) (http://www.discover-trieste.it/code/15476/Museum-of-History-and-Art-and-Lapidary-Garden) is mainly a musty treasure trove of archaeological plunder, from Roman glass and bronzes to Egyptian mummies and a beautiful collection of Greek vases, but the little-frequented Orto Lapidario (Lapidary Garden) beside it is a little gem.

We next visit **Castello di San Giusto** (http://www.turismofvg.it/Castles/San-Giusto-Castle). This was built between 1470 and 1630 and is pleasingly castle-like. There are mighty ramparts to walk for city vistas and modest collections of armor and furnishings.

Outdoor concerts and films are presented in the huge courtyard in summer. The castle has an amazing view overlooking the Adriatic Sea as well as the city of Trieste.

The **Mariano Temple of Monte Grisa** (Località Contovello, 455) makes for a strange sight. This unusual triangular-shaped church is known by the locals in Trieste as the 'little cheese'. Situated on Il Carso, a short distance north of the city, it has breathtaking views.

The **Basilica di San Silvestro,** the city's oldest church, stands atop Trieste's landmark hill, the Colle Capitolino. Much work has been done on the building through the centuries, but it's still possible to see remnants of the frescoes that once decorated the church. The church was closed in the 18th century and is now a national monument.

Apart from the churches, there are a couple of other places to visit. One is **Miramare Castle** (Viale Miramare) (http://www.castello-miramare.it/eng/home/home.php) which was built by Archduke Maximilian, the brother of Franz Josef, the emperor of Austria. In 1864, Maximilian sailed to Mexico where he became emperor until he was shot in 1867.

The sparkling white castle sits by the water on a headland and the interior is equally impressive. We see Maximilian's chambers and those of his consort, Carlota of Belgium, the guest rooms, and the Duke Amadeo of Aosta's apartment. The original furnishings, ornaments, furniture, and objects dating back to the middle of the 19th century are still intact.

Inland from here is **Grotta Gigante** (http://www.grottagigante.it/page/grotta) which according to the Guinness Book of Records is the world's largest show cave. The cave is accessed by a downhill tunnel then 500 stairs in flights of steps lead down to the main chamber, which is 98.5 meters-high.

The **Opicina tram** which departs from Piazza Oberdan is part of the public transport system, but it is also a tourist attraction. This starts as a conventional tram but then later it is pushed up the steep hills of the green and rocky Carso. Get off at the obelisk for good views of the city or to walk the Napoleon's Walk, or continue to the terminus in Villa Opicina.

The city's harbor is amongst the main landmarks within Trieste and it is always a hub of activity. For something a little more historic, Trieste is well known for its **Roman amphitheater**, which was built some 2,000 years ago.

Museo della Risiera di San Sabba (San Sabba Rice Mill) (via Giovanni Palatucci, 5) was the only concentration camp in Italy during WWII equipped with a crematorium. Many thousands of prisoners were sent to other concentration camps, and thousands of people were murdered here by the Nazis.

You can visit the "Hall of Crosses" where those arrested for racial and political reasons waited to be deported to other concentration camps of the Reich. You can also see the "micro-cells" in which Italian, Slovene, and Croat partisans were held, many of them destined for elimination. The Museum's "Memorial Hall" houses a statue dedicated to the martyrs of Auschwitz.

We had heard about the Caffe San Marco (Via Cesare Battisti, 18) so sought it out. This is the most splendid of the city's historic coffee houses with an Art Nouveau interior combined with a bookstore. There is glossy dark wood paneling, golden walls, marble-topped tables, great coffee, and impeccable service. This is a former hangout of resident authors such as James Joyce, and you can still feel that café society atmosphere.

Before leaving, we climb the 280 steps to the top of the **Victory Lighthouse** for some of the best views across the city.

Back west

Back towards Venice, approximately 20 minutes to the west of Trieste, is the charming town of **Sistiana** which is a wonderful coastal resort complete with a harbour and several beautiful beaches. Several hotels and resorts have been established here and there is also a selection of bars, restaurants, and beach shops.

Our next aim is to reach the sleepy, prosperous town of **Udine** (http://www.italia.it/en/discover-italy/friuli-venezia-giulia/udine.html) which is well worth a visit. The Palazzo Patriarcale from 1517 is now open for visitors to explore. Via Mercatovecchio, the main street is picturesquely cobblestoned and lined with beautiful buildings, villas, and shops.

Several important buildings and monuments are located around the Piazza Della Liberta, including the town hall housed in the 1440s Loggia del Lionello, and a clock tower that was built around the same time.

The 13th century cathedral is a very handsome and imposing structure but both the exterior and the interior received a radical transformation in the 18th century. It does, however, contain some excellent paintings.

The nearby small Oratorio della Purita has some nice paintings while *the Museo Diocesano e Gallerie del Tiepolo* has some magnificent frescos and a very attractive library.

While here, we travel 15 km east to the small town of **Cividale** (http://www.bestsmalltownsitaly.com/town/cividale-del-friuli-friuli-venezia-giulia-north/) in the foothills close to the Slovenian border. Cividale plays a very important role in the history of the Lombards because it was the first town they invaded during the military campaign which brought their King Alboin, in 569 A.D., to conquer Northern Italy.

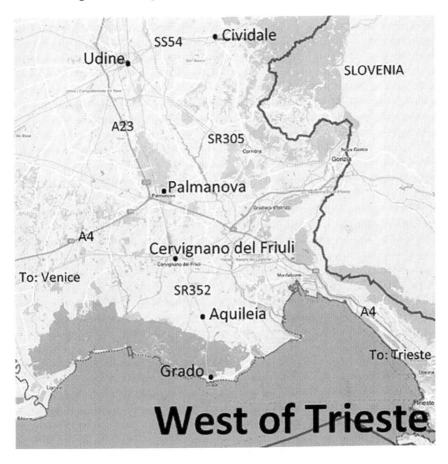

The small 8th century sanctuary in the Santa Maria church houses a remarkable collection of frescoes and stucco figures from the Lombard period. The fresco on the western wall that represents Christ between two Archangels is of great value. Flanking the entryway are statues and decorations carved directly out of the native limestone in an early Lombard Romanesque style.

We visit the historical center of the town dominated by Piazza del Duomo, and find the *National Archaeological Museum* which is housed in the Palladio designed Palazzo dei Provveditori Veneti. This has finds from the Roman, early-Christian, early-medieval, Romanesque, and Gothic periods and a rare collection of Lombard gold coins.

Also worth seeing is the Cathedral which was built in the 15th century over an 8th century building. The *Christian Museum*, annexed to it, houses outstanding examples of Lombard sculpture.

Before leaving, we stop at the impressive Devil's Bridge which spans the Natisone River. There was a timber bridge here from the 1200s and a stone structure was built in the 1440s. Tragically this was blown up in 1917 but a replacement was constructed to a similar design in 1919. Another attempt was made to blow this up in 1945 but the damage was repaired and except for the parapet the bridge remains as it was nearly 600 years ago.

The final visit is to **Aquileia** (http://www.italia.it/en/travel-ideas/unesco-world-heritage-sites/aquileia-the-ruins-and-the-basilica.html). We go back to the main road near Palmanova then continue on to Cervignano del Friuli but still find it a bit hard to find, but the effort was certainly worthwhile.

With its immense archaeological site and its Patriarchal Basilica, it is an artistic and historical treasure trove which has now been recognized as a UNESCO World heritage Site. It was once the fourth most important city in the Roman Empire but after being attacked and almost destroyed by Attila, it gradually dwindled into a small provincial town.

The basilica was founded in the 4th century and was worked on for more than a millennium. The stunning floor mosaic was not discovered until the beginning of the 1900s when the flooring that had been laid in later centuries was removed.

Apart from the basilica, the old Forum, the *macellum* or indoor produce market, the baths, the mausoleum, residential complexes, defensive walls, the circus (or racing arena), and the amphitheater are all still visible in part today.

6 LOMBARDY, MILAN AND THE LAKES

I see **Milan**, the capital of Lombardy, as Italy's most dynamic city. Residents consider it the most sophisticated and high-tech city in the country; it has the highest wages, and arguably is the city to find 'the Good Life'. Visitors quickly notice it has many banks and major industrial companies, but perhaps less obvious is the fact that it is the center for Italy's publishing, fashion, and advertising industries.

While this draws many business visitors to the city, Milan is often overlooked by those seeking the so-called Italian Art Experience. As a tourist, this is not the place to go if you are looking for sunny piazzas and lazy afternoons, but there are enough neoclassical buildings in the inner core and a serious interest in music and art to be interesting to most visitors.

Milan was the Western Roman Empire's capital for a short but significant 109 years from 286 A.D. Its important position was reconfirmed by Napoleon in 1786 when he declared the city his center of the Cisalpine Republic.

Milan is not a particularly scenic city but it makes up for this by providing a lifestyle and visitor experience that includes everything from the delicate Lombardian culinary specialties to a great fashion sense, a surprising cultural art and opera enthusiasm, and an edgy contemporary art scene.

Having a car in the major Italian cities can be a problem so we arrive in Milan by train at the mammoth **Stazione Centrale**, with its walls of marble, granite, and basalt. This is a few kilometers from the center of town. Trams, buses, and the Metro provide services from here to Piazza del Duomo.

Our plan is to find a hotel near the station and use this as a base for exploring the city. When we are done, we will jump on the shuttle bus that links the station with Malpensa Airport for our flight home. Finding a hotel is surprisingly easy and we are quickly ensconced in a basic room at reasonable cost.

Piazza del Duomo is the heart of Milan and our destination this morning. The day is warm and sunny so we decide to walk the three kilometers from the hotel. This is a great decision. We walk down Via Vittorio Pisani to Piazza della Repubblica, take a quick look at the Arch of Porta Nuova, a remnant of the medieval city walls which are unfortunately squashed between modern buildings, and then through the lovely **Giardini Pubblici** park.

This has the Hoepli Planetarium, the *Museo di Storia Naturale (Natural History Museum)* (http://www.milanmuseumguide.com/museo-storia-naturale/), *Gallery of Modern Art* (http://www.milanmuseumguide.com/galleria-arte-moderna/), and a small zoo. It is a great place for a morning or afternoon stroll with its tree-lined paths, sunny lawns, and bubbling stream.

The coffeehouse here is a good stop before going south-west to the start of Via Manzoni which leads to the wonderful Teatro alla Scala, perhaps the world's most famous opera house.

We make a quick detour down Via Montenapoleone in the fashion district, one of Italy's great shopping streets but quickly realize that most prices are out of our reach. It appears that service here depends on how much the salesperson thinks you plan to spend.

There are shops by Gucci, Salvatore Ferragamo, Mario Buccellati, and many more then afterwards the Café Cova is a place to sip your espresso in an elegant room.

The people here are beautiful with their sun-tanned skins, long eyelashes, groomed hair, and natural grace. Their clothes fit their bodies and the colors have been carefully selected. We feel like slobs in our jeans and sneakers. We wonder how long these locals have spent looking carefully in the mirror to achieve this perfect harmony between themselves and their clothes.

There is little doubt that the boutiques and jewelry shops in Via Montenapoleone, Via Manzoni, and Via della Spiga offer the best of Italian fashion and design but you need to exchange a small fortune to acquire it. The smaller side streets in this district are lined with imposing residences whose enormous doors conceal courtyards filled with classic statuary, fountains, and lush gardens.

There are two museums around here that are worth a visit. The *Museo Bagatti Valsecchi* (Via Gesù, 5) (http://www.museobagattivalsecchi.org/en/index.html) is an historic house museum with patterned ceilings, paintings by old masters such as Giovanni Bellini and Giampietrino, majolica (a tin-glazed pottery), Renaissance glass, 15th century furnishings, ivory, objects in precious metals, and armor.

The *Museo Poldi-Pezzoli* (http://www.milanmuseumguide.com/poldi-pezzoli/ on Via Manzoni has paintings by some of Italy's greatest painters such as Pollaiolo, Botticelli, Giovanni Bellini, and Mantegna displayed in an elegant setting of antique furnishings, tapestries, frescos, and woodcarvings. There are also displays of weaponry, glassworks, ceramics, and jewelry.

La Scala Opera House (Piazza della Scala) (http://www.teatroallascala.org/en/) does not look particularly impressive from the outside but the uncluttered elegant interior is stunning. We are unable to get tickets for a performance so have to be satisfied with a group tour of the building. If you don't want to do this, you can still buy a souvenir at huge cost in the La Scala shop.

Across from the opera house is the much-photographed statue of Leonardo da Vinci and it is then only a few steps to one of Milan's most famous landmarks, the huge **Galleria Vittorio Emanuele II** (http://www.visitamilano.it/turismo_en/).

This is undoubtedly one of the most impressive shopping centers in Europe. The towering building with its vaulted glass ceilings and marvelous architectural details has a huge central dome, wrought-iron globe lamps, and an impressive decorative tile floor. It contains outlets for some of the world's iconic brands and a number of bars, bistros, and restaurants. The Savini restaurant is considered by many to be the pick of the bunch for Lombard cuisine.

We are now drawn to the **Piazza del Duomo** at one end of the building, and its impressive marble, lacy Gothic **Cathedral**. There are many cathedrals in Europe but few can compete in size or flamboyance with this edifice. We think it is awesome. From the front, there are belfries, statues, gables, and pinnacles wherever you look.

The building was started in 1386 and many architects have contributed to the startling façade. The inside is equally impressed. The size is gigantic and soaring pillars divide it into five naves. Entry to the cathedral is €3 (November 2018) and this includes entry to the museum, but we pay an extra €9 to visit the roof where we walk through an architectural forest before gazing over the city and surrounds.

Back at ground level, we spend some time in the plaza, gazing at the remarkable façade, admiring the well-dressed locals who can never be confused with the myriad tourists, and avoiding the peddlers who are waiting to scam you with offers of food to feed the pigeons. Beneath the plaza is one of the city's busiest metro stations.

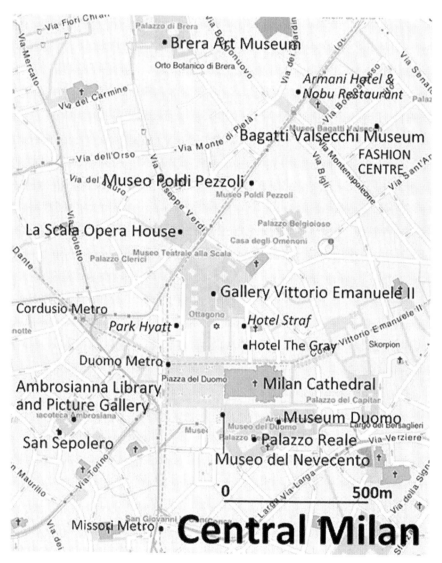

The plaza is also home to other attractions. Just to the south of the cathedral is the *Duomo Museum* (http://museo.duomomilano.it/en) where there are paintings, tapestries, terra cotta scale models of the cathedral, wooden models, graphic material, and artifacts. Tickets are €3 which includes entry to the cathedral.

Next door is the *Palazzo Reale* (http://www.milanmuseumguide.com/palazzo-reale/) an art museum with changing exhibitions in a beautiful building with ceiling friezes, opulent mirrors, refined furnishings, and a sweeping staircase. One of the grandest spaces is the Hall of the Caryatids. It was here that grand royal receptions were held and where the glitterati of Europe gathered to dance and drink in opulent surroundings. The cost to see exhibitions varies considerably.

Here too is the *Museo del Novecento* (http://www.milanmuseumguide.com/museo-del-novecento/) which houses a dedicated exhibition displaying Milan's superb collection of 20th century art. It is directly connected to the Palazzo Reale by a suspended walkway. There are some unusual views of the Duomo from here.

A little to the east, is the San Bernardino alle Ossa (Via Carlo Giuseppe Merlo 4), a relatively unassuming-looking church best known for its ossuary, a small side chapel containing numerous human skulls and bones of people who died in the Middle Ages.

Immediately west of the Piazza del Duomo, is one of Milan's hidden treasures. During the Middle Ages, **Piazza Mercanti** was the commercial and governmental center of Milan. Today, the intimate pedestrianized square seems to take you back to that time thanks to its historic architecture. Palazzo della Ragione, which was built in 1228, the Loggia degli Osii, commissioned in 1316, and Palazzo dei Giureconsulti from 1272 are all here.

We are into art galleries at the moment so the next stop is at the nearby *Ambrosiana Library and Picture Gallery* (Piazza Pio XI, 2) (http://www.milanmuseumguide.com/ambrosiana/) which was founded in the early 17th-century and was only the second public library in Europe. You can see a remarkable collection of art including works by Botticelli, Raphael, and Leonardo da Vinci.

It is incredible to see the da Vinci notebooks up close and the lighting in the gallery gives an excellent view. There are several video presentations including one on the *Portrait of a Musician* by da Vinci where the tiny brush strokes that make up the painting are clear and we have greater appreciation of the painter's skill when looking at the final portrait.

Also here, is The Atlantic Codex, a collection of papers that Leonardo da Vinci kept with him at all times. There were 1119 sheets of sketches drawn between 1478 when Leonardo was still working in his Florentine hometown and 1519, the year of his death in France. Here are the artist's thoughts on various matters, from mechanics to hydraulics, mathematics, astronomy, inventions, machinery, and more. The ticket for the exhibition costs €17 but it also includes a tour inside the gallery. It is closed on Mondays.

This gallery has inspired us so we walk the half kilometer or so to the *Brera Picture Gallery* (Via Brera 28) (http://www.milan-museum.com/brera-pictures-gallery.php). This is one of Italy's finest galleries with works by Lombard, Venetian, and other artists. The Brera began life as a simple warehouse for artworks Napoleon looted from churches, monasteries, and private collections.

There are masterpieces from many of the classical painters, and great works by 20th-century artists as well. We are particularly impressed by Mantegna's *Dead Christ* and his strange use of perspective. There is a glass encased room where you can see the pieces being restored. The gallery is closed on Mondays. You can buy tickets on line to avoid the possible long queue. Tickets are €16.

Most Milan visitors have heard about Leonardo's *Last Supper* (Piazza Santa Maria delle Grazie, 2) (http://www.milan-museum.com/leonardo-last-supper-cenacolo.php) and have this on their 'to do' list. I had seen it some years ago but was keen to repeat the visit but I was not prepared for the new procedures. You now have to make reservations ahead of your visit and only 25 people are admitted at the one time.

You pass through antechambers to remove pollutants from your body then after viewing the painting for 15 minutes you walk through two filtration chambers as you exit. You may be wondering is all this worthwhile?

Well, it depends on your point of view. The painting's history is fascinating. The mural was painted by Leonardo in 1497 and it soon began to deteriorate. By 1556 it was being described as already "ruined". In 1652 a doorway was cut through the now unrecognizable painting, and this was later bricked up.

A restoration of the painting was attempted in 1726 by Bellotti, who filled in missing sections with oil paint then varnished everything. Another restoration was attempted in 1770 by Giuseppe Mazza who stripped off Bellotti's work then basically repainted the original painting.

In 1821 Barezzi, an expert in removing frescoes was called in to move the painting to a safer location but unfortunately, he badly damaged a section before realizing that Leonardo's work was not a fresco. Barezzi then attempted to reattach damaged sections with glue. Three further cleanings and stabilizations occurred in the 20th-century then from 1978 to 1999 a major restoration project was carried out.

Some have suggested that all that is left of the original *Last Supper* is a "few isolated streaks of fading color". In my view, if you want to see an original work by Leonardo, there are many better examples. The painting is in the church of Santa Maria della Grazie to the west of the main downtown area. Leonardo's Last Supper Tickets can be booked only as a part of package. Combined tickets with the Brera Picture Gallery are €36.

While in this area, don't miss visiting the small but extremely impressive **Chiesa di San Maurizio al Monastero Maggiore** (Corso Magenta, 15) (http://www.milanosecrets.it/CULTUREEVENTS/CultureSanMaurizio.aspx). The church doesn't look much from the outside but the interior is filled with outstanding frescos from the early 16th century. Rarely have church painting and architecture harmonized so well. There is free entry but it is closed on Mondays.

The adjoining *Civic Archaeological Museum of Milan* is housed within the ex-convent of the Monastero Maggiore. The inner cloisters reveal the remains of a Roman dwelling from the 1st -3rd century.

The city has several other interesting museums worth visiting. Many of these are in the **Castle Sforzesco** (http://www.milanocastello.it/ing/home.html), an ancient fortress near the center of the city which we now visit. The original construction on the site began in the 14th-century then the castle was developed in the 15th and 16th centuries into one of the biggest citadels in Europe.

The large park behind the castle is a pleasant place to stroll or relax. There are broad winding paths, nice lawns, and beautiful trees. A lake, a huge statue to Napoleon III, and an old stadium are also found here.

The best known of the current civic museums is the *Pinacoteca del Castello Sforzesco* (http://www.milanocastello.it/ing/pinacoteca.html), with an art collection which includes Mantegna's *Trivulzio Madonna*, Leonardo da Vinci's *Codex Trivulzianus* manuscript, and Michelangelo's last sculpture, the *Rondanini Pieta,*.

At age 89, Michelangelo was working yet again on one of his favorite subjects, this *Pieta* when he died. It may be unfinished but this representation of Mary and Nicodemus bearing the body of Christ is considered to be one of Michelangelo's most remarkable works.

The Castello complex also hosts a whole collection of other museums but I don't think any of these are world-beaters. Entry to the museums is €5. Entry to the castle is free.

My favorite museum, however, is some distance south of here. The *Leonardo da Vinci National Museum of Science and Technology* (Via San Vittore, 21) (http://www.museoscienza.org/english/) is a vast complex where I could easily spend a whole day. It is the largest museum of science and technology in Italy.

The museum's collections include 15,000 technical, scientific, and artistic objects representing the history of Italian science, technology, and industry from the 19th century to the present. Perhaps the most interesting section is the da Vinci Gallery which displays copies and models from the Renaissance genius. Leonardo's ability was outstanding and this museum shows just that. The museum opens Tuesday to Sunday. Admission is €10 adults, and under 26 and seniors €7.50 (November 2018).

Near here is another church worth visiting. The **Basilica Sant'Ambrogio** (http://www.sacred-destinations.com/italy/milan-sant-ambrogio) is universally acclaimed as a masterpiece of Romanesque architecture. A church was consecrated here in 387 A.D. and when it was rebuilt in the 11th century it became the model for all Lombard Romanesque churches.

Over the next few days, we wander through the streets of central Milan discovering new attractions and a great shopping district near the Brera Museum. This is one of Milan's most charming districts. It teams with intimate cafés and restaurants, modern art galleries, shops, antique stores, and students.

You will love the pedestrian-only Via Fiori Chiari and Via Madonnina where there are bric-a-brac, clothing, and leather stores. We also visit the **Monumental Cemetery** (http://www.significantcemeteries.org/2011/11/milan-monumental-cemetery-italy.html) where there are Greek temples, obelisks, and Liberty-style buildings similar to Buenos Aires' famous Recoleta Cemetery. The cemetery is full of chapels, commemorative monuments, and pieces of statuary, many of which are of great artistic value.

Another place we find of some interest is the **Rotonda della Besana** (Via Enrico Besana, 12). This is a late baroque building complex and former cemetery, built at the start of the 18th century. It consists of a colonnade portico enclosing a garden and the deconsecrated church of San Michele ai Sepolcri. It now serves as a park and venue for cultural events.

Then there is **Navigli**, a district of canals which were once used for commerce but now the picturesque area that grew up around them is home to artist's studios, craft shops, jazz clubs, bookshops, and restaurants. In summer, some areas are pedestrianized so it's nice to walk. In particular, we suggest visiting the Vicolo Lavandai, a beautiful corner despite recent construction, where washerwomen used to wash clothes.

The round **Basilica di San Lorenzo Maggiore** (Corso di Porta Ticinese 39) (http://www.sacred-destinations.com/italy/milan-san-lorenzo-maggiore) with its soaring columns was built between the late fourth and early fifth centuries. Inside, the Chapel of Saint Aquilino, with its breathtaking mosaics, is a highlight.

In front of the basilica, there are 16 ancient columns from the 3rd century B.C., which remind us of the ancient origin of the city. This area is often occupied by young, alternative-style looking young people but they don't seem to worry visitors.

Spazio Forma (Via Meravigli, 5) is the city's only space dedicated to photography. Exhibitions highlight the history and some famous practitioners and there are also occasional shows devoted to fashion and design photography. Housed in a former tram shed, the center runs courses and workshops (in Italian) and has an excellent bookshop. It is open from 11 a.m. to 9 p.m.

Museo dell'Ottocento (Villa Belgiojoso Bonaparte, via Palestro 16) a neo-classical villa, formerly known as the Villa Reale, is a conspicuous display of wealth. There are English-style grounds, complete with pond and footpaths, which add to the appeal. It's little wonder that Napoleon chose to live here in 1802.

The ground floor has neo-classical paintings, sculpture, and bas-reliefs. In the ballroom and former living areas on the first floor, are paintings from the Romantic period as well as some Futurist works. The second floor showcases the Grassi and Vismara collections, the latter including works by modern Italian and international masters.

Civico Museo di Storia Naturale (Corso Venezia 55) is in a striking red stone neo-classical building within the leafy grounds of Giardini Pubblici which was constructed to house the collections left to the city by aristocrat Giuseppe de Cristoforis. It's a great rainy-day museum: the displays cover botany, mineralogy, geology, and paleontology.

Eating and drinking

It's a good idea to steer clear of the touristy restaurants around the Piazza del Duomo, the fashion district, and those within sight of the Castello Sforzesco as these are designed for tourists and many will serve food that is overpriced and of less than perfect quality.

The Armani Nobu restaurant (Via Pisoni 1) (02 7231 8645) is Japanese with Latin American influence. There is a casual lounge bar, with a selection of sushi on the ground floor and table service on the first floor with a sumptuous menu.

Il Luogo di Aimo E Nadia (Via Privata Raimondo Montecuccoli 6) (024 168 86) has been awarded two Michelin stars. This is a family-run traditional Tuscan restaurant and the tasting menu is the best way to sample the food. Tuscan suckling pig with apple compote and chestnut flour cake is popular with the locals as is the impeccable service.

Sadler (Via Ascanio Sforza 77) (025 810 4451) serving modern Italian cuisine in an art-filled room also has two Michelin stars. Reinventing traditional dishes in bold ways is the forte here such as goose liver, raisins, nuts, toasted pan brioches, bitter chocolate sauce, zest of orange, and coffee.

Cracco (Via Victor Hugo 4) (028 767 74) is another restaurant with two Michelin stars. It serves Italian nouveau cuisine such as egg yolk spaghetti with garlic, olive oil, and chili so expect your taste buds to be challenged. Dishes can be accompanied by some of the world's finest wines.

There are also many cheaper options offering good value for money. Typical of these is La Ricetta di Mamé (Via Vigevano, 34) (02 8324 1707), a bright space with an open kitchen, casually hand-written menus, and chalkboard. The recipes are actually quite traditional, tied always to region and season.

Un Posto a Milano at Cascina Cuccagna (Via Cuccagna 2) (02 5457 785) is a *cascina* (farmhouse) in the city. It opens for lunch, dinner, or drinks, and you can shop for organic produce at the Tuesday markets. There is a wonderful mingling of types and generations and you can sit under umbrellas hung with candles.

Milan Facts

Malpensa (http://www.milanomalpensa-airport.com/en/passenger-guide) is the largest airport in the Milanese area with domestic and International connections. The airport is well connected with the city. The journey takes roughly one hour by car on the A8 autostrada and there are also shuttle services (Malpensa Bus Express, Malpensa Shuttle Air Pullman) that connect it with **Stazione Centrale** (Central Station) and Linate Airport. It is also connected by train to Central and Cadorna stations, with intermediate stops at Garibaldi and Bovisa (Malpensa express).

Linate Airport (http://www.milanolinate-airport.com/en) is very close to the center and is considered particularly convenient for business people. Connections take just a few minutes to Piazza San Babila with the urban bus line number 73. Linate is also serviced by private shuttle buses that link the airport with Central Station, Fiera Milano city, Rho fair center, and also Malpensa airport.

The low-cost airline airport **Orio al Serio**, approximately one hour's travel from Milan, can be reached by car on the Milano-Venezia A4 or by shuttle bus (Autostradale, Locatelli Air Pullman) that connects it with Central Station.

In all of the airports, there are numerous taxi, car-rental, and chauffeured car services.

The tourist information office **InfoMilano** is at Galleria Vittorio Emanuele II, corner Piazza della Scala. The phone number is +39 02 884 55555. There is another tourist office at the Central Railway Station.

There are many ways to explore the city. You can walk, take a historic tram, or sightsee from the roof of an open-top bus, or from the deck of a canal boat. There are a tram (https://tramilano.com/) and bus (https://www.hop-on-hop-off-bus.com/milan-bus-tours) **hop on-hop off** routes which reach more than 60 points of interest throughout the city. The service is available every day.

Milan has four **Metropolitana** (subway) lines. You can purchase a single trip ticket, a ten-trip carnet ticket for those using the Metropolitana occasionally, or a tourist pass for anyone wishing to explore the city in depth. A single ticket costs €1.50 and a Day ticket €4.50.

MilanoCard (https://www.milanocard.it/) is a tourist & travel card which includes free public transport, a free personal driver, and free entry or discounts at more than 500 Milan tourist attractions. Valid for 24, 48 or 72 hours MilanoCard enables you to do everything in Milan at a vastly reduced cost. A 24-hour card costs €8, a 48-hour card €14, and a 72-hour card €19 (November 2018). There are other options that include specific add-ons.

Another option is the **Milan Pass** (https://themilanpass.com/) which gives transport and free access to Milan's most important museums and attractions for 48 hours for a cost of €69. If you are particularly interested in museums the **Tourist Museum Card** at €12 gives unlimited 72-hour access to 8 city museums, and discounts on other city events and attractions.

Outside the city

Milan has been enjoyable but it's now time to explore further afield. We find a car rental agency close to our hotel and drive 35 km south to **Pavia** (http://www.italia.it/en/discover-italy/lombardy/pavia.html). This is the capital of a fertile region known for agricultural products. Between 568 and 774, it was the capital of the Kingdom of the Lombards.

Once again, my lack of historical knowledge comes forth but I soon learn that the Lombards originated in southern Scandinavia and moved south over several centuries. By 570 they had conquered all the principal cities north of the Po River except Pavia, but this fell in 572. Little remains from that time but the Lombard influence can be seen on later buildings.

We see the Cathedral that was begun in 1488 and not completed until 1898, St. Michael's church which was rebuilt from around the end of the 11th century, and The Basilica of San Pietro in Ciel d'Oro, which was begun in the 6th century, although the current construction is from 1132.

Pavia's most famous building is the Certosa (http://www.prolococertosadipavia.it/index.php?option=com_content&view=article&id=15:fortourists) or monastery, founded in 1396 and located eight kilometers north of the city.

This was once located on the border of a large hunting park belonging to the Visconti family of Milan. The massive building is rich with Lombardesque decorations and sculptures. The church, the last edifice of the complex to be built, was to be the family mausoleum.

The façade of the church is famous for its exuberant decorations. An elegant portal leads from the church to the Small Cloister with its small garden in the center. This is still a working monastery and we tour through an example of the little houses the monks occupy and purchase some of their beauty products and liqueurs.

Brescia (http://www.italia.it/en/discover-italy/lombardy/brescia.html) is the second largest city in Lombardy. It is an industrial center and parts of the city are uninspiring and even scruffy. The center of Brescia, with its historic squares and lanes, is manageable on foot and very attractive but there is a new commercial district outside the historic center, called Brescia Due.

This has been an important regional center since pre-Roman times and there are a number of Roman and medieval monuments to see. The Piazza del Foro marks the site of the Roman-time forum and a Roman temple built over earlier Republican-era buildings was discovered here in the 19th century and has been partially reconstructed. Alongside is the town's Roman theater.

The medieval monuments are more extensive. The Old Cathedral is a Romanesque church, striking for its circular shape. The main structure was built in the 11th century on the ruins of an earlier basilica, which in turn was founded on Roman buildings. The new cathedral, started in 1604, is in a Palladian style.

Piazza della Loggia is the prettiest square, the seat of the local administration, and the location of the town's main tourist information office. The medieval Town Hall is a massive 12th and 13th century building with an original city tower with a belfry. The monastery of San Salvatore, now a World Heritage Site, is one of the best examples of High Middle Ages architecture in northern Italy.

Further down Via Musei is the *Museo della Città* which houses archaeological finds and collections from Brescia's past. It's housed in a monastery complex, Santa Giulia, which has a long and rich history and incorporates the Church of San Salvatore, begun by the Lombards in the 8th century.

On the side of Cidneo Hill, there is a Corinthian temple. We climb to the medieval castle complex on the hill and find towers, ramparts, gardens, courtyards, drawbridges, and several underground tunnels. It houses the *Ancient Arms Museum*, the *Risorgimento Museum*, and a model railway exhibit. From the highest point, there are good views of the city below.

Back to the west, **Bergamo** (http://www.italia.it/en/discover-italy/lombardy/bergamo.html) is an attractive hill town with a long history. The town is split in two and it is the upper town with the most interest. This was founded by the Celts and became a Roman municipality in the 2nd century B.C. Many of the town's stone fortifications are medieval Venetian built over Roman foundations.

We leave the car in the lower town and walk nearly one kilometer to Piazza Vecchia in the upper town then discover that there is a funicular railway between the two.

The square houses the town hall, an 18th century fountain, the Palazzo della Podesta which is now a small museum with limited English explanations, the 52-meter high Civic Tower which offers splendid views, the Palazzo della Ragione with its sun dial, and the town library which was the previous town hall. A vaulted arcade leads to Piazza del Duomo where the Bergamo Cathedral is located. All around are circuitous streets and imposing medieval architecture.

The Romanesque cathedral was founded in the 12th century but it was given a baroque interior at some later stage. The choir dates from the 16th century. One of the highlights is the Flemish and Tuscan tapestries on display.

Facing the cathedral is the baptistery. It was originally built to a Campione design but was rebuilt in the 19th century. Here too is the15th century Colleoni Chapel with its pink and white inlaid marble façade and attractive ceiling frescos from the 18th century. It looks dainty from the outside, but inside the great domed ceiling, with its exuberantly painted frescoes is startling.

Bergamo has some very impressive Venetian walls which are over six kilometers long, and more than four centuries old. As well as walking on the walls, don't miss the chance to walk inside the walls and to visit the casemates of San Michele and San Giovanni.

The Accademia Carrara (Piazza Carrara, 82) in the Lower Town hosts one of the richest collections in Italy with around 2,000 paintings from the 15th to the 18th century. The Galleria d'Arte Moderna e Contemporanea, a modern art gallery, is on the opposite side of the road in a partially restored 14th century monastery that was previously used as a barracks.

It is definitely worth taking the little funicular railway up the mountain to the fortress of San Virgilio, perched on a precipice overlooking the city. Seen from above, the Renaissance domes, towers, and piazzas, laid out with geometric precision, seem even more magnificent. The view of Bergamo Citta Alta is best at sunset when the sun is behind you and the colors on the buildings turn warm amber.

It is only a short drive from here to **Lecco** (http://www.italia.it/en/discover-italy/lombardy/lecco.html) which lies at the end of the south-eastern branch of Lake Como. We walk some little alleyways around Piazza Roma which give us a taste of what Medieval Lecco might have been like. Some are stepped, some cobbled, and some lead to unexpected small squares. We are fascinated.

Lake Como

This is Italy's most popular lake and one of my favorite places in the world. Internationally, it is also the most well-known of the Italian Lakes now partly because of George Clooney's villa on the lake. Lake Como (http://www.discovercomo.com/) is shaped like an inverted Y giving it a long shoreline. The lake is surrounded by beautiful villas, resort villages, and hiking paths and it is popular for boat trips and water activities.

Ferries crisscross the lake and a bus system connects villages around the lake. For those needing to go higher, several funiculars will take you into the hills.

We decide that this area is too attractive to rush so we get off the highway and wander along the lakeside road. There are small villages after small villages, each with villas built by the wealthy, and more reserved family homes. We make many stops. There are pine trees and flower-filled gardens and everywhere there are gorgeous views across the lake.

It's now through Varenna and Colico before turning west then south. **Varenna** (http://www.lakecomoitaly.org.uk/varenna/) is considered by some to be the most picturesque town on the lake. A leisurely stroll along its steep winding alleys shows us charming homes with flowering balconies and lace-curtained windows. Women are sitting outside along the street shelling beans, mending clothes, and talking with neighbors.

Just above town is the ancient castle where Theodolinda, Queen of the Lombards, is said to have died in the 7th century. Two famed villas to visit here are Villa Cipressi (http://www.hotelvillacipressi.it/en/), with terraced gardens cascading right down to the shore, and Villa

Monastero (http://www.villamonastero.eu/index.php/en/), an ancient monastery and patrician villa with a botanical garden.

The western side of the lake seems even more attractive than the east. **Menaggio** (http://www.discovermenaggio.com/) is a popular destination, particularly for holidaymaker's keen on outdoor activities. There is an eighteen-hole golf course close to town, and plenty of good walking in the area, from easy strolls to tough mountain hikes, as well as opportunities for swimming, water-skiing, mountain-biking, and riding.

Menaggio makes an extremely good center for visitors because of its transport links. Ferries arrive here from the northern and southern ends of the lake, and cross the waters to Varenna and Bellagio, while buses run to Lake Lugano, and along the Como lakeside, making it easy to visit all of Lake Como's attractions. The town itself has a pretty little lakeside promenade and harbor, and a town square with some cafés.

Just to the south is the Villa Carlotta (http://www.villacarlotta.it/home.php?lang id=2), an immense 18th century palazzo with an art gallery and a garden remarkable for its collection of colorful flowers in spring.

The gardens are worth visiting at any time of the year to see century-old cedars and sequoias, huge planes and tropical plants, the Rock garden and the Ferns valley, the Rhododendrons wood and the Bamboos garden, and the agricultural tools museum.

On the southern shore is **Bellagio** (the pearl of the lake) (http://www.bellagiolakecomo.com/), a beautiful village on a headland. We visit here by ferry from Menaggio. Its narrow-cobbled streets, breathtaking views, lovely homes, and glorious villa gardens, help support the claim by some that this is the most beautiful town in all of Europe.

I am not into those sorts of claims but it is certainly attractive. Bellagio and Varenna get very crowded so we don't find them to be the best places to stay, but they are great to visit outside of peak times.

The town spills down a series of stone staircases to a long plaza open to the water and lined with shops and cafés. While here, you should visit Villa Melzi (http://lakecomotravel.com/lake-como/villas/villa-melzi/) just to the south of the town. We had seen the white columns that flank the landing stage in front of the villa, and the classical style of the house from the lake and find it equally appealing on land. The wide rolling lawns and ornamental pavilions and pools stretch along the shore providing picturesque vistas.

Tremezzo (http://www.lakecomoitaly.org.uk/tremezzo/) is another lovely west lakeside town with a classic lakeside promenade, as well as wonderful old villas, many now hotels. Here is what could probably be the most famous lakeside building, *Villa Carlotta* (http://www.villacarlotta.it/home.php?lang_id=2). Built in the 17th century, this place has nice interiors and a great garden. There are trees and shrubs from all over the world, making it a must-see for any garden lover.

Further south, **Cernobbio** (http://www.visitsitaly.com/lombardia/cernobbio/) is a small, chic resort frequented by the wealthiest Europeans with an old town that has a delightful collection of picturesque houses and narrow alleys. Nearby, the Villa D'Este (http://www.villadeste.com/en/13/home.aspx) is considered to be one of the grandest hotels in all Europe with rooms almost like museum galleries. The garden is one of the finest in Italy.

Finally, we come to the town of **Como** (http://www.italia.it/en/discover-italy/lombardy/como.html) with its walled old town. Piazza San Fedele has many 400-year-old buildings and the Como cathedral on the site of the Santa Maria Maggiore basilica is one of the masterpieces of the area. There is much to see including a series of 16th century tapestries and several remarkably good paintings. There is also a beautiful rose window best viewed in the afternoon.

Streets radiate from here and we walk them all. At the top of Via Cantù there is the Porta Vittoria, a spectacular standing tower. Nearby, is the austere church of San Abbondio and behind it is the Baradello Tower.

From here, we walk back down the hill and visit Como's third great basilica, the early Romanesque San Corpoforo. Before leaving Como, take the *funivia* up to Brunate for a truly spectacular view. If you're a hiker, you might like to take the footpath up to Monte Boletto.

We are close to Switzerland here and that offers many exciting possibilities but we decide to go to the Italian part of **Lake Maggiore** instead. The lake is shared with Switzerland and like Lake Como, there is great natural beauty and villas with lush gardens. The resort-studded western shore is the most scenic.

Stresa (http://www.visitstresa.com/About_Stresa.htm) is the main center. This has become a first-class international resort and its setting is unparalleled. So too are its accommodation options with the lakeside *Grand Hotel des Iles Borromees* the leading resort.

North of Stresa near the resort of Pallanza, is the Giardini Botanici at Villa Taranto (http://www.villataranto.it/en/). This magnificent garden spreads over 20 hectares and contains more than 20,000 species of plants. The formal gardens are laid out with ornamental fountains, statues, and pools.

Back in Stresa we relax overlooking the lake. There are a few fishing boats with their elongated prows drawn up on the shingle beach and pink and green nets hung up to dry. We watch boats come and go, bringing in tourists who fall upon the souvenir stalls, and see a few fish jumping in the lake as we sip our coffee.

Next day, we leave the car behind and take to the water. There is a chain of tiny islands in the lake and several have lavish villas and gardens worth seeing. The most impressive is the Borromeo Palazzo on Isola Bella (http://www.visitstresa.com/Isola_Bella.htm). The views from here are remarkable, the white peacocks in the garden fascinate, and the six grotto rooms are outstanding.

Isola Madre (http://www.isoleborromee.it/eng/isola-madre.html) also has interest. The 17th century palace contains rich furnishings, a doll collection, and a marionette theatre while the Orto Botanico has a wide range of tropical and temperate plants.

People keep telling us about **Lake Orta** (http://www.orta.net/eng1/indexe.htm), a little further west. The area around Lake Orta has long been a favorite with tourists in the know, thanks to the quiet beauty of the landscape, its fascinating history, and its wealth of artistic treasures - principally Romanesque and Baroque architecture.

Orta village sits on a tiny promontory ringed with thickly wooded streets. Its narrow streets pass charming old houses and lead to the lakeside Piazza Motta. A 16th century town hall faces the lake, and all around are outdoor cafés.

It is well known for the nearby Sacro Monte. You can walk or drive here to see the 20 rococo chapels containing life-size terra cotta figures depicting scenes from the scriptures. The site was added to the UNESCO World Heritage List in 2003.

Offshore is the Island of St. Giulio (http://www.isolasangiulio.it/), which you can visit after a 10-minute boat ride and which is today a place of great mysticism. There is a lovely walk around the cobbled pavement and you should read all the wall mounted plaques, each one has a different message about what silence brings to life. The major building is the Basilica of San Giulio which was originally founded by St. Giulio in 390 and is now occupied by Benedictine nuns.

The island has a few stunning private villas, palm trees, a restaurant, and a shop. The church is a treasure house of art works covering a number of centuries. Little wonder that many Italian couples choose this fairy tale destination to be the scene of their wedding.

7 VERONA AND THE DOLOMITES

We have stayed with friends and used Conegliano as a base for exploring Venice and surrounds and now it proves to be a good starting point for our travels through the northern Veneto and the Dolomites.

Conegliano (https://en.rail.cc/conegliano/city/l/12551) is a cheerful and attractive historic town in wine-producing country close to the foothills of the Alps. The historic center is compact, and while the surrounding new development has more recently sprawled, it still retains a welcoming small-town feel.

Conegliano main square

Leaving the station, an avenue leads to a flight of steps climbing up to an arcade which leads through to a little piazzetta with a well. This small space acts as a kind of grand entrance onto the town's theatrical main square, Piazza Cima.

In most towns, this would be the site of the town's cathedral, but Conegliano's sloping piazza is dominated by a neo-classical theater, called the Teatro Accademia. It is flanked by the town hall, with busts of Garibaldi and Vittorio Emanuele II.

One of the joys of Conegliano is a walk up to the castle on its hill. On the way, we take in three other little sights. The first is the Convento di San Francesco, a former monastery with a pretty cloister which can be visited during opening hours. The second is the Brolo di San Francesco, a pleasant little garden which belonged to the monastery. Next stop is the Chiesetta della Madonna della Neve, a tiny church with a rediscovered fresco halfway up the hill.

Conegliano's castle, the Castello, still has battlements and a couple of towers standing. A pleasant green garden fills the space inside the fortified walls. A café-restaurant is located in a tower, with outdoor tables and we sit and relax with views over the green countryside rolling towards the Alps.

The town museum is located in the main tower complex, and if you climb up to the very top there is a nice view in every direction. Inside there are small historical displays and an art collection.

This is great wine country and the surrounding hills are patched with vineyards. There are several defined wine routes from here and they take you through Merlot, Cabernet, Prosecco, and Raboso country. There are many cellars to visit and we enjoy a pleasant sunny afternoon visiting several of them.

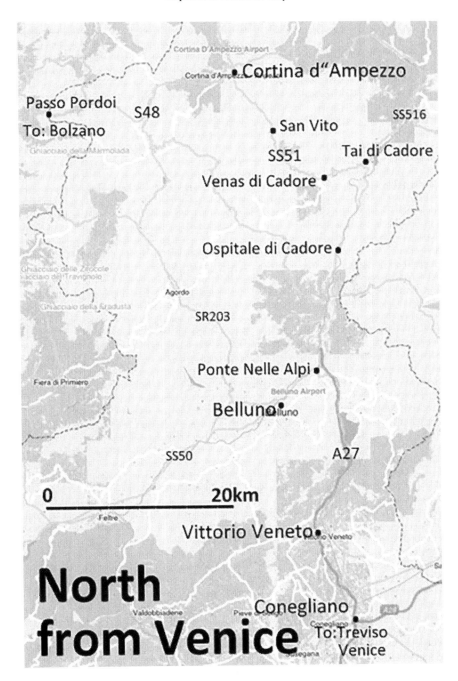

It's time to move on so we drive north to **Vittorio Veneto** (http://www.venetoinside.com/en/discover-veneto/surrounding-in/treviso/context/surroundings/surrounding/vittorio-veneto/) which lies in a picturesque position at the foot of the Prealpi. The name of the city was chosen in honor of the king, Vittorio Emanuele II, and was formed when the two ancient centers of Serravalle and Ceneda united. The final battle of the First World War was fought here.

Serravalle is an old, walled district with many fascinating 16th century houses; a rather dull cathedral with an altarpiece by Titian; and the Loggia Serravallese (1462) which houses a small museum. We walk the center of town and find it very interesting. Ceneda has an 18th century cathedral with little appeal and the remains of the 15th century San Martino Castle.

The last of the major towns before you enter the Dolomites is **Belluno** (http://www.italia.it/en/discover-italy/veneto/belluno.html). This has a lovely position on the Piave River and it provides good access into the mountains. The tourist office gives us leaflets on hiking and ski resorts but we are time limited so we opt to stay in town. Piazza dei Martiri, is the heart of the modern town while the more interesting Piazza del Duomo is the old town center.

The yellow-stone Gothic cathedral has an elegant interior while the Rettori Palace is a frilly Renaissance building now hosting the town administration. The Torre Civica is all that's left of a medieval castle. Also, here is the *Civic Museum*, with some fine works from the 15th to 18th centuries. Piazza del Mercato, which is now hemmed in by porticoed buildings, was once the ancient Roman forum.

SS51 now heads north towards **Cortina d'Ampezzo** (http://www.italia.it/en/discover-italy/veneto/poi/cortina-dampezzo.html). This chic resort town has hosted a Winter Olympics and is a great center for exploring the snowy Dolomiti. Cortina draws nature lovers in summer and skiers in winter. The scenery is spectacular and the surrounding ranges contain numerous peaks that rise above 3300 meters.

Cortina has three town museums, all housed in one building. There is a modern art gallery, a paleontological museum, and a section dedicated to the historic communal administration of Cortina. Unless you are a museum freak, you can give them a miss.

There are dozens of cable cars starting at various points along the valley floor. The most spectacular ride is on the Freccia nel Cielo which departs from behind the Olympic stadium. This has three sections and it reaches the top at Tofana di Mezzo at 3214 meters. You don't have to be a skier to enjoy this trip.

The **Faloria-Cristallo** area surrounding Cortina is known for its slopes and fresh-snow runs. The area has a beautiful setting and it offers a total of 120 km of ski trails and 52 lifts, all of which are part of the grand Dolomiti Superski circuit.

If down-hill skiing is not your thing, you can still enjoy cross country skiing, off track skiing, telemarking, excursions with "snow shoes", and you can even descend by sled. The Olympic Ice Stadium provides opportunities to ice skate, play hockey and curling, and practice many other winter sports.

Mountain climbers will enjoy the Dolomites rocky cliffs, and the pastures and forests of the Ampezzo basin are the destinations for those who like to go trekking, Nordic walking, and mountain biking. You should never get bored because there is a comprehensive 300 km network of trails.

One of the greatest drives in Europe, the Strada della Dolomiti, is 110 km of twisting and turning along a road showing the results of great engineering design. We leave Cortina on road SR48 then, later on, take SS241 into Bolzano. Glorious photo opportunities wait around each of the dozens of hairpin turns. The highest point on the drive is at Passo

Pordoi. It takes 2.5 hours to do the trip fairly slowly but I feel it has been rushed.

Bolzano (http://www.bolzano-bozen.it/en/bolzano.htm) has some similarities to Innsbruck. This arcaded old town of 100,000 people, with a great open-air market on Piazza Erbe, is worth a stroll and a stop at its Dolomite information center.

In the high-tech, modern *South Tyrol Museum of Archaeology* (http://www.iceman.it/en) we see Bolzano's Ice Man, the 5,000-year-old body of a man found frozen with his gear in 1991. This is probably the most important Stone Age find helping us understand the life of these people.

The city lies in a broad valley basin at an altitude of 265 meters, with three beautiful Alpine high plateaus of rolling hills encircling it. The renowned Via dei Portici with its arcades begins at the western side of Piazza Municipio - Rathausplatz. Via dei Bottai - Bindegrasse is one of the most typical streets in the historic center characterized by its original signs in wrought iron of the numerous artisans' shops.

At the northern end, we visit the Maximilian house, built in 1512 in late Gothic style. This was the seat of the administrative offices of Emperor Maximilian I. Now it houses the *Natural History Museum of South Tyrol* (http://www.museonatura.it/en/default.asp).

The 13th century Castel Roncolo sits atop a small cliff upriver from the town and looks like the most livable medieval castle you can imagine. The central courtyard is hung with staircases and open wood balconies, while many rooms retain all sorts of wonderful medieval frescoes.

Europe's largest high alpine meadow, Alpe di Siusi, separates two of the most famous Dolomite ski resort valleys; Val di Fassa and Val Gardena. The meadow is 13 km wide, 30 km long, and it rises over 2000 meters.

Alpe di Siusi is dotted with farm huts and from mid-June to the end of July there are wildflowers. It is surrounded by Dolomite peaks and is much appreciated by hordes of walkers. The Sasso Lungo Mountains at the head of the meadow provide a dramatic backdrop.

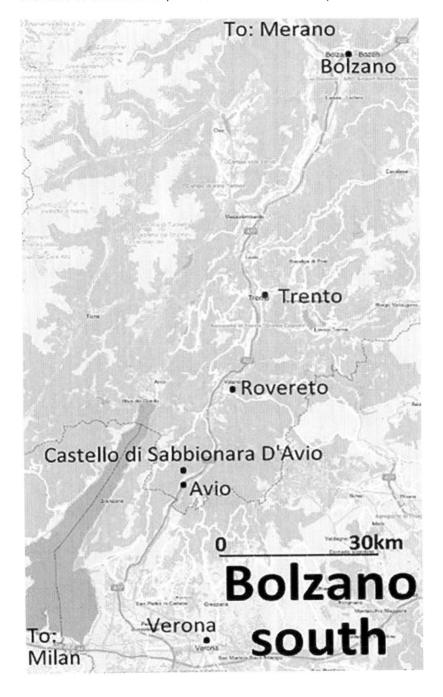

The country around here has so impressed us that we decide to go further north to the garden city of **Merano** (http://www.meranerland.com/en.html) which seems halfway between vine-covered slopes and glaciers. This was once the Tyrol's leading city and since the late 18th century the town has attracted royalty and other important visitors. To house them grand Victorian hotels were built and many of these still offer royal treatment to guests today.

The area has been inhabited since the 3rd millennium B.C. but what you see today is from a much later era. Among the town's landmarks are the medieval city gates, the Gothic St. Nicholas' Church, and the St. Barbara's Chapel, both dating to the 15th century, and the Steinerner Steg stone bridge which crosses the Passer River and is from the 17th century.

The area is well known for its wines, both white and red, and vineyards extend right into the town. There are also extensive orchards. The main shopping street is lined with arched arcades with high end boutiques but as you walk beneath the low ceilings it is easy to imagine the presence of ancient Romans, emperors, and counts.

Just a few kilometers north of the city is **Tirolo**, a small town in lush terrain. There are dozens of castles, manor houses, and monasteries in the region and many are open to visitors. There is a footpath from the center of town which takes you to a small terrace overlooking the Passitio River Valley and this provides great views of the massive Schloss Tirol and the turreted Gothic Schloss Brunnenburg (https://www.merano-suedtirol.it/en/tirolo/artikel/brunnenburg-castle-in-tirolo-45/) dominating surrounding mountains.

The first Tirol castle was built before 1100. The second construction dates to 1139/40. A third phase of construction took place in the second half of the 13th century. In the 19th century, the castle was restored and the keep was rebuilt in 1904. It now houses the *South Tyrolean Museum of History*. A museum tour includes the southern palace with its famous Romanesque portals, and the former dungeon.

Heading south again, stop before you reach Trento at the *Museo degli Usi e Costumi della Gente Trentina* (Ethnographic Museum) (Via Mach 2, San Michele All'Adige) (http://www.museosanmichele.it/), one of Italy's best and largest museums of culture and popular traditions. It fills 41 exhibit rooms on four floors. Its specialty is the agricultural traditions and methods of the Alps, and it includes tools and implements for haymaking, timber cutting, cheese making, beekeeping, and a complete water mill for grinding grains.

Trento

We now head south along A22 to the city of Trento (http://www.visittrentino.it/en). The city has a picturesque Medieval and Renaissance historic center, with ancient buildings worth visiting. Start sightseeing at the **Cathedral of Saint Vigilius**, a Romanesque-Gothic building of the 12th century. This is remarkable for the combination of Lombard Romanesque style with the high vaulted ceiling more common to later Gothic architecture. Under the cathedral are the remains of an early Christian basilica (6th century), with a fine mosaic floor.

The Piazza Duomo, on the side of the Cathedral, with its frescoed Renaissance buildings and the Baroque Fountain of Neptune forms a delicate, civilized enclave contrasting dramatically with the startling expanse of jagged mountains in the background.

Here too is the Palazzo Pretorio (https://www.visittrentino.info/en/guide/must-see/palazzo-pretorio-e-torre-civica_md_2399) from the 12th-century, with a bell tower. It was the main Bishops' residence until the mid-13th century. Inside the palace is the *Diocesan Museum*, which documents the development of local artistic styles and techniques, especially in wood carving and sculpture as well as displaying religious items.

Look up as you follow wide **Via Belenzani,** which runs north from the Piazza del Duomo, to see some of the best of Trento's painted façades. This is my favorite street in town, with its series of palaces painted with historical, classical, and mythological motifs, and exhibiting faux architectural details. Near the north end of the street, on the right, is the 16th century Palazzo Municipale, with the 15th century Casa Geremia opposite.

Elsewhere in town, the 1520s Church of Santa Maria Maggiore (http://www.visittrentino.it/en/cosa_fare/da_vedere/dettagli/dett/chie sa-di-s-maria-maggiore) has some history. This was the site of the preparatory congregations of the Third Council of Trent (1562 –1563) where the Catholic Counter-Reformation was launched. In the choir of the Renaissance church are a beautiful organ gallery from 1534 and a fresco from 1563.

The Castello del Buonconsiglio (http://www.buonconsiglio.it/index.php/en/Buonconsiglio-Castle/castle/Visit/Introduction), was where the ruling prince-bishops of Trento resided from the 13ᵗʰ century to the end of the 18ᵗʰ century.

The castle is vast, and this is where the Famous Council of Trent met and effectively put up a wall between Catholicism and the Protestant churches. It now includes a museum and the notable Torre dell'Aquila, with the *Cycle of the Months* fresco painted around 1400. The Castello houses the *Museo Provinciale d'Arte*, which displays sculptures, period furniture, archaeological, and ethnological collections. Also here, is the *Museo del Risorgimento* where exhibits relate to Italy's struggle for unification and liberation from the Austro-Hungarian Empire.

Another tower of interest is *Torre Verde* which is along the former transit path of the Adige River. This is said to be where persons executed in the name of the Prince-Bishop were deposited in the river. We now visit the Palazzo delle Albere, a Renaissance villa next to the river built around 1550. It now hosts a modern art museum.

The *Museo delle Scienze di Trento* (Museum of Sciences of Trento) (Corso del Lavoro e della Scienza 3) (http://www.muse.it/) is in a stunning building. The dramatic outline of its soaring glass walls is designed to echo the silhouettes of the surrounding mountain peaks and slopes. it is filled with hands-on, multimedia, and sensory experiences that bring the artifacts and the subject to life.

The *Museo dell'Aeronautica Gianni Caproni* (Museum of Aeronautics) (Via Lidorno 3) is Italy's oldest aviation museum. It is next to the Trento Airport and is dedicated to the memory of Gianni Caproni, the Italian aeronautical engineer and aircraft designer. More than two dozen aircraft are exhibited in the museum.

Viticulture has been a business here since Roman times. Pinot Grigio and Chardonnay grapes are grown here, and the high, cool slopes provide marvelous bright, sharp, light and aromatic vintages. There are also good *spumante* or sparkling wines, and the reds from the northern part of the region are pleasant.

Just to the east of Trento lies Castello di Pergine. This mediaeval castle has been converted into an elegant hotel and restaurant, within attractive grounds and walled gardens, and hosting several cultural events during the warmer months. The castle includes 20 guest rooms, and three towers which are also available for accommodation.

South of Trento is **Rovereto**, with its 14th century Castello providing beautiful views of the town below and the mountains rising from the Adige Valley. Inside the castle is one of the region's best museums of the two world wars and their effect on local towns. Near the center of town, the *Museo Civico* explores local silk manufacturing and has worthwhile collections of Greek and Roman artifacts, as well as local dinosaur finds.

It is now south to the city of Verona. We pass through Avio and on the slopes of Monte Vignola see the **Castello Sabbionara** which was a true fortress and has now been delicately restored. It can be visited and is open Wednesday – Sunday 10 a.m. - 6 p.m. (March - September), and Wednesday - Sunday 10 a.m. - 5 p.m. (October and November). In August, it also opens on Tuesdays.

Built in the 11th century and enlarged in the 13th century, it was on the line between the constantly warring neighboring powers of Venice and Austria. We admire the splendid frescoes of the Veronese school on the walls of the Guard House, and the Room of Love on the top floor of the keep.

Verona

Above us stands a balcony; around us a crowd. The balcony is bare but most of us can hear the words, "But, soft! What light through yonder window breaks? It is the east, and Juliet is the sun!" Verona was the setting for the most famous love story in the English language, Shakespeare's *Romeo and Juliet*. It is hard not to get caught up in the moment. But this is perhaps one of Europe's great cons.

It is not known if a Romeo or a Juliet ever existed. Certainly, if they did, Juliet did not live here at this house we are admiring. In fact, it is believed to have been a brothel in the 19th century and it was acquired by the city in 1905. Shakespeare never visited Verona so his story is of an imagined location.

The city realized that it was on to a potential winner so it established this attraction to keep visitors happy. Unfortunately, the whole thing is a contrived sight. That doesn't stop millions of visitors coming here and it doesn't stop us. We do draw the line, however, at visiting the so-called Juliet's tomb which has become a money-raiser for a Franciscan monastery.

Aside from Juliet, the remains of Verona's past are much in evidence today and they are a great attraction for visitors. It is hard not to be impressed by the **Arena di Verona** (Piazza Brà, 1) (http://www.arena.it/en-US/HOMEen.html), an elliptical amphitheater resembling Rome's Coliseum, dating from the first century.

It is the first thing we see as we enter the central city. It's only slightly smaller than the Coliseum in Rome but its setting within a huge piazza makes it even more striking.

It has been hosting spectacular events for 2000 years: gladiatorial contests, medieval jousting, circuses, and bull fights. During July and August, it becomes an opera house where more than 20,000 people enjoy music by Verdi and Mascagni. The acoustics are amazing and microphones are not used at most performances. I'm told that the performances of *Aida* are stunning. That's a good reason to go back.

The arena is on one side of a gigantic square where we also find the neoclassical town hall, the Renaissance palace called the **Gran Guardia** (http://www.tourism.verona.it/en/enjoy-verona/art-and-culture/monuments-and-sights/gran-guardia-palace), a large fountain, and many restaurants. We walk down **Via Mazzini**, the most fashionable street in Verona. There are no touristy products or souvenirs here, just elegant fashion on a par with Rome and Milan. Prices are out of our budget.

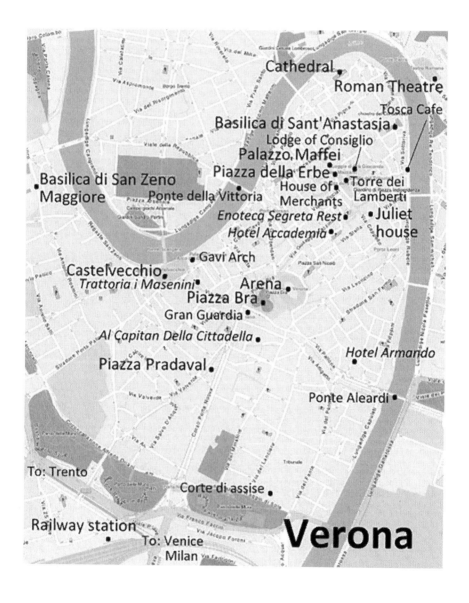

Verona is good for walking or biking but it is difficult to negotiate by car so we park in an underground parking station. The Adige River meanders through the city and most points of interest are on a peninsula on the west bank.

The pedestrian street eventually opens out to the **Piazza delle Erbe** (http://www.verona.com/en/guide/verona/piazza-delle-erbe-verona/), a lively square flanked by medieval and Renaissance palaces. This was formally the Roman city's forum but now it is packed with shoppers and sightseers. The view is just stunning. Everywhere, there are buildings of interest.

The **Torre dei Lamberti** (Via della Costa, 1) (http://www.tourism.verona.it/en/enjoy-verona/art-and-culture/monuments-and-sights/lamberti-tower) which soars to 80 meters dominates the scene and there is a lift to the first level then a sturdy staircase to the top. You can climb the whole way but be warned, there are many, many stairs.

The early 14th century **House of Merchants** was built to house the local merchant's association. It has been restored a few times during its history, and many of the original elements of its architecture have been altered, but it is still an important example of medieval architecture. Today, the building houses a bank.

On the western side of the square is the **Palazzo Maffei** with its three-floor Baroque façade. The first floor has five arches with elegant balconies above. The top of the façade is designed as a balustrade with six statues. There is a restaurant facing the square and you can enter the courtyard and take a look at the imposing columns inside.

The Casa Mazzanti is also marvelous. In the center is a fountain from the 14th century and a Roman statue called the *Virgin of Verona*.

Under an archway to a side street is the Piazza dei Signori with a statue of the poet Dante in the center. Again, the view is stunning. Here is the **Palazzo del Governo** (http://www.tourism.verona.it/en/enjoy-

verona/art-and-culture/monuments-and-sights/palazzo-del-governo)
and behind Dante sits the **Loggia del Consiglio** with its frescos and
statues.

Under another archway is the **Arche Scaligere**
(http://www.verona.com/en/guide/verona/arche-scaligere/), outdoor
Gothic tombs surrounded by wrought-iron fences and gates. There are
fascinating things to see in all directions.

It would not be Italy without some magnificent churches. Two are
nearby. We visit the **Basilica di Sant'Anastasia** (Piazza Sant'Anastasia at
Corso Sant'Anastasia) (http://www.tourism.verona.it/en/enjoy/history-
heritage/churches-holy-places/basilica-of-sant-anastasia), Verona's
largest.

It was started in 1290 and its façade is still not complete and probably
never will be. It is, however, the finest representative of Gothic design
in the city and the interior has been decorated by many 15th and 16th
century artists.

Verona's red and white striped **Cathedral** (http://www.sacred-destinations.com/italy/verona-cathedral) also deserves a visit. It was begun in the 12th century but over the centuries, it has been the subject of several interventions and today it is a blend of Romanesque and Gothic styles. A door in the cathedral gives access to two other churches and the remains of a 4th century basilica.

We were keen to see the **Basilica di San Zeno Maggiore** (Piazza San Zeno, 2) (http://www.sacred-destinations.com/italy/verona-san-zeno) which is said to be one of the most significant Romanesque churches in northern Italy. The building is from the first part of the 11th century, the massive rose window in the façade is from the early 13th century, and the 48 bronze panels on the magnificent doors are from the 12th century.

The **Castelvecchio** (http://www.historvius.com/castelvecchio-museum-457/), a 14th century castle, stands near the Adige River. This stronghold, complete with its own fortified bridge across the river, was so mighty that it survived the centuries intact until the Nazis bombed it in World War II. It is now an art museum with some excellent 15th century sculptures and several painting masterpieces from the Middle Ages.

If you are not into art it is still worth wandering the maze of halls, passageways, stone staircases, and ramparts. Close by is the **Arco dei Gavi**, a first-century Roman triumphal arch.

The *Archaeological Museum* (Rigaste Redentore, 2) (http://www.tourism.verona.it/en/enjoy-verona/art-and-culture/monuments-and-sights/roman-theatre-archaeological-museum) is located on the hill in the ex-convent of San Gerolamo (15th century). It contains a wealth of Roman artifacts found all over Verona and as a bonus the museum has a great view over the river and the city.

The adjacent **Roman Theater** in its splendid setting was built towards the end of the 1st century B.C. and is used for musical and other activities.

Another Roman structure worth seeing is **Porta Borsari** (Corso Porta Borsari) an ancient Roman gate which dates to the 1st century A.D., though it was most likely built over a pre-existing gate from the 1st century B.C. This was the city's main entrance and was therefore richly decorated.

Away from the main tourist area is the **Giardino Di Palazzo Giusti**. This is undoubtedly one of the most beautiful Renaissance gardens in Italy and is well worth a visit. It is a spacious garden featuring flower beds, fountains, statues, a cypress-lined avenue, and one of Europe's oldest labyrinths. It dates from the late 16th century but has been redesigned since then.

There is much more to see. Verona is a beautiful city for wandering. For a city that reached its peak under the medieval Scaligeri princes, it is doing very well today. It is undoubtedly among the great cities of Italy although most international visitors devote all their time in this area to Venice rather than Verona. In my mind, this is a mistake.

There is no disputing the attraction of Venice. A large number of visitors, famous, infamous and ordinary have been visiting for centuries. Verona is a contrast and much more a living city. You need to see both.

There is plenty of accommodation but like many Italian cities, it tends to be expensive. The *Accademia Hotel* at Via Scala 12 in the center of the shopping district is a large first-class tourist hotel. It lacks a bit of atmosphere but is clean and has good service. The three-star *Armando Hotel* is acceptable and is better value. The historic center is just a few minutes' walk from the hotel and the rooms are modern, spacious and clean.

Eating and drinking

Our most recent brief visit hardly makes me an expert on Verona restaurants and things change all the time but everyone is raving about Café Tosca (Via Ponte Nuovo, 8) (366 592 2835), one of the most elegant bars in the city. It is a great place to stop in for a coffee with a pastry or to have a glass of wine with some delicious *focaccia*.

Verona's oldest restaurant, Ristorante 12 Apostoli (Corticella San Marco, 3) (045 596 999), is a tourist trap or unique experience depending on your point of view. You will certainly never forget the interior ambiance of the restaurant, the amazing basement wine cellar, and archaeological exhibit.

Al Capitan Della Cittadella (Piazza Cittadella 7/a) (045 595 157) is a country-style restaurant set in a former palazzo. It has excellent fish dishes and a comprehensive list of local wines.

Trattoria I Masenini (Via Roma 34) (045 806 5169) is a basic welcoming restaurant with two dining rooms decorated in simple, warm colors. The menu offers regional dishes alongside typical Italian fare, as well as house specialties.

Enoteca Segreta (Vicolo Samaritana) (045 801 5824) has an excellent location, good food, and pleasant service. The two-level restaurant will be full of locals not tourists but the staff all speak English and are very helpful. The food has a homely feeling to it and the wine selection is excellent.

Verona has one more claim to fame. The cake known as *Pandoro* was created here and has since been patented in Italy. The light and fluffy star-shaped sweet cake with a dusting of icing sugar on top is now well-known as a Christmas cake in many parts of the world.

The **Verona Card** (http://www.tourism.verona.it/en/information/travel-your-way/verona-card) gives free or discounted access to museums, churches, and other attractions in Verona as well as free travel on AMT buses. Visitors can buy either a one- or a two-day card. The card is sold at museums, churches, and tourist information offices.

The cost is €18.00 for 24 hours and €22.00 for 48 hours (November 2018). The time starts from the first moment you show the card in a monument/museum or on the bus. It is a standard price with no special categories of price for students or over the 60s.

Elsewhere

Founded in the 2nd-century B.C., **Vicenza** (http://www.italia.it/en/discover-italy/veneto/vicenza.html), which is east of Verona, prospered under Venetian rule from the early 15th to the end of the 18th century. Among the public buildings erected in Roman times that survive are the remains of the theater, now incorporated in a more recent structure, and sections of the aqueduct to the north of the city.

The city has a beautiful, compact town center and attractive villas and viewpoints in the hills a short walk away. I am told it is one of the country's wealthiest cities. It was inscribed on the UNESCO World heritage Sites in 1994. In 1996, the site was expanded to include the Palladian villas outside the core area.

The work of Andrea Palladio gives the city its unique appearance. A total of 26 buildings known to have been designed or constructed by Palladio or attributed to him, make up the World Heritage site - 23 in the city itself and three villas in its immediate environs.

If you arrive by train, the railway station is to the south-west of the town center. It's a short walk to the old town gate, Porta Castello, but first, you can visit the Giardino Salvi just outside the gateway. This is a shady park, with many statues and the Palladian Loggia Valmarana. Inside the gate and off to your right, is Palazzo Porto Breganze, designed by Palladio, but never finished.

Around Verona

The Corso Andrea Palladio is the main street in town and it is largely pedestrianized. This allows us good views of the many palaces along here. The street ends at Plaza Matteotti where we see the Palazzo Chiericati, which now houses the *Civic Museum*, and tour the Teatro Olimpico, the oldest indoor theater in Europe and Palladio's last work.

The theater is open throughout the day. The building was modeled on ancient Roman theaters, with a curved amphitheater, graded stepped seating, and lavish ornamentation.

We wander back into the center and discover Piazza dei Signori. Here we find one of Palladio's most famous works, the Basilica. The huge Gothic hall is used for exhibitions. Across the square is the Loggia del Capitaniato which remains unfinished, the 16th century Monte di Pieta, and the church of San Vincenzo. You can't miss the slender Torre di

Piazza which was started in the 12th century. A tourist office is near here and they have a good map and other information.

Two other structures worth seeing are away from the city center. Villa Rotonda (http://www.villalarotonda.it/en/homepage.htm) is Palladio's strict neoclassical take on an ancient temple designed as a home. Also, near here is Villa Valmarana, a 17th century Palladian-style villa with remarkable 18th century frescoes inside by Giambattista and Giandomenico Tiepolo. Both can be visited by taking bus Number 8 from downtown.

The Palladio links have inspired an architecture study center and museum, the *Centro Internazionale di Studi di Architettura Andrea Palladio*. This displays architecture exhibitions in a palazzo designed by Palladio, the Palazzo Barbaran da Porto.

Mantua (http://www.italia.it/en/discover-italy/lombardy/mantua.html) is south of Verona. It was one of the main cultural and musical hubs of northern Italy but is now often neglected by visitors who are focused on other places. This leaves Mantua agreeably crowd-free. A visit is worthwhile because it has several architectural treasures and artifacts, elegant palaces, and medieval and Renaissance cityscape.

Marooned between artificial lakes on three sides, the old town has remained almost unspoiled, and of medieval dimensions. The town's center has three spacious and lively piazzas that join together and reflect development over seven centuries. The cathedral with its Baroque façade has a splendid, grand interior.

In 2008, Mantua became a UNESCO World Heritage Site based on its Renaissance planning and architecture. We visit the Renaissance-style Palazzo Te (Viale Te) which hosts the *Museo Civico*. As you enter the vast square cloistered courtyard of Palazzo Tee it can take your breath away. This beautiful building has its original frescoes preserved, giving the appropriate ducal magnificence to hall after hall and room after room

The Palazzo Ducale (Piazza Sordello) is a residence made up of a number of buildings, courtyards, and gardens. It is a majestic, overwhelming maze of gardens and galleries, chapels, and courtyards, statues, staircases, and frescoes. Approach via the Piazza Sordello, which is flanked by the Palazzo del Capitano and the Magna Domus – two of the most ancient buildings, with distinctive spiky silhouettes.

On a corner of the Piazza Sordello, is a beautiful little 15th century house with a small, square front garden. In the center is a wonderfully realistic yet strange bronze statue of a court jester. This is Rigoletto, a character from Verdi's opera of the same name.

A number of local companies offer sailing trips, which range from around €10 for a 1.5-hour trip up to €20 for a five-hour excursion to San Benedetto Po. If you're feeling really nautical, you can even sail all the way to Venice for the day.

Because the area is largely flat, it is ideal for exploring by bicycle in spring or autumn, when the weather can be ideal. Starting from Mantua, a 20 km round trip can take in the fabulous Bosca Fontana Nature Reserve with gorgeous views of the city.

It is worth going west from Verona to see **Lake Garda**. This is the largest in Italy. Its wider part to the south is surrounded by morainic hills that were left when the glaciers receded, while the northern part is enclosed by the mountains that create its fjord-shape. You should find a congenial base and spend leisurely days exploring the lake, picking out what each little town has to offer.

There is much to see but there are two sights not to be missed. The Vittoriale degli italiani (http://lakegarda.gardasee.de/museum/vittoriale.html) is a hillside estate in the town of Gardone Riviera.

It is where the Italian writer and nationalist Gabriele d'Annunzio lived from 1922 until his death in 1938. What you think of this place will depend a lot on your point of view. Some find it monumental, others think of it as a folly. It probably is a bit of both.

Visits to d'Annunzio's house are by 25-minute guided tour only, so we join a group. The rooms are said to reflect his passions, his obsessions, and fears. They are amazing and crammed with books, statues, rugs, drapes, ornaments, and a myriad of rare and beautiful objects, many connected with the women in his life. One room is an Arabian tent with gold and black damask walls.

The *Museo della Guerra* (War Museum) records d'Annunzio's WWI antics. Interesting artifacts including the actual biplane he flew on a propaganda raid over Vienna in 1918. Also, you can see his rare Isotto Fraschini car, a motor-torpedo-boat housed in its own building, and bizarrely, the front half of the light cruiser *Puglia*, built into the terraces of his extensive gardens. There is a bar in the gardens which sells snacks and drinks.

In the same area, The Heller Botanic Garden is just a short walk uphill from the waterfront. The garden is also known as the Giardino Hruska Botanico after its founder, Arthur Hruska, who was the dentist of the last Tsar as well as being a botanist. He began laying out this tropical haven between 1910 and 1971, taking advantage of the sheltered spot and mild climate to plant many exotic species.

Today, the garden is run by a foundation set up by the artist Andre Heller, and works of modern art are dotted among the plants, pools, and streams. The garden is open daily between March and October from 9 a.m.-7 p.m.

The second sight not to miss is in **Sirmione**, an historical center which is located on the Sirmio Peninsula. The busy historical center with its narrow winding lanes is pedestrianized. Today, holidaymakers swarm off the ferries, ignore the history, eat at waterfront cafés, line up for multicolored cones of local ice cream, and elbow their way through the tiny, winding streets.

As well as the usual trinket shops, Sirmione has thermal baths and a health center with hot springs and treatments. The Romans built two castles, two harbors, a settlement, and the gigantic villa that rises on rocks at the end of the headland.

On the foundations of the old eastern harbor, the famous Scaliger Castle (http://www.sirmioneitaly.com/history.php) was built in the 13th century. It is a charming, graceful yet strong and imposing bulwark, defended by a moat and crossed by drawbridges. It includes a rare example of medieval port fortification. It is a real fairytale castle from the exterior but the interior lets it down. Even so it is well worth a visit as you can explore the ramparts, admire views over Lake Garda, and climb the tower.

While in town, you should also visit the large, impressive ruined Villa Romana, out at the end of the headland. The ruins (closed Mondays) are surrounded by the lake and olive groves and the archaeological finds in the small museum are interesting.

Almost all the businesses in Sirmione are aimed at tourists and, unfortunately, most of the restaurants are also tourist standard. Like several other Italian resorts, Sirmione bans visitors from walking around its streets wearing swimming costumes.

Desenzano, the largest of the lakeside towns, is just a short ferry ride from Sirmione. It has a rich old quarter, lively cafés, surprisingly good restaurants, and a 12th century castle looming above the port. You should also see the ruins of a substantial Roman villa, with fine mosaic floors.

The tiny, arcaded Venetian harbor, almost landlocked, is one of the most picturesque on the entire lake, lined with tables for eating outdoors. A hundred meters along, the port quayside is busy with ferries, catamarans, and hydrofoils.

Bardolino, elegant and potently pretty, relaxed but classy, has a 19th century feel to the esplanade with its Edwardian villas and decorative wrought-iron gates. Umbrella-shaded tables cluster at the water's edge while cool, dark wineries line the main street. This lower end of the lake, with its Mediterranean flavor, adequately lulls the visitor into a sense of relaxation.

Riva is at the northern end of Lake Garda and is a pleasant tourist destination. The pretty public gardens by the waterfront have a quaint, middle-aged 'resort' air to them. The town is large enough to support a market and shops; although the lakeside area is packed mostly with gelaterias, cafés, and restaurants aimed squarely at tourists. The waterfront is dominated by one of Garda's fortresses, the Rocca, which contains the town's museum.

Malcesine is pretty, atmospheric, and packed with tourists. The town, on the eastern shore of the lake, is charming, with a maze of historic alleys. A castle with towers to climb guards the waters, and is open to visitors, while mountain slopes rear up behind the clustered buildings. A cable-car takes you right up to the high grassy summit of the Monte Baldo ridge, where you can refresh yourself at several café-restaurants.

8 TURIN AND AOSTA

Piedmont and the Valle d'Aosta are two regions tucked away in the north-west corner of Italy. They are often overlooked by visitors but the area has the best alpine peaks in the country and there are medieval castles, Roman ruins, fashion, and the home of Fiat. Turin is the only major city in these parts and it, of course, is well known because of the controversial Shroud of Turin.

The surrounding Piedmont countryside is largely agricultural while further north there are some good ski resorts, and tunnels through the Alps to France. This Alpine flavor is part of the reason Piedmont feels so un-Italian. Few regions can offer towering mountains, authentic villages, historic towns, ravishing lake resorts, and ancient abbeys and castles within so small an area.

Like Tuscany, Piedmont is a favorite destination for wine buffs. The region produces world-renowned selections such as Barolo, Barbaresco, Barbera, Dolcetto and Moscato D'Asti. However, it's also a perfect destination for travelers hoping to enjoy some fine dining along with their drinks, and its local dishes where butter replaces olive oil and mushrooms and white cheese substitute for vegetables are celebrated throughout Italy.

Turin

Turin (http://www.turismotorino.org/index.aspx?lingua=EN) is a major industrial city with high-tech industries as well as car production but the city has one of the most favorable natural settings in Italy. It is located at the junction of the Po and Dora Rivers and it is in the foothills of the Alps so there are magnificent views of snow-capped mountains in the distance.

Many of the outer suburbs are pretty horrible but its inner core is well-laid out and there are historic churches, squares, palaces, and museums. The wide elegant boulevards lined with imposing mansions with Mansard roofs and French doors remind us very much of Paris.

There is also much history. Much of the city's history is associated with the House of Savoy, a dynasty that lasted for 900 years. It may have reached its peak in 1861 when Vittorio Emanuele II was proclaimed king and Turin became the first capital of a unified Italy for four years.

This is the home of Italy's car industry, its first cinema, and some say chocolate; it's the place in which vermouth and Nutella were invented, and it gave birth to the Slow Food movement.

We arrive in Turin by train and exit the station onto **Via Roma**, the city's main shopping street. This leads north to Piazza San Carlo and eventually to Piazza Castello and knits together many of the city's grandest old palaces and squares. Both of these squares deserve some of your time.

Turin has a very walkable city center and an extremely friendly public transport system if you need to go further afield.

Piazza   San   Carlo (http://www.visitatorino.com/en/piazza_san_carlo.htm) is the center of the city. The huge square was designed in the 17th century and despite being heavily bombed during World War II it remains a great place to see and to relax with a coffee. The square has two churches – San Carlo and Santa Cristina.

North of here is the Science Academy Building (Via Accademia delle Scienze 6) from the 17th century. This houses the excellent *Museo Egizio*

(*Egyptian Museum*) (http://www.museoegizio.it/pages/hp_en.jsp) with its world-class collection.

This was the world's first real museum of Egyptian artifacts and it remains one of the most important today. The collection of 30,000

pieces was largely amassed by the Piedmont Savoy kings but was enlarged by excavations between 1900 and 1935.

Some will argue that none of this should be here but the reality is that some of the prized exhibits have probably been safer here than if they had remained in Egypt. There is statuary, funerary art, a reassembled tomb, and a rock temple all in surprisingly good condition.

The building once contained the *Galleria Sabauda* (Via XX Settembre, 86) (http://www.turismotorino.org/cultura/EN/ID1300/galleria_sabauda) with one of Italy's richest art collections but this has now moved to a new home.

This contains the royal art collections amassed by the House of Savoy so it is appropriate that it is now housed on four floors of the new wing of the Royal Palace. There are plenty of paintings by local Piedmontese artists but also many by others such as van Dyck, Botticelli, van Eyck and Rembrandt.

In the next block, we find the amazing brick **Palazzo Carignano** (Via Accademia delle Scienze 5) (http://www.visitatorino.com/en/palazzo_carignano.htm). The history of this graceful palace with its undulating Baroque façade is closely related to the political and social movement during the 19th century for the unification of Italy. The first king of united Italy, Vittorio Emanuele II was born in this building and later it served as Italy's first parliament building.

Today, the palace is occupied by the *National Museum of the Resurgence*, a large part of it dedicated to the eccentric revolutionary leader of the Risorgimento - Giuseppe Garibaldi. We also see the well-preserved circular chamber where the first parliament of the newly-united Italy was held.

There is a collection of plazas and buildings just north of here that can take ages to explore. Piazza Castello runs into Piazza Reale and Piazza

San Giovanni. Galleria Subalpina, a pedestrian passage from Piazza Castello to Piazza Carlo Alberto is one of the most elegant places in the city. The opera house, the famous cathedral, and the Royal Palace are all here.

The Renaissance **Cathedral** (Piazza San Giovanni) (http://www.comune.torino.it/chiese/sangio.htm), dedicated to John the Baptist, was built during the 15th century and it is adjacent to an earlier bell tower. The Chapel of the Holy Shroud, the current resting place of the *Shroud of Turin*, was added to the structure in the 17th century. Unfortunately, both were damaged during a fire in 1997 but they are now restored.

A few Roman structures can be seen around the Cathedral. The most impressive are the remains of an ancient amphitheater, and the majestic **Porta Palatina** (http://www.italia.it/en/media/virtual-tours/virtual-tour.html?no_cache=1&stuid=159). The latter is an ancient structure with four arched entrances in a high wall, flanked by two impressive towers that served as one of four Roman city gates. The nearby Piazza della Repubblica is home to a huge open market.

The splendid **Royal Palace** (Piazzetta Real, 1) (http://www.visitatorino.com/en/turin_palaces.htm) is a gorgeous nouveau-riche residential complex constructed during the 16th century.

The palace features a graceful façade and refined interiors with glitzy halls, and impressive paintings. There are tapestries, Oriental vases, the royal armory, and elegant gardens laid out by master landscape architect Le Nôtre.

Right next to the western wing of the palace, is located the church devoted to San Lorenzo. The church's interiors are richly decorated with multicolored marble, various statuettes, and fetching frescoes.

On the opposite side of Piazza Castello, we see the attractive **Palazzo Madama** (http://www.visitatorino.com/en/palazzo_madama.htm). This was the home of the regent Queens of Savoy. It has an elaborate Baroque façade and is a mix of medieval and baroque rooms. This houses the *City Museum of Ancient Art*, with varied displays.

We had been told about the **Mole Antonelliana** (Via Montebello 20) (http://www.museocinema.it/mole.php?l=en) so we head east to find it. This must be one of the strangest structures anywhere. It consists of a squat brick base and a steep cone-like roof, which supports several Greek temples, piled one atop the other.

There is a needle-like spire at the very top, rising 167 meters. Begun in 1863 and designed as a synagogue, the Mole is now home to Italy's *National Film Museum*. It is more a tribute to film than a true museum but the sleek, dimly lit interior does contain some famous costumes while Temple Hall screens Italian movies in strange settings.

Even if you skip the museum, you can still ascend to an observation platform at the top in a glass elevator. The views when you arrive are stunning. Admission to the museum is €10 and admission to the panoramic lift is €7. A combined ticket is €14.

Not far away on Via Po is the *Museum of Decorative Arts of the Pietro Accorsi Foundation* (http://www.fondazioneaccorsi-ometto.it/en/museum/page/the-palace/) which is housed in an historical palace from around 1684. The 27 rooms of the museum house thousands of objects which originally furnished the house.

The priceless exhibits cover the full gamut from precious metalwork, porcelain, glass, and ivory, to furniture and paintings. Opening hours are Tuesday to Friday 10 a.m. to 1 p.m. and 2 p.m. to 6 p.m., and Saturday and Sunday 10 a.m. to 1 p.m. and 2 p.m. to 7 p.m. Entrance to the museum including a guided tour is €10.

If paintings by Canaletto, Canova, and Matisse interest you then you must head to the *Pinacoteca Giovanni e Marella Agnelli* (Via Nizza, 230/103) (http://pinacoteca-agnelli.it/visit/en/). This daring art gallery, which opened in 2002, was a gift to the city from the president of the Fiat automobile company.

Situated in the Lingotto neighborhood, this art site has a permanent collection by well-known artists and it also holds temporary exhibitions.

There are some Renoirs, Picassos, and others considered to be world-class.

Monte dei Cappuccini is a place in the hills, just above the Gran Madre church, which is the perfect spot to look down on the city. You can see every detail of Piazza Vittorio and the Mole, but it's also isolated and quiet. Visit in the winter and you'll love the amazing light displays put on every Christmas.

The **Basilica of Superga** (http://www.basilicadisuperga.com/en/) is a church at the top of the Superga Hill. It was built in the early 18th century. The complex can be reached on foot, by car, or by the Superga Rack Railway. The church is quite beautiful and unique. It contains the remains of some of the most prominent members of the House of Savoy.

The guided tour of the crypt is a must. While here, we visit the memorial where in 1948 the entire AC Torino soccer team perished when their plane crashed into the side of the mountain in fog.

The **Roman Quarter** west of the main central area is worth a visit. There are no sensational sights here but the narrow streets lead you to some old walls and columns and there are many trendy shops pubs, cozy restaurants, and bars in the area.

While in this area we visit **Santuario Basilica La Consolata** (Piazza della Consolata) (http://www.turismotorino.org/cultura/EN/ID5247/santuario_della_con solata_%28maria_consolatrice%29) with its splendid interior. Much of it comes from the 17th century and it combines Baroque and Italian Rococo styles.

An older Romanesque tower still stands beside the Basilica. The churches' lovely silver Madonna and Child image is paraded through Turin every June in recognition of the Virgin's protection of the city.

Parco del Valentino (http://www.pianetatorino.it/valentino.htm) (Valentino Park) is very popular with the locals. From the terraces of the park, there are good views across the river. In the center of the park stands the 17th century horseshoe shaped *Castello del Valentino,* home to the Politecnico di Milano, the University of Architecture, and this is a good place to get a coffee.

Also worth seeing is the *Borgo Medioevale,* a replica of medieval mountain castles of Piedmont and the Aosta Valley. The park is also popular at night because of the bars and restaurants here.

Turin is the automobile capital of Italy so it is appropriate that the beautiful *Museum of the Automobile* (Corso Unità d'Italia, 40) (http://www.museoauto.it/website/en) is here. The museum has a collection of cars from something like 80 brands. Highlights are a 1914 Rolls Royce Silver Ghost, many old Fiats, and racing cars by Ferrari and Alfa Romeo. It can be enjoyed by just about anyone.

For something quite different, we take a guided tour of underground Turin. Beneath the hectic and bustling city lies another mysterious and unknown world where time seems to stand still. Fifteen meters below the city, the tunnels of the citadel and the sub-cellars of the Baroque palaces are waiting to let us discover their mysteries.

Another way of seeing some more underground areas is to visit the *Pietro Micca Museum* (via Guicciardini 7a) (http://www.visitatorino.com/en/civic_museum_pietro_micca.htm). This tells you all about the Siege of Turin in 1706 and takes you into the maze of underground tunnels that were constructed at that time. Unfortunately, there are no explanations in English and English guides are rare but if you call ahead you might be lucky.

North of the center is Parco Dora, a former factory district once home to the production lines of Fiat, Michelin, and carpet manufacturer, Paracchi. Now completely transformed, the park's centerpiece is a skeleton of soaring girders, creating a vast space for kids to skate, play basketball and football, and turn out in their thousands for events.

Turin has lots of street markets, all around the city, that serve thousands of people every day. **Porta Palazzo Market**, a 5-minute walk from Piazza Castello, is one of the biggest, cheapest, and most diverse markets in Europe. You will find a treasure chest of knick-knacks, cheap second-hand and vintage clothes, paintings, electronics, furniture, bikes, and foodstuff. The markets are open every weekday morning and all day long on Saturday. On Sunday, Porta Palazzo houses a smaller flea market.

Alternatively, go to **Piazza Benefica Market** and grab discounted designer gear and other bargains. The market is actually in Giardino Luigi Martini where, from Monday to Saturday, the most stylish market of the city takes place. Many stalls offer a good selection of designer clothes, shoes, accessories, and bags at about half the price of the stores.

You will see bull heads in the streets of Turin called toretti. The toretti are water fountains shaped like bull heads which deliver free fresh water all day long.

The **Torino Card** (http://www.visitatorino.com/en/turin_card.htm) is a pass that gives free entry to over 130 attractions in Turin and Piedmont, including museums and royal residences. Other benefits include free travel on public transport in the city and free trips on the panoramic lift in the Mole Antonelliana. Passes last for 48 or 72 hours and cost €35 or €42.

Turismo Torino run the TurismoBus Torino (http://www.turismotorino.org/internaCB.aspx?idA=889&idE=30), a hop-on, hop-off tour bus with three routes which covers the main attractions. Route A operates daily from March to November and at weekends otherwise. Routes B and C operate from April to early November. A 3-route pass for 2 days costs €30.

Free Tour Turin (http://www.freetourturin.com/) has two different free walking tours of the city. The non-profit association is run by young persons who are travelers themselves, and who are really passionate about meeting people coming from all over the world to visit their city.

Turin holds Italy's premier food show, Il Salone del Gusto which now claims to be the world's largest food and wine fair. It is held every two years in October and is sponsored by the Slow Food Movement. It is held in the Lingotto building, once the former Fiat factory, which has been rebuilt into a modern complex, with theaters, a convention center, shopping arcades, and a hotel.

Eating and drinking

Del Cambio (011 546 690) is one of the most elegant, historic restaurants in Italy now meticulously restored to its former glory. Enjoy Piedmontese specialties (although the menu also includes a few fish dishes) surrounded by a gold and red velvet decor. On the first floor, there is a bistro to the rear and the Cavour bar serves a selection of faster, more reasonably priced options.

Porto di Savona (011 817 3500) opened in 1863 when Turin was the capital of Italy so this is one of the city's oldest restaurants. It is situated on the city's beautiful Piazza Vittorio and the warm 19th century tavern has period furniture and tiled floors. The menu includes many old favorites and some new items.

Eataly Lingotto (011 1950 6801) is large food emporium with a large section dedicated to slow food, the international movement born in Turin. Dotted throughout, are informal restaurants and cafés, each serving tasty dishes prepared with high-quality seasonal and local ingredients.

The Circolo dei Lettori (The Readers' Circle) (011 432 6827) was formerly a private members club where Turin's intellectuals, writers, poets, and artists used to meet. Today, the large restaurant is open to anyone. On the menu are regional dishes including *finanziera*, a hearty dish of veal offal and cockscomb cooked with Marsala wine, vinegar, and herbs.

Porta Rossa (Via Passalacqua 3b just off Piazza Statuto) (011-530 816), will delight fish enthusiasts as a large part of its menu is dedicated to seafood. The wine selection has been carefully thought-out but prices are still very reasonable. The atmosphere is relaxed and intimate despite the central location.

Solferino (Piazza Solferino 3) (011 535 851) is a classic restaurant serving traditional cuisine, which has been renowned and popular for 30 years. You can eat inside in air-conditioning or outside at lunch or dinner time.

Dai Saletta (Via Belfiore 37) (011 668 7867) is an authentic trattoria in the middle of the city. With its checkered tablecloths and Italian flags, the restaurant is famous for traditional dishes such as *tajarin* or *brasato al barolo*. The wine list features wine from small local producers.

Osteria di Pierantonio (011 674 528) is a stone's throw from the Lingotto conference center. A lunch time crowd is attracted by its reasonably priced set lunch served at tables spilling onto the street. Homemade desserts include *bônet*, an exquisite regional dish similar to crème-caramel.

Villa Somis (Strada Comunale Val Pattonera 138) (011 631 2617) is located in a beautiful art nouveau villa on top of the hill with a fantastic view of the city from the terrace. It is a lovely setting, and they serve a really ambitious cuisine. One alternative is a set menu of 3 courses which you leave to the cook.

The gentrifying southern district of San Salvario still offers the best bars in town, particularly around the crossroads of via Sant'Anselmo and via Giuseppe Baretti. Many are intimate bars with live music and DJs. I really like La Cuite (Via Baretti 11/G), a wine and cocktail bar full of young people and serving tapas at reasonable prices.

A few minutes around the corner is ORSO (Via Claudio Luigi Berthollet 30/G), a 2014 coffee "laboratory" serving a variety of Arabica and Robusta coffees from around the globe. It's linked to artisan gelateria Mara dei Boschi (Via Berthollet 30/H) which has mouthwatering, cream-free, delights.

Turin Facts

The **Turin airport** (http://www.aeroportoditorino.it/en) is located about 16 km north of the city. A railway links the airport with Dora GTT Turin Station in 19 minutes (€3). From Dora GTT you can reach the Porta Susa station, the Metro, and the center of Turin. The bus service SADEM between the center of Turin and Turin Airport has a bus every 15-30 minutes and includes stops at the railway stations of Porta Nuova and Porta Susa. It costs €7.50.

Turin is connected to the main Italian and foreign **railway** systems and it is an important link between France and Switzerland. The main Turin railway stations are Porta Nuova (http://www.grandistazioni.it), Porta Susa (Tel: 011.538513 booking office), Lingotto (Tel. 011.3173897 booking office) and Stazione Dora.

The most efficient way to get around the city is by **public transport** (buses or trams), especially in the city center, because moving by car becomes really difficult both for parking and for the Restricted Traffic Area. Turin has a widespread network of buses and trams and there is a single driverless underground railway line. There is a €1.50 travel charge for 90 minutes. The Turin public transport company is the GTT (http://www.gtt.to.it/cms/en) and there are many details on this web site.

Taxis are available, but they are expensive compared to many cities and cannot be hailed on the street.

The **Sassi-Superga tramway**

(http://www.gtt.to.it/cms/en/touristfacilities#tramway) is an historical means of transport which connects the Sassi tramway station (situated in Piazza Modena) with the Superga tramway station on a route of 3,100 meters and with a rise of 425 meters. Tickets can be bought in the Sassi tramway station and you can also visit the tramway historical museum which is here.

Ristocolor and **Gustotram** are restaurant-trams which takes you on a journey through the city center while comfortably seated and which gives you the opportunity to taste Piedmontese cuisine served with appropriate wines (http://www.gtt.to.it/en/touristfacilities).

Outside the city

Our first trip outside Turin is to the town of **Nichelino**, 10 km to the south-west. Stupinigi Palace (http://www.visitatorino.com/en/palazzina_stupinigi.htm) was originally intended as a Royal Hunting Lodge but then it was extended into a summer residence for Vittorio Amedeo II.

The final building has a total of 137 rooms and 17 galleries and was the Savoy's equivalent of Versailles. The fantastic and astonishing building has finally re-opened its doors to the public again after many years. Visits are strictly guided only.

Within the giant, sinuous X-shape, local authorities have collected furnishings, paintings, and other decorative elements from dozens of Savoy palaces to create here a sort of museum of 18th and 19th century decor. It is sad, however, to see the work that would be needed to completely restore this grand home. The woods and agricultural land surrounding Stupinigi have been preserved as the Parco Naturale.

Castello di Rivoli, (Piazzale Mafalda di Savoia) (https://www.castellodirivoli.org/en/), is one of Europe's most important contemporary art museums in the small town of Rivoli, east of Turin. The unfinished 18th century castle stands on top of Rivoli Hills. Entry is €6.50 adults and €4.50 for seniors and students. Every Saturday and Sunday a free shuttle connects Piazza Castello in central Turin to Castello di Rivoli, via Porta Susa railway station.

Corso Francia (France Road) is one of the world's longest streets and was built because of the desire of the House of Savoy to connect the Royal Palace in the center of Turin with Rivoli Castle. You can reach it by bus or taxi.

The **La Venaria Reale** (http://www.lavenaria.it/web/), outside the town of Venaria, 10 kilometers north- east of Turin, is a restored mid-17th century Baroque building built for Duke Carlo Emanuele II di Savoia and is now a UNESCO World Heritage Site. Since reopening in 2009 it has become one of the most popular spots in Italy. The enormous palace contains some of the most outstanding examples of European Baroque architecture: the enchanting Salone di Diana, the solemnity of the Galleria Grande and the chapel of Sant'Uberto, and the immense complex of the Scuderie, designed by the 17th century genius, Filippo Juvarra.

Admission is adults €25 which gives access to the Reggia, the gardens and the exhibitions, allows a 10% discount at the estate's cafés, restaurants, snack bars, and bookshop, and reduces the price of garden activities. Other tickets are available.

Out of town

After spending a few days exploring Turin, it is time to rent a car and travel elsewhere. We first go south to see the late medieval town of **Alba**, the truffle and wine capital of Piedmont. It has a 12th century Romanesque cathedral whose lofty dimensions and its 1512 wood-carved chorus suggest Alba's early importance.

Alba has been built on the site of ancient Roman Alba Pompeia and remains of some edifices with marble and mosaics can still be seen. The city once had many towers but only a few from the 15th century remain. The city has a thriving economy, which includes the confectionery industry's world-renowned Ferrero Company.

Our aim is to travel westwards on minor roads to eventually reach Saluzzo. **Verduno**, a small village surrounded by vineyards, nestles beneath its early 16th century castle. It is famous for producing some of the world acclaimed Barolo Wine and for great food. This is more than enough reason to visit.

The fairly unassuming Il Falstaff restaurant is a local favorite. Trattoria Dai Bercau, La Cascata, and Casa Ciabotto are all alternatives with good food, wine and service. There is also a small restaurant in the castle. The atmosphere in the village is great and you can find nice hotels as well.

Cherasco is a fascinating town which it is easy to fall in love with. With its broad streets, it gives the impression that time stopped after Napoleon came through in 1796. Napoleon was very impressed calling it the "most beautiful spot in Italy". There is a collection of splendid buildings many from the 17th century when noble families fleeing the plague in Turin built fine houses along the arcaded main street.

The town's specialty is snails, and it is no coincidence that Cherasco is recognized as the Italian capital of snail farming and has been the home of the International Institute of Heliculture for the last 30 years. Trattoria Pane e Vino, Locanda del Prof, and Pasticceria Barbero are three restaurants where the food can be recommended.

Cherasco is also famous for antiques and antique shops. Italian and French antique dealers and collectors meet here, surrounded by ageless objects for sale in the various markets specialized in antiques, ceramics, glasswork, old books, toys, and models.

Some of the sight-seeing attractions are the 14th century Visconti Castle, the Romanesque church of St. Peter, and the 1672 church of St. Augustine with its Baroque altar. The Palazzo Salmatoris has beautiful architecture and is used today for various cultural events and shows. The civil museum of Cherasco is housed in the beautiful 17th century Palazzo Gotti di Salerno. Its most interesting exhibit is its coin collection.

Cherasco has a handful of good restaurants including slightly refined La Gargotta del Pellico, Taverna San Martino, with a very quaint and atmospheric setting, and Le Quattro Stagioni d'Italia with its large enclosed courtyard.

Saluzzo in the Po Valley is a major discovery. During the Renaissance, the town had its own court and today it still has cobbled streets and a castle. It is one of the most delightful towns in Piedmont and has succeeded in preserving the architectural and urban features of various eras within its ancient walls.

All along steep Salita al Castello are narrow medieval houses sandwiched between grander Renaissance dwellings with frescoed façades. Elsewhere, there are flowering terraces, inviting cafés, and fascinating antique shops.

We see the 15th century cathedral on a cobbled square which has a façade decorated with rose-windows and statues. The interior contains a magnificent Baroque high altar. The Dominican church of San Giovanni, begun in 1330 has a noteworthy façade. The present Town Hall is the former Jesuit College.

We now head north to **Pinerolo** which In the Middle Ages was one of the main crossroads in Italy. The Cathedral dates from the 9th century and has an attractive bell tower. From here it's up the Chisone Valley. We stop at a small village for a drink and see immobile old men slumped in folding wooden chairs near the square. We hear the distant tolling of church bells floating past as they roll down the long valley. There are few other noises and very little moves.

Now it's on to **Sestriere** which is only 17 km from the French border, and a host of good ski resorts. These make up the Milky Way skiing area which hosted the 2006 Winter Olympic Games. The village is completely surrounded by mountains, and here you find one of the biggest ski resorts in Italy. In the summertime, it is possible to play golf on Europe's highest 18-hole course. The road climbs and twists and turns then after crossing the ridge we now go down the valley of the Dora Riparia.

The Roman town of **Susa** (http://www.italia.it/en/travel-ideas/the-mountains/the-susa-valley-and-its-villages.html) has a cathedral, the triumphal Arch of Augustus which was erected in 8 B.C. to celebrate a peace treaty between the Gauls and the Romans, a castle and the remains of a Roman amphitheater, and interesting aqueduct. The town attracts visitors because of its important Roman ruins and medieval monuments, and because Susa has easy access to amazing countryside.

Probably the most spectacular sight in the valley is the fortified **Abbey of Sacra di San Michele** (http://www.sacradisanmichele.com/eng/test_display/index/id/16/cat/8/), perched atop a rocky outcrop, overlooking the village of Avigliana. Someone suggested that the stony bulk, elaborate carvings, and endless staircases, give Sacra di San Michele abbey a movie-set air somehow more appropriate to a Tibetan monastery than to a Christian abbey.

It is believed that it was started in 983 and rebuilt in the 1100s. Access is up a forbidding staircase carved out of the solid rock. Inside, the feeling of being part of something ancient and monumental is overwhelming. The frescoes within are some of the most priceless in Piedmont.

We now travel north-east, bypassing Turin, and see the sanctuaries of Sacro Monte and Santuario di Oropa. Sacro Monte (sacred mountain) (http://www.varese2008.org/sacro-monte-di-varese.html) is an extraordinary collection of 45 chapels. Each houses a fresco with scenes from the life of Christ. This has been a place of pilgrimage since the 15th century.

The Sanctuary of Oropa is a group of Roman Catholic buildings in the municipality of Biella. These include the Ancient Basilica, the royal apartments of the House of Savoy, a big library, the Royal Gate, and the more recent Upper Basilica. The Sacro Monte di Oropa, a devotional path, is not far from the sanctuary and is now composed of twelve chapels.

The Aosta Valley

The Aosta Valley is dramatically beautiful and has a long history which has left many fortresses, castles, towers, and mansions, often splendidly conserved. Many are in dominant sites, guarding the valley or points of strategic importance.

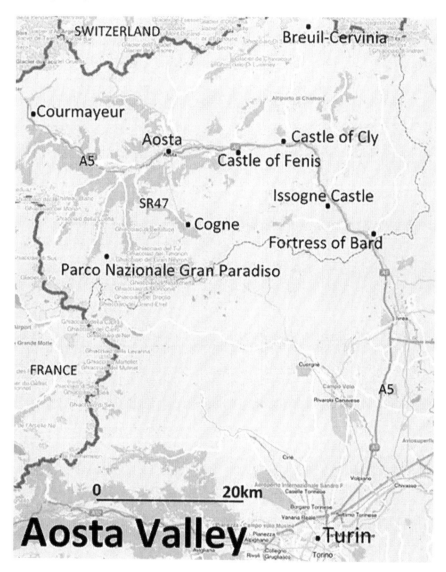

The first major site we see is the austere **Fortress of Bard** (http://www.fortedibard.it/en) just after we leave Piedmont. A structure was built here in the 11th century as a toll station and it was fortified in the 13th century. Napoleon destroyed it in 1800 but it was rebuilt in the 1830s. It is now the *Museum of the Alps*.

There are many more places to see. **The Castle of Issogne** (http://www.in-italia.com/italy/aosta/issogne-castle/) is the next. The site has been inhabited since Roman times but the present building is from the early 16th century.

From the outside, it seems massive and severe but inside, the court rooms and colonnades are magnificently decorated. In fact, this is more a house than a fortified castle. There is an amazingly impressive wooden staircase and entry with carved wood and beautiful frescoes adorning the entire walls.

Much of the outer walls of the 1250s **Castle of Cly** above the town of Chambave are still in good condition and you can visit in summer. The impressive building is surrounded by a Romanesque chapel and some residential buildings, stables, and cellars.

A few kilometers further, the **Castle of Fenis** (http://www.italia.it/en/discover-italy/aosta-valley/poi/castles-in-valle-daosta.html) is one of the most famous castles in the Aosta Valley because of its extraordinary architecture and the evocative power of its towers and turreted walls. It is now a museum and is one of the most visited places around here. It opens April to September 9 a.m. to 7 p.m. daily, and October to March 10 a.m. to 1 p.m. and 2 p.m.to 5 p.m. except Monday.

Aosta

The Valle d'Aosta provides stunning views of Mont Blanc. Cable cars take you over the border into France but these are not for those suffering from vertigo. The main town around here is Aosta (http://www.aosta-valley.co.uk/destinations/aosta-town/) which is laid out in a grid pattern thanks to the Romans. Walking around the pedestrian-only historic center is easy.

The Arco d'Augusta built in 24 B.C. honors Augustus, who gave his name to Augusta Pretoria, the town's original name. The Roman Theatre is being restored, while the Roman Forum can be visited beneath ground level. The Cheese Tower is alongside the amphitheater and other Roman ruins are scattered about.

Some of the original city walls plus the four towers that stood at its corners are still standing, and elsewhere the Praetorian Gate and the remains of a cemetery, baths, apartments, and more can be seen. There is also a well-preserved Roman bridge, still paved with river rocks.

The town is also enriched by its medieval relics with the 11th century cathedral and its double façade the most interesting. Inside there is a plaster sculpture of the Last Supper. There are two bell towers, built for different buildings, and ancient stained-glass windows. We see the wonderful mosaic floor, carved choir stalls, and the Museum, which houses Gothic masterpieces that were placed here for safe keeping.

The 11th century Church of St. Orso, dedicated to the patron saint of Aosta, still has many of its original frescoes. The bell tower, the church, the cloisters, and a lime tree provide memories of medieval times.

Just to the west, the **Parco Nazionale del Gran Paradiso** (http://www.pngp.it/en), Italy's first national park, is an oasis for ibex, golden eagle, and chamois. The park is named after the mountain which is located in the park. It encompasses 700 square kilometers of beautiful alpine terrain. The valley floors are forested and there are alpine meadows at higher altitudes with rocks and glaciers higher again.

The most popular gateway to the park is Cogne. The town center is surrounded by four valleys and there is a large meadow at the southern edge. During the summer, hiking and mountain biking are popular. Two places in the area worth seeing are the Lillaz Waterfalls which are nice falls in a beautiful setting, and the Giardino Botanico Alpino Paradisia a beautiful, calm garden which can be a feast for all the senses.

There are hotels and restaurants in Cogne and elsewhere. April to October are the favored times for visitors. The northern part of the park has higher mountains, more spectacular views, and plentiful hotels and picnic areas but serious hikers like the southern valleys.

Aosta Valley's picturesque Observatory and Planetarium (http://www.oavda.it/english/index.htm) in the Saint-Barthélemy Valley can be visited. While you can go on daytime visits, I would recommend the night time visits which consist of two-hour sessions of sky viewing with the naked eye and by using telescopes. The observatory opens from April to August: from 4.30 p.m. to 9.30 p.m. and from September to March from 3 p.m. to 9 p.m.

There are shows at the Planetarium on Saturdays and during July, August, and September there are also shows on Sundays.

We go north for a day trip to **Breuil-Cervinia** (http://www.cervinia.it/pages/BREUIL CERVINIA i en/432), more than 2,000 meters above sea level and with a great view of one of the most famous mountains in Europe, the Matterhorn. We are not in the Swiss resort of Zermatt, but instead, we are still in Italy.

There is great skiing especially for beginners and those who like wide pistes. This is a small village with a lovely atmosphere and stunning scenery.

Finally, we go west from Aosta to **Courmayeur** (http://www.italia.it/en/discover-italy/aosta-valley/poi/courmayeur.html). This is located at the foot of Mont Blanc, the highest mountain in Western Europe. It is one of Europe's most famous ski locations, and it also contains the Giardino Botanico Alpino Saussurea, which claims to be Europe's highest botanical garden. In the summer months, Courmayeur is a popular destination for hikers.

It is a traditional, old Italian mountaineering village that has retained much of its character. The village has a charming traffic-free center with cobbled streets and well-preserved buildings which has a great evening atmosphere. As the lifts close, people crowd the many bars while others patronize the small shops which sell smart clothes, nice food, and books.

Nearby, are the thermal springs of Pré-Saint-Didier. For over 150 years the thermal spas were one of the main attractions of the Valle d'Aosta and now, once again, the facilities are open. The facilities range from whirlpool baths to relaxing baths with still water, toning cascades, themed saunas in wooden chalets, aromatic steam baths, a mud treatment area, color therapy rooms, and aromatherapy rooms.

9 EMILIA-ROMAGNA

This is one of northern Italy's lesser known regions yet it is strategically placed between Venice, Milan and Florence. It is an area that was known to the Etruscans and to the Romans and is considered by many to be the food capital of the country. It was once summarized as the region of slow food and fast cars and it certainly has both.

There is some lovely countryside and there are several towns and cities which demand some of your time. Curiously, it is overlooked by many visitors to Italy. We will start in the south-east and move slowly to the west.

Rimini

We start our exploration at Rimini (http://www.visit-rimini.com/), one of Italy's most popular beach resorts with 15 kms of fine sandy beach. The seaside promenade, Lungomare Augusto Murri, is lined with restaurants, hotels, and nightclubs. We are somewhat surprised to find Rimini is also an art center and that it has an interesting historic center, Roman ruins, and museums.

Good sandy beaches spread north and south of town. One of the popular attractions is Rimini Terme, a thermal spa with treatment facilities, heated salt water pools, and a wellness center.

Rimini has several interesting Roman remains of which the main town gate, which was erected in 27 B.C., is the oldest. There's a Roman bridge that was built in 21 A.D., and part of a 2nd century Roman amphitheater that could hold over 10,000 spectators. We visit Piazza tre Martiri, the site of the old Roman Forum, and see the early 16th century temple, Tempietto di S. Antonio da Padova, and the clock tower, built in 1547.

Piazza Cavour is the main square. In its center is the circular Pigna fountain built in 1543 but incorporating some Roman remains. Around the square are several interesting buildings including a 13th century palace, the town hall, the old fish market, and a neoclassical theater. Behind the theater is the mildly interesting and much-altered 15th century fortress, Castel Sismondo, which is now used for cultural events.

Viserba, 4km to the north, is an old fishing port and popular holiday resort. Its popular park, Italy in Miniature, has 272 Italian architecture scale reproductions representing all of Italy's regions. While in this area, we decide we must leave Italy for a day and visit San Marino.

San Marino

The Republic of San Marino was founded in 301 A.D. and is the most ancient European Republic. It sits at 700 meters above sea level on Mount Titano and is completely surrounded by Italy. San Marino is well worth the visit for its shopping, scenery, monuments, museums, works of art, and typical tourist spots.

The pedestrian area has narrow streets, interesting squares, and several churches. There are also a thousand stores and boutiques making shopping an important visitor activity.

The first things we see are the Porta di San Francesco, the Church of San Francisco and the attached Convent of Friars Minor founded in 1361. The *San Marino State Museum and Art Gallery* is housed in the two cloisters of the courtyard. In the center of town is the Palazzo Pubblico where the Council has met for hundreds of years.

One of the highlights of the city is the view from the Towers Terrace with the Romagna Coast on one side and the ancient Republic on the other. The First Tower (Guaita Tower) dates back to the 10th-century. Some parts of the tower were used as a prison until 1970. It now provides the best view of San Marino. On the second and highest pinnacle of Mount Titano, stands the Cesta Castle which was built at the end of the 11th century.

Today, this houses the *Museum of Archaic Arms*. The Third Tower called Montale, dates back to the end of the 13th century. We stop to see La Pieve, the Basilica, built in the early 19th century, in neo-classic style with a portico of Corinthian columns. The massive bell tower, originally in Romanic style, was rebuilt in the 1600's. Internally, the Basilica has three aisles and seven altars.

The *National Museum* (http://www.sanmarinosite.com/en/things-to-see/museums/national-museum/) is in an antique building in the historical city center called Palazzo Pergami Belluzz.

For stamp and coin collectors San Marino is interesting. Its stamps and coins are in great demand and are an important source of income for the country. The first stamps were issued in 1877. While I didn't try to buy any of these, I did pick up some interesting modern ones to add to my collection.

Local money dates to 1862, the year in which San Marino signed a monetary agreement with the Italian Monarchy, allowing it to issue its own currency. Only 280 of the first five-cent, copper coins were issued. Today, the Italian and San Marino Euros circulate in both countries without distinction even though San Marino is not a member of the European Union.

North along the coast

There are a string of small towns and nice beaches along the coast north of Rimini. This area is very popular in summer but for the rest of the year, it is rather quiet. The nucleus of **Bellaria-Igea Marina** is a fishing village that dates back to at least medieval times when there was an inn for pilgrims and other travelers.

Today, the village is best known for 7 kilometers of beautiful beach, great hotels, fine restaurants, and numerous recreational opportunities. Travelers looking for a place to jog, cycle, or simply enjoy being outdoors will love the Sentieri per l'Uso. This is a 14-kilometer trail that runs along the river.

Cesenatico dates back to 1302 when the harbor was dug and the fortress was built in order to defend it. In 1502, Leonardo da Vinci designed the Canal Harbor. The hamlet 'Cesenatico Centro' is situated on the west side of the harbor and represents the historical core of the city. It is a both touristic and a residential area at the same time.

Cervia is a seaside resort with 10 kilometers of sandy beaches. See Bagno Fantini, which has an astounding number of world-class facilities, including a spa. Cervia is very small, and you can walk around the city center. Piazza Garibaldi is the main square and it houses both the cathedral and the town hall and is lined with cafés.

The *Museum of Salt* (Via Nazario Sauro, 24) (http://musa.comunecervia.it) is a building on the banks of a canal that documents Cervia's history as an important salt-producing city. During the winter, the population of the resort falls drastically and many places close.

Ravenna

Ravenna (http://www.sacred-destinations.com/italy/ravenna) is the main town north of here. This has a great history. In the 5th century, it was first the capital of the Western Roman Empire then later the Visigoth Empire. In the 6th, 7th and 8th centuries Ravenna was the capital of the Byzantine Empire. It was one of the greatest cities on the Mediterranean.

Even today, it doesn't pander to tourists but it is still a pleasure to explore. The train and bus stations are both on the eastern edge of the city and Via Farini leads directly to the Piazza del Popolo, the city's heart. The local economy has boomed because of a big chemical industry and the discovery of offshore gas deposits, but the town center is quiet, with its pedestrian-friendly core and locals on bicycles.

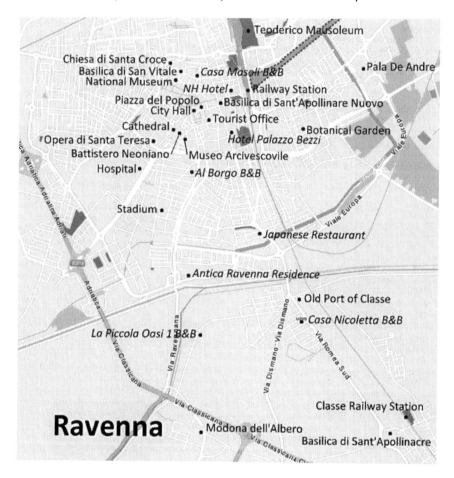

Today, it has eight early Christian buildings inscribed on the UNESCO World Heritage List. Despite all this, Ravenna looks like many other Italian cities except that its churches have low Byzantine domes rather than soaring spires. One thing, however, sets it apart. The city's mosaics from the 6th, 7th and 8th centuries are certainly the finest in Western Europe and the most splendid outside Istanbul.

If you want to see all the important buildings and mosaics, you need to spend at least a day and a night in Ravenna and do some planning on when to visit the various sites. The tourist information office stocks maps and useful information including lists of the sights with their opening times. If you are arriving in Ravenna by train, you can walk into the historic center in about ten minutes.

We see our first mosaics at the **Basilica di Sant'Apollinare in Classe** (http://www.ravenna-info.com/sant-apollinare-in-classe.htm), a church about six kilometers south of the central city. The apse of the church contains exceptional turquoise and gold mosaics.

We see further examples back in the city center at the unpretentious 5th century **Mausoleum of Galla Placidia**. Translucent window panels bring the blue, green, gold, and orange mosaics alive. The low arches and domes are lined with fifth-century mosaics made of the tiniest of tiles. The UNESCO citation calls this "the earliest and best preserved of all mosaic monuments, and at the same time one of the most artistically perfect."

We debate about paying to see anymore but then succumb at the nearby *Basilica of San Vitale*. The mosaic of Christ astride the world, flanked by saints and angles is outstanding and makes this 6th century domed church something special. This is one of the most important examples of early Christian Byzantine art and architecture in Western Europe. Apart from a few Baroque frescoes added to the dome, the entire decoration is in mosaic, but they look like paintings.

Also worth seeing, is the **National Museum of Ravenna** (Museo Nazionale di Ravenna) which is situated here in the cloisters of the former Benedictine Monastery. There are Roman monuments, carved ivory, pottery, textiles from the Coptic to Renaissance periods, icons, weapons, and more but it needs someone to bring it into the 21st century. You can buy a combined entrance ticket which also gets you into the Baptistery of Bishop Neon and the Mausoleum of Theodoric.

We go to the center of the city at Piazza del Popolo and feel a Venetian vibe. This charming piazza is lined with attractive historic buildings. The most outstanding is the Palazzo Comunale (Town Hall), originally built in the 15th century. There are cafés with outdoor tables, and it's a lovely place to sit and relax.

We succumb again to see more mosaics in the 5th century **Neoniano Baptistery** (http://www.sacred-destinations.com/italy/ravenna-battistero-neoniano). The baptistery belonged to a cathedral that no longer exists. Intricate mosaics line its entire dome, culminating in a large mosaic medallion at the top picturing the Baptism of Christ by John the Baptist.

The adjacent present cathedral building is from the 18th century while the campanile is from the 10th or 11th centuries. The *Archiepiscopal Museum* (Piazza Arcivescovado, 1) in the 6th century Archbishop's Palace is famous for its ivory throne of Maximian, one of the most famous carved ivory works of all times.

As we leave the city, we see the **Mausoleum of Theoderic** which was built in 520AD as his burial place. It is entirely made of Istrian stone and the upper level is topped by a big monolithic dome with twelve square arches bearing the names of eight apostles and four evangelists. This remarkable piece of late Roman architecture is capped by a single stone more than 10 meters in diameter. It is the only UNESCO-cited attraction here without a single mosaic tile.

Ferrara

We leave Ravenna to its dusty but fascinating history and take the road to Ferrara through Argenta. This is near the Valli di Campotto natural oasis, and the Comacchio Lagoon. Much of the Comacchio Lagoon is today a wildlife sanctuary and Argenta is the home of the *Marsh Museum* which offers many facilities for bird study.

Ferrara (http://www.italia.it/en/discover-italy/emilia-romagna/ferrara.html) has history, interesting buildings, and more from a point in time some 900 years later than Ravenna. This is almost a perfectly preserved medieval and Renaissance city, with barely a car or a tourist to be seen. We immediately notice the bells coming from the churches and hundreds of bicycles that are a major transport mode in the city.

The city was dominated by the Este family who built a powerful duchy. They built palaces, castles, and churches, became associated with Pope Alexander VI through marriage, and finally gave it all up as Pope Clement VIII took over the city as his personal fiefdom. Today, the city is on the UNESCO World Heritage List.

The walled city has much of its history intact and we quickly warm to its charm. It has palaces fronting narrow streets, doors opening to reveal arcaded courtyards, and churches where bells ring as they have for 500 years. The walls are massive enough for paths, trees, and lawns and there are some great views over the town.

It's a good idea to explore the city's network of medieval and Renaissance streets with a map as these picturesque streets are quite extensive. A wide boulevard divides the medieval quarter from the Renaissance side. In the Renaissance city, all is space and dignity: parks, palazzi, and grand houses. In the medieval quarter, there is a jumble of roads, packed with churches, cloisters, old palaces, and ordinary houses.

Maps and other information are available from the tourist information office in the courtyard of the Castello Estense. If you arrive by train, you can walk into the historic center in about twenty minutes, or catch a local bus.

Perhaps the top attraction is the 12th century **cathedral** which is a mixture of Gothic and Romanesque styles. It has a triple façade with a magnificent porch and a bell tower that has never been finished. The interior was completely refurbished in the 17th century in a grandiose classical style but it is rather dark and the art-work can be difficult to see. The grandiose *Last Judgment* by Bastianino (16th century) is probably the artist's masterpiece.

There are three palaces and a castle worth seeing in town. The **Castello Estense** (http://www.castelloestense.it/en?set_language=en), a moated four-towered castle was home to the Estes. It started as a menacing massive fortress but two hundred years later it had white marble balconies, and fine, frescoed rooms which can still be seen today.

It is used for provincial administration offices but you can still view many of its once lavish rooms by paying a fee. It's worth paying a small extra to climb the Torre dei Leoni, a tower with views over the town center, and you can go down into the small and gloomy prison cells.

Opening hours vary throughout the year. From October to February they are 9.30 a.m. - 5.30 p.m. Monday closed. From March to May, and

September they are 9.30 a.m. - 5.30 p.m. every day. In June, 9.30 a.m. –
1.30 p.m. and 3 p.m. – 7 p.m. every day. In July, and August, 9.30 a.m. –
1.30 p.m. and 3 p.m. - 7 p.m. Monday closed.

The **Palazzo dei Diamanti** (http://www.palazzodiamanti.it/895/palazzo-dei-diamanti) is another Este building which today houses a collection of
museums. Its name comes from a friend of the Este family. It was once
lavishly decorated but now it contains mainly frescoes and sculpture.

Finally, the **Schifanoia Palace**
(http://www.ferraraterraeacqua.it/en/ferrara/discover-the-area/art-and-culture/villas-historical-residences-and-theatres/palazzo-schifanoia) now holds the *Civic Museum of Ancient Art*, a diverse
collection of coins, medals, bronzes, plates and pottery, and
archaeological finds.

You can walk or bike over 9 km of Ferrara's walls, which were
commissioned by Duke Ercole I d'Este and built between 1493 and 1505
with walking paths. Elsewhere, there are hidden squares and churches
which you will only find when you get lost.

The *Museum of Italian Judaism and the Shoah* opened in December
2017 in the old prison as the city's newest attraction. This shows that
before the Lombards, Normans, and the Spaniards arrived in the
peninsula, the Jews were already there – and were already Italians. The
project is being built in stages and construction is on-going. It opens
Tuesday to Sunday from 10 a.m. to 6 p.m. and Thursday. to 11 p.m.

There are quite a few little restaurants and bars dotted around the
central cathedral area. You need to try *Salama al Sugo*, a local delicacy
that looks quite awful but tastes good.

The Palio di Ferrara horse race will be run late May in 2018. The
weekends before are full of medieval games and competitions. First
recorded in 1259, it claims to be the oldest of these kinds of horse races
in the world.

Bologna

It is only 50 km to Bologna (http://www.bolognawelcome.com/en/), the capital of this Emilia-Romagna region and a city of young people. The city's university is the oldest in Europe and is renowned for both its medical school and business school.

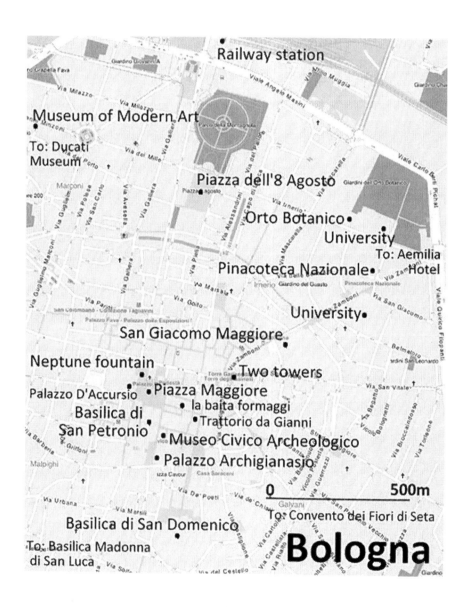

The university gives the city an edge and it is no surprise to find a lively art and culture scene. The city also has several important sights but we plan to leave these until tomorrow.

We discover that Bologna's best hotels are too expensive for us so we search for something more reasonable. This proves difficult and we finally settle on a plain choice without many frills for around €150/night.

We celebrate our arrival with an aperitif in one of the many bars and cafés on the main square. Most offer a selection of nibbles to accompany your *prosecco*. Or try a *brachetto* – a slightly sweet, sparkling red wine.

After dinner, we go looking for a nice café and have no difficulty in finding several with a young crowd and a vibrant atmosphere. Students have also influenced the profusion of funky clubs and well-stocked bookshops which we see around town.

Today, our first stop is at the tourist office in **Piazza Maggiore**. Immediately we are surrounded by sights. This is the oldest part of the city and this huge pedestrian square is surrounded by some impressive medieval and Renaissance buildings.

The 14th century **Palazzo d'Accursio** (old town hall) (http://www.bolognawelcome.com/en/places-to-see/history-art/params/CategorieLuoghi_7/Luoghi_250/ref/Palazzo%20d%27Accursio%20o%20Comunale) has retained its splendor and there are a couple of museums inside.

We don't want to start the day with a museum so we head across the plaza to the adjacent Piazza del Nettuno with its well-known **Neptune Fountain** which has become the symbol of the city. When it was first built in 1566, it was very controversial but we doubt if it raises any eyebrows these days.

On the other side of the square is the **Basilica di San Petronio** (http://www.bolognawelcome.com/en/places-to-see/history-art/params/CategorieLuoghi_34/Luoghi_129/ref/Basilica%20of%20San%20Petronio) a huge Gothic building which has never been completed. It is said that the Pope stopped the construction when he was told that the structure was planned to be larger than St. Peter's in Rome. The scale of the building is indeed massive and some of the 22 art-filled chapels are interesting.

Most of the present building dates from the 17th century but there has been a church here for over 1000 years. The building does not look very impressive from the outside but the Baroque interior has several interesting works of art. Entry is free. The building is dedicated to the fifth-century bishop and patron saint of the city, St Petronius.

The *Museo della Storia di Bologna* (Museum of the history of Bologna) (via Castiglione 8) is an institution focused on the long history of the city. It is housed in the medieval Palazzo Piepoli and the permanent exhibition has multimedia exhibits and graphic panels along with archaeological findings and artworks, including paintings by the Carracci family, Guercino, Balla, and Marinetti as well as sculptures by Lucio Fontana and Arturo Martini.

The city is well pedestrianized and easily explored by foot. Immediately to the east is the *Museo Civico Archeologico* (http://www.museibologna.it/archeologicoen/) an archaeological museum in an elegant Palace. There are important local pieces from the Etruscan period, some Greek and Roman sculptures, and a major Egyptian collection spread over several floors.

Next to this is the **Palazzo Archiginnasio** which was home to Bologna's famous university until 1805. Today, it is a huge public library but you can also take a tour to visit the impressive wooden Anatomy Theatre where medical students once watched instructors and you can watch actors.

If you walk south you reach the **Basilica di San Domenico** (http://www.italyguides.it/us/italy/emilia-romagna/bologna/churches-basilica/basilica-of-san-domenico.htm) from the 13th century. We admire the tomb of St. Domenico, a Renaissance masterpiece by a group of sculptors that included a young Michelangelo. It is said that the *San Procolo* here was a preview for his later *David*.

It is impossible to miss the **Garisenda Tower** and its larger cousin the **Asinelli Tower** so we now walk north towards them. The two 'twin' towers (http://www.bolognawelcome.com/en/places-to-see/history-art/params/CategorieLuoghi_10/ref/Towers) stand at the point where the old Roman Aemilian Way entered the town in Piazza di Porta Ravegnana.

These towers are believed to have had important military functions but with their imposing heights, they would also have signified the social prestige of noble families. In the late 12th century, at least one hundred towers dotted the town's skyline, but today only twenty have survived the ravages of fire, warfare, and lightning.

The Asinelli Tower was built in the 12th century by the Asinelli family. It is 97 meters high with a lean of about two meters and an inner staircase of 498 steps. It is quite an effort to reach the top but the view over the city is excellent. The cost is €3. There is a fantastic view of the red roofed-streets fanning out below.

The Garisenda Tower, built around the same time, is much smaller (47 meters) but with a greater lean due to an early and more marked subsidence of the foundation. It is believed to have been initially higher, but some 12 meters was knocked off it in the 14th century. This tower cannot be climbed.

We still have more to see and the day is rapidly passing, so we head north-east along Via Zamboni to the **San Giacomo Maggiore church** (http://bolognaitaly.ca/attractions/sangiacomomaggiore.html). Placed in one of the most attractive squares of Bologna, it was built between 1267 and 1315 and it was restored at the end of the 15th century. The interior has a wide and bright nave and it holds some famous art treasures, among them the Bentivoglio Chapel.

This is on the edge of the university district so we proceed to the *Pinacoteca Nazionale di Bologna* (National Art Gallery) (Via della Belle Arti 56) (http://bolognaitaly.ca/museums/pinacotecanazionale.html). This gallery has many works from the painters of the Bologna school that flourished from the 14th century. Some of the best works are by Guido Reni including a revealing portrait of his mother. There are also paintings by Vitale de Bologna and other Italian masters such as Raphael.

While talking art, the *MAMbo* (Museum of Modern Art at Via Don Minzoni 14) (http://www.mambo-bologna.org/en/) will interest some readers. Currently, it also houses the art collection from the Museo Morandi so you get more for your money. Note that the museum does not open until noon and is closed on Mondays.

The university is considered the oldest in Europe and was founded in 1088. Its big student population helps this area a youthful vibe and the surrounding streets are somewhat scruffy but crammed with bookshops, bars and Laundromats. The university theater and museum are well worth seeing.

Bologna Old City is one of the largest in Europe and this area is enriched by elegant and extensive arcades. In total, there are some 38 kilometers of arcades in the city's historical center, and these encourage us to walk throughout the area. The Portico of San Luca with 606 arches, the longest in the world at 3.5 km, connects Porta Saragozza (one of the twelve Gates in the ancient Walls) with San Luca Sanctuary.

While the arcades are obvious, Bolognas 55 km network of canals, most now covered over, that make up Bologna's own "Little Venice" are not so well known. You can get a glimpse of one in Via Piella by opening the small graffiti-covered hatch in the wall for a view on to the Reno Canal.

Basilica di Santo Stefano, also known as Sette Chiese (Seven Churches) is worth seeing in Piazza Santo Stefano, an elegant broad square that's perfect for a coffee stop. From the wonderful square, the façade of three churches may be seen: the church of the Crucifix (on the right), the church of the Calvary (in the center), and the church of Saints Vitale and Agricola (on the left). The first one dates back to the period of the Lombards and now preserves the 1019 crypt, and in the third you can see the remains of 6th-century mosaic floors.

The **Basilica Madonna di San Luca** (Via San Luca 36) (http://www.bolognawelcome.com/files/PDF/3ante_san_luca_ENG-WEB.pdf) may not be worth the 3.7 km climb but at least there is an attractive porticoed route. There are some nice frescos around the altar and a highly-valued icon of the Virgin Mary. The view over the rolling countryside is nice.

Motor cycle enthusiasts will be interested in the *Ducati Museum* (Via Cavalieri Ducati, 3) (http://www.ducati.com.au/company/visit_us/index.do). The museum, to the west of the city center, is adjacent to the Ducati factory and shows all the models that have made the brand famous worldwide. A factory guided tour is interesting and a good way to learn all about the production processes.

Car enthusiasts will enjoy the excellent *Ferruccio Lamborghini Museo* (http://www.museolamborghini.com/index.php?lang=en) in the town of Funo di Argelato just north of Bologna. If you are lucky, your guide could be the charming Fabio Lamborghini, nephew of the famous industrialist who can tell you intimate family stories about the large collection.

One of the principal attractions in the city is food. Local producers gather weekly on Saturday morning in Piazzetta Pasolini, via Azzo Gardino e Giardino Klemlen to offer high-quality fruit and vegetables, cheese, cured meats, bread, beer, and street food. From May to September this also operates on Wednesday evenings.

Since reopening in 2014, the barn-like Mercato di Mezzo in the city's traditional market district of Quadrilatero has become a new foodie destination. This makes a good lunch spot and there are several outlets offering delicious meals such as tortelloni with taleggio and walnuts. Eataly World (https://www.eatalyworld.it/en/), is a sprawling complex of 40 restaurants, grocery stores, food laboratories, and cooking classrooms on the edge of town. If you have an interest in food, don't miss it.

You should enjoy a meander around the food stores and markets of the three streets immediately east of Piazza Maggiore - Via Clavature, Via Pescherie Vecchio and Via dei Orefici. These, and a few others, form a picturesque cluster of narrow lanes packed with opulent small stores bursting with food. This is a good place to find *mortadella*, the local sausage.

This is where you will find Trattoria da Gianni (Via Clavature) a small, intimate trattoria, tucked down an unmarked side alley. This is one of Bologna's most popular restaurants which focus on Bologna and regional specialties. Also here, is La Baita Formaggi (3 Via Pescherie Vecchie), the most renowned cheese shop in the city, and at lunchtime shoppers can stop off for a proper meal of *affettati* (cold cuts).

Every cobblestone square seems to feature tables where you can sit under startling church or palace facades. These are great places to enjoy a dark, strong coffee in a tiny cup or sample the local gelato which comes in as many flavors as you can imagine.

For those readers into shopping, Via dell'Indipendenza is lined with Italian brands and international chain stores. For a more traditional selection of up-market leather goods manufacturers, clothing retailers and perfumers, head to Via Massimo d'Azeglio off Piazza Maggiore.

There are several routes south of Bologna to Florence and we take the most western one (S64) to **Porretta Terme** (http://www.termediporretta.it/en/porretta-terme-2/). Located 400 meters above sea level and it is surrounded by beech, fir, chestnut, and pine forests. Porretta Terme owes its fame to its spa waters which have been used for 2000 years. There is a large modern hotel located near the "Puzzola" Spa Park and several others in town. Every Saturday morning, the underground springs of Porretta Terme open to the public.

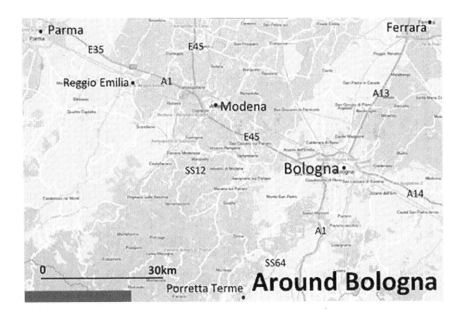

Around Bologna

Modena

There are two more cities that we want to see, so we now wind through delightful country to the north-west to Modena (http://www.emiliaromagnaturismo.com/en/locations/modena-mo/details?ID=1028). This is the home of Ferrari and Maserati so it is not a complete surprise to find a modern city largely rebuilt after the bombings of World War II. This is not to say that the city has no soul or history.

The **Cathedral** (http://www.lifeinitaly.com/tourism/emilia/modena-cathedral), in fact, is one of the most impressive in northern Italy. The 12th century Romanesque building marks one of the earliest appearances of rounded arches and its façade has an impressive rose window, and great Romanesque reliefs, most notably, the *Creation* and *Temptation of Adam and Eve* reliefs on the west façade.

Art works inside include two 15th and 16th century terra cotta nativity scenes, a 13th century marble parapet portraying the Passion of the Christ, a 14th century wooden crucifix, and mosaics. Inside the cathedral, the gallery above the crypt is outstanding while the crypt itself is a forest of columns. It opens daily, 7 a.m-12:30 p.m. and 3:30 p.m.-7 p.m. Entry is free.

The 87 meter-tall, slightly-leaning bell tower was started in 1167 and added to in 1319. Inside there are some frescoes. It is open Sundays and holidays from April - July and Sept - Oct, from 9 30 a.m. to 12:30 p.m. and 3 p.m.-7 p.m.

After the Pope took over Ferrara, the Este family moved to Modena and established a duchy in the last few years of the 16th century. They managed to bring some art from Ferrara with them then built up the collection while they were in Modena. This is displayed today in the *Galleria Estense* in the Palazzo del Musei. There is a bust by Bernini, paintings by most of the Bolognese school of artists, and works by El Greco and Velazquez.

Also here, is the **Bibliotheca Estense**, one of the best libraries in southern Europe with over 500,000 printed works. We pay the small entry free to see some of the ancient volumes which are kept under glass.

While I will never own a Ferrari, I visit the Enzo Ferrari House Museum (Museo Enzo Ferrari) (Via Paolo Ferrari, 85) (https://museomodena.ferrari.com/il-museo), a short walk from the historic center. It houses a display of Ferrari and other exotic cars. Inside the childhood home of Enzo Ferrari are a series of videos about the history of the cars, photos, and memorabilia. There's also a café and store. The museum is open daily, 9:30 to 6 p.m. or until 7 p.m. from April to October.

I find visiting the *Galleria Ferrari* (https://museomaranello.ferrari.com/) in Maranello, around 18 km from Modena, an interesting experience. There are engines, antique cars, the latest model Ferrari cars, racing trophies, and more on display. Visitors can now test their driving skills in semi-professional Formula 1 simulators at both Ferrari Museums. A shuttle bus to the museum in Maranello departs from the Modena museum every 90 minutes, starting from 9. 40 a.m.

There is another car museum worth visiting. One of the most beautiful collections of Maserati's is hosted in a typical farm house located in Cittanova di Modena (Via Corletto, 320). The Maserati Collection was first established by the Maserati brothers and was later expanded. It has remained almost intact to this day. It currently includes 23 motor vehicles.

The whole Emilia-Romagna region is known throughout northern Italy as a gastronomic hotspot and Modena is probably its epicenter. The city produces the 'best' Lambrusco wine and balsamic vinegar and we pick these up together with the ingredients for a wonderful picnic at the morning outdoor market on Via Albinelli. Mercato Albinelli is a fabulous, historic food market full of fresh and local fare, this is a 'must-visit'. It keeps alive the tradition and heritage of the ancient market that since the Middle Ages has spiced up the city.

Naturally, there are some excellent restaurants including the famous Chef Massimo Bottura's modern Italian restaurant **Osteria Francescana** which was the World's No. 1 Restaurant in 2016 and again in 2018. In 2017 it was No. 2. according to a list compiled by William Reed Business Media. But also try the backstreets which are crammed with some of the best restaurants no one's ever heard of!

Another must-visit place is what is considered to be the oldest deli in the world – *Hosteria Giusti*. We find a little park and indulge in a long-lunch under the trees while watching local children at play and elderly residents walking their dogs.

Continuing west, we come to smart and well-to-do, **Reggio Emilia** (http://www.italia.it/en/discover-italy/emilia-romagna/reggio-emilia.html). It has a handsome historic center and great restaurants. The town has existed for 2200 years but much of what you see today was built by the Este family during the 400 years it controlled the town, from the 15th to the late 18th century.

We walk from Piazza del Monte, where we find Palazzo del Monte di Pietà, to nearby Piazza Camillo Prampolini, which has the most important municipal and religious buildings. The Cathedral with its unfinished façade is here as is the Baptistery and the City Hall. The Basilica of San Prospero and the Church of St. Augustine are two other places worth seeing.

Piazza Fontanesi is probably the place I enjoy most. The trees in the piazza provide shade. There is a fruit & vegetable market some mornings, and there are plenty of bars for aperitif, and restaurants for a delightful evening meal. There are outdoor concerts in the summer.

The Valli Municipal Theatre is simply breathtaking. Elaborate frescoes adorn the ceiling, the main stage curtain is painted, and the gilded box seats with their red velvet chairs are magnificent. If you have the opportunity to see a concert, ballet, or opera live within these historic walls, consider yourself one of the lucky ones.

Bicycles are the preferred mode of transportation here. If you feel like going for a ride, Reggio Emilia has the longest city bike trails in Italy. For lunch or dinner, try Il Pozzo (Viale Antonio Allegri 7). Their outdoor courtyard is quite enchanting and their selection of food and wine is a bit pricey but outstanding.

Reggio makes a practical base for exploring the Apennines to the south. A village not to be missed is **Quattro Castella** which takes its name from four castles rising on four hills. There is a great concentration of archaeological finds here.

Parma

While Modena was home to opera star Pavarotti, Parma (http://www.italia.it/en/discover-italy/emilia-romagna/parma.html) was the home of Toscanini and an attraction for Verdi who was born close by. Parma rose to prominence in the 16th century as the seat of the Farnese duchy, then later it came under the control of the French Bourbons. Even today, you can see that this is a prosperous region. Parma is as famous for its art and architecture as it is for its cheese and ham.

Parma is about mid-way between Bologna and Milan and the railway station is about 10 minutes walking distance from the city center. Parma is also linked with other Italian and European cities by bus.

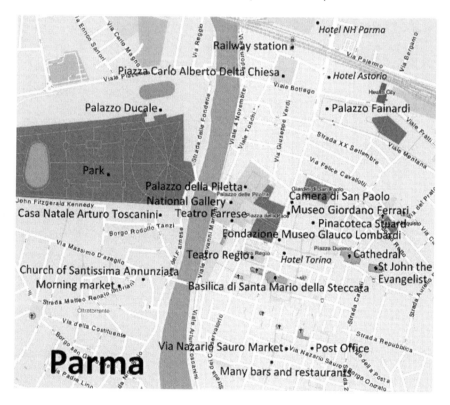

Parma's Cathedral (http://www.sacred-destinations.com/italy/parma-duomo) from the 12th century is a great example of Romanesque architecture. It has an unusual octagonal dome and the bell tower is topped by a gilt copper angel. Inside, there are some beautiful frescoes. The pink marble octagonal Baptistery has doors that are elaborately decorated.

The 10th century abbey church of Saint John the Evangelist had to be rebuilt in the early 16th century after a fire but it has an interesting façade and a bell tower. The Palazzo della Pilotta from 1583 is next on our list. It houses the Academy of Fine Arts, a library, gallery, museum, and theater. You enter through the cathedral-like Teatro Farnese. Built in the 1600s and blown up in World War II, the stunning wooden theater was reconstructed in the 1950s.

The artworks in the Galleria Nazionale (Piazza della Pilotta - 9/A) are worth seeing. The collection starts with medieval panel paintings of saints and martyrs and continues into portraits of the 19th century. Highlights include High Renaissance works from the Florentine school, Canaletto's gold-bathed cityscapes of Venice, and Da Vinci's sketch of a young girl's face, *La Scapiliata*. It opens Tuesday to Saturday 8 30 a.m. to 7 p.m.; Sunday and holidays 8 30 a.m. to 2 p.m.

The Festival Verdi at the gilded 19th century Teatro Regio is Parma's annual music gala. During the rest of the year, the theater has everything from opera and ballet to jazz and experimental dance. To see the opulent interior, noted for its painted ceiling, tapestry-like curtain, tiers of colonnaded loggias, and massive French chandelier, you can take a guided 30-minute tour, available mornings and afternoons.

On Strada Matteo Renato Imbriani, alongside the stone arches of Santissima Annunziata church, the morning market is an emporium for fresh local fruits, vegetables, jams, juices, butter, cream, grains, wines, — and especially ham hocks and cheese blocks.

A market of a different kind can be seen on Via Nazario Sauro at the monthly Saturday art and antiques market. At other times, the tiny passage holds multiple vintage shops. Via Luigi Carlo Farini is a lively strip of bars and restaurants.

Because this area is so well-known for food, we take a Food Valley Gourmet Tour. Here we experience how Parmigiano Reggiano is made, we see the process for making Parma Prosciutto then we lunch at a winery. After lunch, we head off to witness the love that goes into making Aceto Balsamico. All in all, it is a good day.

10 ESSENTIAL EXPERIENCES IN NORTHERN ITALY

I claim little expertise in art, architecture, opera etc. so am very grateful to the visitor centers, museums, professional societies, and other experts who have helped with the preparation of this section.

Art

Most people visit Italy with some basic knowledge of art. Once there, it is difficult to ignore the wonderful art that is found everywhere. Perhaps most well-known is the Renaissance art but don't ignore both earlier and later periods.

Northern Italy was home to the **Etruscans** for several centuries. Their original styles were later heavily influenced by the Greeks. The most famous Etruscan works are in terra-cotta but they also worked in bronze. The **Romans** also copied heavily from the Greeks.

Etruscan remains are mostly found in museums, the best in the Tuscan towns of Florence, Volterra, and Cortona. Roman art is also around but the best examples are not in our area of interest.

The **Byzantine** period is best illustrated by the churches in Ravenna which are covered in stylized mosaics and the Basilica di San Marco in Venice with its domes and amazing mosaics. **Romanesque sculpture** was popular for a time but most has not survived.

There are, however, a few examples that are of interest including the Door of St Ranieri (1180) on the Il Duomao in Pisa, the 48 relief panels of the bronze doors on the Basilica San Zeno Maggiore in Verona, and the friezes, statues, and painted frescos at the Baptistery in Parma. Aosta's Collegiata dei Santi Pietro e Orso still has part of an 11th century fresco cycle.

Now we start to recognize some famous names. **Giotto** was probably the greatest Gothic artist. You can see his *Ognissanti Maesta* (1310) in the *Uffizi Gallery* in Florence and his fresco cycles in Padua's Scovegni Chapel and in Florence's Basilica di Santa Croce. **Ambrogio Lorenzetti** is another important figure and you can see his works in the *Uffizi Gallery*, and Siena's *National Picture Gallery*.

The pre-Renaissance and Renaissance periods of the 15th and 16th centuries saw many artists doing remarkable works. Sculptors **Ghiberti** and **Donatello** were important and their best works can be seen in Ghiberti's *Gates of Paradise* in Florence's Baptistery, and Donatello's bronze and marble statues in several Florence museums and Siena's Duomo and Baptistery.

Michelangelo was a genius in sculpture and painting. His most famous sculpture, *David*, is in Florence's *Galleria dell'Accademia*, several works are in the *Bargello Museum*, *Pietas* are in the *Duomo Museum* and the unfinished *Rondanini Pieta* is in Milan's *Museum of Ancient Art*. The only Michelangelo painting in Italy is in the *Uffizi Gallery*. One of his most famous works is within the Medici's family tomb in Florence's Medici Chapels.

Leonardo da Vinci stands head and shoulders above others as a genius with a diversity of achievements that we associate with the Italian Renaissance. He was much more than an artist but some of his fine art works can be seen in northern Italy where he spent most of his life.

His *Annunciation* and *Adoration of the Magi* can be seen in the *Uffizi Gallery*, his *Portrait of a Musician* is in the *Biblioteca Ambosiana*, Milan, and the *Vitruvian Man* is in the *Accademia*, Venice. There is a *Self-Portrait* in the *Royal Library*, Turin, while the remains of his famous *Last Supper* are in the Refectory, S. Maria delle Grazie, Milan.

Raphael produced a body of work that influenced later European painters. His only significant work in northern Italy, however, is a sketch in Milan's *Pinacoteca Ambrosiana*.

Titian produced works full of color and he explored the effects of light on darkened scenes. His works are everywhere In Venice from canvases in the *Accademia* to altarpieces decorating churches.

Antonio Canova was Italy's top neoclassical sculptor. You can see his work in the *Brera* in Milan and in Venice's *Museo Correr*.

Architecture

Italian architecture shows a wide and diverse range of styles over the years which chronicle community changes. The following can be considered the most important periods or styles.

Classical: Classical architecture comes from the Greeks. This influenced the Roman Empire who began to construct buildings using strict mathematical principles. Roman urban planning was highly significant and this can still be seen in the street layouts of several cities and in buildings in places like Aosta (a gate and theater stage) to Brescia (an ancient temple and theater) and Verona (a magnificent ancient amphitheater still used for performances).

Medieval: This style developed after the fall of the Roman Empire and was influenced by Byzantine style and characterized by the round arches on buildings. A late example of this style is the Ponte Vecchio in Florence.

Romanesque: This period went from approximately 800 A.D. to 1100 A.D. This was an important period in Italian architecture when the Leaning Tower of Pisa, the Basilica of Sant'Ambrogio in Milan, and Siena's cathedral were built. They have the tiered loggias and arcades that would become hallmarks of the Lombard Romanesque.

Gothic: Here pointed arches were used instead of round ones, buildings had bigger windows, and there were other influences from Moorish architecture. The Doges Palace in Venice is a fine example of this work. The true, French-style Gothic flourished only in northern Italy, and the best example is Milan's massive cathedral begun in the late 14th century.

Venice's Frari is a bit airier and boxier; Padua's Basilica di Sant'Antonio is largely Gothic, but with a Romanesque façade and Byzantine domes. In palace architecture, the Venetians developed a distinctive style with an Eastern flair. This is seen in countless palaces across Venice, especially in the Ca' d'Oro, Ca' Foscari, and the Palazzo Ducale.

Renaissance: Italian architects and engineers constructed buildings with symmetrical arrangements, used columns and pilasters, domes, and painting in the ceiling of chapels. The Rialto Bridge in Venice and Florence Cathedral are good examples of this style.

The undisputed master of the High Renaissance was Andrea Palladio who worked in a much more strictly classical mode of columns, porticoes, and other ancient temple-inspired features. In Venice, Jacopo Sansovino's loggia and Libreria Sansoviniana lining St. Mark's Square are a classic.

Neo classicism: This has many similarities to High Renaissance. Order, balance, elegance, and harmony with the landscape are all apparent in the creations of Palladio. He is best known for the villas he built on the flat plains of the Veneto. Nineteen of these villas still stand, including what may be his finest, La Rotunda, outside Vicenza.

Baroque: This is one of the most extravagant styles. In Italy, this style was encouraged by the Popes to give special ornamentation to churches and express holy splendor. The Basilica di Superga in Turin is a good example as is Venice's Santa Maria della Salute.

Modern: Contemporary architects invented a style that improved the materials and technologies of earlier architecture. Some important names are Giuseppi Terragni with the "Casa del Fascio" in Como, Pier Luigi Nervi and Gio Ponti's Pirelli skyscraper project in Milan, and Giovanni Michelucci with the Santa Maria Novella Station in Florence.

Opera

Italian musical theater began in the 17th century at the court of the Medici in Florence, and operatic theater began in 1639. To curb high costs, it became necessary to stage the same show many times and it soon became fashionable to go to the theater.

The most famous Italian opera writers are Rossini, Donizetti, Bellini, Puccini, and Verdi, who all expressed the feelings and anxieties of Italian society of their day. The discontent that pervaded Italy after the Unification, for instance, is wonderfully encapsulated in *Don Carlos* by Verdi.

There are many opera theaters in northern Italy, nearly always in splendid 17th – 19th century buildings. The most important are the world-famous **La Scala** in Milan and the **Fenice Theatre** in Venice. Opera is also held in other venues such as Verona's Arena. But don't be surprised to find theaters and opera houses in some of the smaller centers.

Some of the most famous opera singers include Luciano Pavarotti, Mirella Freni, and Renata Scotto.

Museums

Italy's museum heritage is sometimes described as the largest in the world because there is something like 1,500 museums across the country. Art has made its way into Italy's finest and most beautiful museums and some collections include some of the world's most prestigious artworks.

While there are some science and other specialist museums, it is the art museums that dominate the scene. In many Italian museums, you can find guides, long opening hours, welcome centers, and sales points. Here are a few of northern Italy's best museums.

The **Uffizi Gallery** is one of Italy's most popular museums and is one of the top things to see in Florence. The Uffizi has an amazing collection of art works by many of Italy's Renaissance masters. Because it's so popular it's best to book in advance to be sure to get tickets.

The **Peggy Guggenheim Collection** in Venice is Italy's top museum for contemporary art. It's housed in the 18th century palazzo that was the residence of wealthy art patron, Peggy Guggenheim, who collected masterpieces from some of the best-known artists and art movements of the 20th century.

Established in 1865, the **Bargello** in Florence was one of the first museums in Italy and is a premier sculpture gallery. The dozens of statues and busts on display were sculpted by some of the most famous

Renaissance artists including Michelangelo, Donatello, Verrochio, and Giambologna.

The **Galleria dell'Accademia** in Florence is most famous for its art works by Michelangelo, in particular, the large "David" sculpture. Throughout the rest of the gallery are displays of art from the 13th - 16th centuries, a collection of musical instruments, and pieces by other Renaissance artists.

The **Museo Nazionale della Scienza e della Technologia Leonardo da Vinci** in Milan is Italy's largest science and technology museum. In addition to housing the Leonardo Gallery, which contains some of Leonardo da Vinci's original drawings and numerous models of his scientific innovations, the museum has interactive labs and other attractions.

The **Museo Egizio** is a museum in Turin, specializing in Egyptian artifacts. It houses the second largest collection of Egyptian antiquities in the world.

Cathedrals

The **Pisa cathedral** was begun in 1064 and is built in the Romanesque style, with rounded arches. Most of the interior was destroyed by fire in 1595, so there are few medieval features inside the building. One that survived is the giant mosaic of Christ the King (1302) in the apse. Another is the carved marble pulpit (1302-1311) by Giovanni Pisano.

The **Duomo of Milan** took five centuries to build and this magnificent and ornate Gothic cathedral is the third-largest church in the world. It has 135 marble spires, a stunning triangular façade, and thousands of statues flanking the massive but almost fanciful exterior.

St. Mark's Basilica in Venice is the most exotic and Eastern of the Western world's great churches. The onion-domed and mosaic-covered San Marco took much of its inspiration from Constantinople. The candlelit cavern of the 1,000-year-old church began as the private chapel of the doges but is now open to everyone.

The **Basilica di Santa Maria della Salute** is a famous church in Venice., While it has the status of a minor basilica, its decorative and distinctive profile and location make it among the most photographed churches in Italy.

The **Duomo of Florence** was begun in the late 1200s and consecrated 140 years later. The pink, green, and white marble cathedral was a symbol of Florence's prestige and wealth. It's loaded with world-class art and is one of Italy's largest and most distinctive religious buildings.

The **Duomo of Siena**, begun in 1196, is one of the most beautiful and ambitious Gothic churches in Italy, with extravagant zebra-striped bands of marble. Highlights here include a wonderful pavement of masterful mosaics, a pulpit carved by Nicola Pisano, and the lavishly frescoed Piccolomini Library.

Food

We all love Italian food but really there is no national cuisine. Regional traditions still dominate and the differences within the country are significant. As you move around, it is important to try the popular local dishes. Forget pizzas and spaghetti and meatballs and explore the unknown things on the local menu. You are unlikely to be disappointed.

The region around Genoa is notable for its bouillabaisse flavored with spices and its pesto, a sauce made from fresh basil, garlic, cheese, and walnuts which is used on pasta and fish. Seafood is also popular in Venice and a favorite is grilled fish served with a bitter red radicchio lettuce. Fegato alla veneziana (liver and onions) is a typical 'homely' dish.

Around Milan, the cooking is more refined. Osso buco, a shin bone of veal cooked in a ragout sauce and served on rice and peas, is a favorite. So too is cotoletta alla Milanese, a dish very similar to Wiener schnitzel.

Risotto is another favorite, often cooked with saffron and butter and served with Parmigiano-Reggiano cheese.

Tuscan food tends to be hearty with local olive oil in almost every dish. Popular pastas are *pappardelle* and *penne* served with tomato-based sauces. Meat and fish are prepared simply with strong cheeses sometimes served on the side. In the extreme north, there are some unusual dishes. In Piedmont, *fonduta* made from melted fontina cheese, butter, milk, and egg yolks is popular. Further east in the highlands, German and Austrian dishes become popular.

The Emilia-Romagna area probably has the best-rounded cuisine. Pragliatelle and tortellini pastas are notable. So too is lasagna and mortadella sausage. We enjoyed dishes such as cotoletta alla Bolognese, a veal cutlet fried with ham. This is the region that produces the best prosciutto, which is served in super-thin slices, and the delicious Parmigiano-Reggiano cheese.

Wine

Italian wines are known around the world and it is claimed that Italy is the largest wine-producing country in the world. Some wine makers are high-tech, high-volume producers while others work on family plots and produce small quantities each year. Each region has particularly popular wines but throughout northern Italy there are many varieties.

The Lombardy region north of Venice produces renowned wines. Some of the most popular are *Frecciarossa* to go with fish, *Sassella* for red meat and roasts and *Inferno* for meats. Tuscany is famous for its *Chianti* but you should also try the *Brunello di Montalcono* with roasts and game, and *Vernaccia* with fish or chicken. There is also a delightful dessert wine called *Vin Santo* which is perfect for dunking biscotti.

The Emilia-Romagna region is known for its sparkling *Lambrusco* and the delicate red *Sangiovese* and yellow *Albana*. The Veneto produces the ruby-red *Bardolino* and *Valpolicella* to go with meats. This region is also known for its Cabernets. The Dolomite region produces Riesling, Terlano and Traminer for fish and *Santa Maddalena* for red meats.

Piedmont lays claim to the finest wines in Italy. Asti Spumante is probably the most well-known but you should also try *Cortese* with fish and *Barolo* and *Barbaresco* with meat. This is also the home of *Vermouth*, a white wine with herbs and spices which is served as an aperitif. While the Riviera isn't a well-known wine-producing area, it does produce an interesting *Vermentino Ligure* to go with fish and *Dolceacqua* served with meat.

Three other drinks should be on your tasting list. The bright red *Campari* is served with ice and soda. The bright yellow *Limoncello* is becoming a popular liqueur world-wide while *Grappa* can be drunk before or after dinner or added to coffee.

Festivals

Carnevale in Venice is Italy's top carnival or mardi gras celebration. Carnevale season lasts several weeks, culminating on the Day of Carnival or Shrove Tuesday. During carnival season, Venice is filled with costumed characters, entertainment, and food stalls. The main events are centered on Piazza San Marco.

Venice International Film Festival is the oldest international film festival in the world. It takes place every year in late August or early September on the island of The Lido in the Venice lagoon.

Biennale de Arte in Venice is a major contemporary art exhibition that takes place once every two years in odd years. The annual Venice Film Festival is part of it. So too is the Venice Biennale of Architecture.

Opera in Arena in Verona is held at the Roman Arena which is one of Italy's most spectacular settings for outdoor opera performances and concerts. Built in the 1st century B.C., it's the third largest Roman arena in Italy. The Arena di Verona summer opera season usually starts in mid-June and runs through early September.

Festival Shakespeariano in Verona mixes ancient Roman heritage and Shakespearean fame in a theater festival of Shakespeare's plays along with ballets and concerts, from classical to jazz. It is held in the ruins of the Teatro Romano ancient theater. The Royal Shakespeare Company usually performs *Romeo and Juliet* and *Two Gentlemen of Verona*, as well as other plays, in English.

The annual **San Remo Music Festival**, which is held in February, is a very popular song contest held in the city since 1951. It is said that this festival inspired the Eurovision Song Contest, which started in 1956.

There are also many smaller or shorter festivals which can be just as interesting. A few of these are:

Il Palio - Sienna's famous horse race around the central square takes place July 2 and August 16. You might be lucky to get a standing place, but reserved seats are usually sold out in advance. Before the race, there's a spectacular procession with people in medieval costume.

A **Medieval Festival** is held the first week of July in **Brisghella**, an interesting medieval hill town and spa center in the Emilia-Romagna region.

Sagra di Saint Giovanni is the oldest historic event on Lake Como. Tiny floating lamps, a big fireworks display, a boat parade with traditional boats decorated with flowers, and folk dancing and flag throwing competitions are all part of the celebrations. Events are held the weekend closest to June 24.

Luminara of Saint Ranieri is celebrated in Pisa on June 16. The Arno River is illuminated with the flames from over 70,000 candle holders. The historic *Regatta of Saint Ranieri* is the next day.

The **Puccini Festival** celebrates the life of the composer. Giacomo Puccini lived in a villa in Torre del Lago, a small town on a lake near the coast of Tuscany, and he composed many of his operas there. Today there's a new outdoor amphitheater that is the setting for the festival held in July and August.

Partita a Scacchi a biennial festival in Marostica, Veneto turns the checkerboard main piazza in front of the castle into a great place of celebration. After a parade of costumed gentlefolk and medieval-style entertainers (jugglers, fire-eaters, clowns), people dressed as chess pieces fill the piazza's board, and the match begins.

Sagra del Pesce in Camogli takes what is claimed to be the world's largest frying pan (3.6 meters across) and places it on the wide, waterfront promenade of this tiny Riviera fishing town. It is then filled with sizzling sardines and the town is ready to party. The festival celebrates seafood, the town's traditional industry on the second Sunday in May.

11 A BRIEF HISTORY

Thank you to those who helped with this chapter.

The earliest known inhabitants of northern Italy were the Celts and Teutonic tribes.

Around 1000 B.C. the Etruscans appeared. It is not clear exactly where they came from but their religious rites and architecture show a connection with Mesopotamia. They quickly occupied most of northern Italy then moved south and eventually established their capital in Rome which they named Roma.

The Etruscans introduced gold tableware and jewelry, bronze urns, and terracotta statuary and much of Greek and Asian Minor art and culture.

We will, however, probably never really know why they colonized Italy. These early Etruscans left no literature that we can understand, and no texts of religion or philosophy; therefore, much of what is known about this civilization is derived from grave and tomb findings. We do know that when they came to Italy, they brought civilization and urbanization with them.

The Etruscans lived in independent, fortified city-states which would often form small confederacies. These city-states were initially ruled by a monarch but were later ruled by oligarchies that governed through a council and through elected officials.

They were a sophisticated people, with an alphabet based on the Greek alphabet, a powerfully original sculptural and painting tradition, a religion based on human-type gods, and a complicated set of rituals for divining the future, which they handed down to the Romans.

In 510 B.C., Rome witnessed a revolt against the rule of the Etruscan kings. The rebellion failed to achieve final independence for Rome, but it would be the birth of the Roman Republic. The Romans conquered neighboring communities and many of the famous cities of Italy originated as colonies, connected to Rome by military roads.

By 49 B.C., Rome ruled the entire Mediterranean world and most of the wealth and glory was found in Rome. This drained other Italian communities of money and people.

In the 4th century A.D., the Roman Empire fragmented as administrative capitals were established in cities such as Milan and in 394 A.D. the empire split with a "New Rome' established at Constantinople (Byzantium).

The Goths begin the invasion of Rome's northern provinces and are generally welcomed by the population. Shortly afterwards, Alaric, king of the Visigoths attacks Rome itself. Forty years later Attila the Hun invades Italy and in 476 A.D. the last emperor is deposed, the empire falls and the Dark Ages begin.

Ninety years later the Lombard invasion of northern Italy begins. The Lombard's established the "Kingdom of Italy" which reached its peak during the 8th century. In 774 A.D., the Kingdom was conquered by the Frankish King and integrated into that Empire. When the King died, Italy broke up into a series of small warring kingdoms.

The dark ages are a period of war and strife. The Roman Catholic Church strived frantically for more control and in 962 A.D. the Holy Roman Empire was founded under Otto I, king of Saxony. Italy didn't escape the Black Death that decimated Europe in the 14th century, and its population was reduced by a third.

In the 15th century, city-states hold power, with Venice controlling much of the eastern Mediterranean. By the middle of the century, there is a rediscovering of the art and philosophy of ancient Greece and this gives rise to the artistic Renaissance.

Carlos I Habsburg of Spain is crowned Holy Roman Emperor as Charles V in 1519. He wages war against the French largely over Italian territories. In 1527, he marches into Rome and destroys the city, then occupies nearly all of northern Italy. Eight years later Francesco II Sforza of Milan dies, leaving the Duchy in Spanish Habsburg hands.

The Roman Catholic Church's considerable power has been used to accumulate great wealth but it is being challenged by the reformist

Protestant movements sweeping northern Europe. In the mid-16th century the Catholic Council of Trent launches the Counter-Reformation and this ultimately severely reduces the pope's power.

The 17th and 18th centuries are a bad time for northern Italy. Bandits control the countryside and the Austrians and Spanish control the cities and the wealth.

Things start to improve by the mid-18th century when wealthy northern Europeans begin taking the Grand Tour, journeying to Italy to study ancient architecture and Italian old masters. Italy's tourism industry has begun. It doesn't last long, however, as in 1796-1814 Napoleon sweeps through Italy, changing everything.

After Napoleon's demise, we see the beginning of the Risorgimento political movement in Turin and Genoa, which encourages Italian nationalism. This culminates in 1861 with the creation of the Kingdom of Italy under Vittorio Emanuele II, through the military campaign of General Garibaldi. Turin serves briefly as interim capital. In 1870, Rome, the last papal stronghold, falls to Garibaldi and Italy becomes a country with Rome as its capital.

In the years that led up to World War 1, Italy had sided with Germany and Austria-Hungary in the Triple Alliance. In theory, it should have joined these two nations when war broke out in August 1914 but it did not. What Italy did was wait and see how the war progressed.

On April 26th 1915, it came into the war on the side of Britain, France, and Russia. By the end of the war in 1918, 600,000 Italians were dead, 950,000 were wounded, and 250,000 were crippled for life.

In March 1919, Mussolini formed the Fascist Party, which received the support of many unemployed war veterans. These became armed squads known as Black Shirts, who terrorized their political opponents. In 1921, the Fascist Party was invited to join the coalition government. By October 1922, Italy seemed to be slipping into political chaos.

The Black Shirts marched on Rome and to prevent further violence King Victor Emmanuel invited Mussolini to form a government. But Mussolini wanted more and gradually dismantled the country's democratic institutions and in 1925 made himself dictator, taking the title 'Il Duce'. His next aim was to re-establish Italy as a great European power.

In 1935, Mussolini invaded Abyssinia (now Ethiopia) and incorporated it into his new Italian Empire. In 1939, he signed a Pact of Steel with Nazi Germany. He declared war on Britain and France in June 1940 but his forces suffered defeats in North and East Africa and the Balkans and in July 1943, Allied troops landed in Sicily.

This caused Mussolini to be overthrown and imprisoned by his former colleagues and in September, Italy signed an armistice with the Allies. The German army then occupied Italy and Mussolini was rescued by German commandos. For a while he again headed the new government, but in reality, he had little power.

As the Allies advanced northwards through Italy, Mussolini fled. He was captured and shot, however, by Italian partisans and then strung up at a Milan gas station.

In 1946, a national referendum narrowly established the Republic of Italy but it was not until 1975 that the borders we know today were finally established. With the help of the Marshall Plan, the country was rebuilt after World War II but the economic boom reached mainly northern Italy and intensified the contrast within the country. Southern Italy, in particular, became a country of emigration. More than two million Italians moved to northern Italy or to foreign countries.

As a founding member of the **European Union** and a member of **NATO** and the **United Nations**, Italy has established its place in the world in terms of foreign policy. Domestically, however, the country struggled from one crisis to the next. Corruption, the mafia, and the disagreement of many small parties, present problems for the country. 61 different governments in 62 years is evidence of the internal instability.

Despite this, northern Italy has become a world leader in the fashion industry and its tourism industry is thriving. Whether this is enough to keep the country progressing is yet to be seen.

12 WHAT TO SEE AND DO

Riviera

The Italian Riviera is glamorous but in an old-fashioned way. There are chic resorts such as San Remo and Portofino, dramatic beauty and outdoor adventure at the Cinque Terre, and the history and architectural charm of Genoa.

You find rocky and sandy beaches connected by a modern road that hugs the beautiful coastline and connects many of the small fishing villages and resort towns. There is an efficient train service which is a very effective way of getting around without traffic and parking problems.

San Remo
La Pigna is the oldest part of the city. Tiny streets and covered alleyways wind up the hill to the gardens and sanctuary at the top. Madonna della Costa Sanctuary on the hilltop can be seen from most places in San Remo and is a symbol of the city.

Savona
Priamar Fortress was built in 1542 by the Genoese. The fortress was later used as a prison but today you can visit and perhaps see a concert inside.

Genoa
The Porto Antico (Old Port) is a lively spot, filled with waterfront shops and eateries. The dome-shaped Biosfera greenhouse is always popular, along with the Genoa Aquarium, supposedly Europe's second largest. Around Genoa's central squares, such as the Piazza San Lorenzo, see the

Cattedrale di San Lorenzo, the city's beautiful 12th century cathedral and the many museums established in old palaces.

Camoglia

The charming fishing village is a 20-minute drive east from Genoa. Thanks to its picturesque harbor, beautifully decorated churches, and authentic atmosphere, Camoglia is becoming an increasingly popular tourist destination.

Portofino

In contrast to Camoglia, Portofino is anything but a quiet fishing village. For years, this seaside resort has attracted the rich and famous, including film stars and members of various royal families.

Santa Margherita Ligure

This is an old-fashioned kind of Riviera resort with palm trees, an esplanade meant for walking, and some chic shops. Foreign visitors enjoy the balmy climate, attractive views, and comfortable long-established hotels.

The Cinque Terre

This is one of Italy's treasures and fortunately it is UNESCO protected. Riomaggiore, Corniglia, Manarola, Vernazza, and Monterosso are the five towns that form the Cinque Terre and each is extremely attractive. There are walking and hiking options.

Florence

Piazza della Signoria

This is the heart of the historic center and it is a free open-air sculpture exhibit. The *Loggia della Signoria* holds some important statues including a copy of Michelangelo's *David*.

Duomo (cathedral)

The *Cattedrale de Santa Maria del Fiore* is a huge Gothic building which was begun in 1296 and holds 20,000 people. Its exterior, made of green, pink, and white marble, has several elaborate doors and interesting statues. Inside, Brunelleschi's Dome is a masterpiece of construction.

The Baptistery of John the Baptist
From the 11th century, this is one of Florence's oldest buildings. Its exterior is made of green and white marble and it has three sets of amazing bronze doors.

The Ponte Vecchio
Built in 1345, this was Florence's first bridge across the Arno River and it is the only surviving bridge from Florence's medieval days. The *Ponte Vecchio* is still lined with shops selling gold and silver jewelry.

The Galleria degli Uffizi
This holds the world's most important collection of Renaissance art. Artists whose works you'll see include *Michelangelo, Giotto, Botticelli, Leonardo da Vinci, Perugino, and Raphael.*

The Galleria dell' Academia
Here are some of the most important paintings and sculptures from the 13th -16th centuries. Michelangelo's *David*, probably the most famous sculpture in the world, is here.

The Pitti Palace
This was once the seat of the Medici family. You can visit eight different galleries here. There is a huge park on a hillside behind the palace where there are beautiful gardens and fountains.

Tuscany

Lucca
The capital of the Province of Lucchesia is a town rich in tradition and culture. It has a unique town center that is completely enclosed by a massive brick wall dating back to the 16th century. A good way to find your way around Lucca is to follow the 4 km path around the top of the city wall.

Pisa
Tourist interest is dominated by the Leaning Tower but do allow time to see other attractions. Visit the Baptistery (Battistero), which ranks amongst Italy's finest and is enormous.

San Gimignano

This is a town brimming with character and historic attractions. Spend time exploring the streets and piazzas on foot, so that you can soak up the atmosphere. Visit the Piazza del Duomo and sightsee around this church square. A number of tall, medieval towers flank the piazza.

Siena

The 12th century Duomo has a stunning, zebra-striped interior and a lavish floor. It also contains the Piccolomini Library, where there are vibrant frescoes by Pinturicchio. The shell-shaped Piazza del Campo lies at the heart of the city and here the Palazzo Pubblico is open to the public. The Torre del Mangia tower can be visited separately and offers superb views over the city.

Venice

St Mark's Cathedral

The golden Byzantine Basilica was founded in the ninth century. Its fabulous exterior of Eastern appearance is dramatic while the interior is enhanced by wonderful mosaics. It houses many of Venice's greatest treasures, including the venerated icon of the Madonna Nicopeia.
The golden screen behind the high altar is the Pala d'Oro, beautifully crafted with sapphires, emeralds, and rubies and inset with enamels from Constantinople.

The Doges' Palace

This was once home to the elected leader of Venice. The building is a merging of Islamic and Gothic styles and the façade dates from 1365. The first floor has some wonderful paintings by Titian and Bellini. The Palazzo also houses ancient prison cells and an armory. The Bridge of Sighs is an architectural masterpiece that links the Doge's Palace to the prison cells on the opposite side of the small canal.

The Accademia

This is the most important art gallery in the city. It is housed in the former church of Santa Maria della Carita and the adjoining Scuola.

The Peggy Guggenheim gallery

This collection of modern art is probably the most distinguished in Italy. There are works by a wide variety of artists, including Pollock, Picasso, Kandinsky, and Dalí. The sculpture garden is particularly impressive.

The Ponte Di Rialto

This single-stone arched bridge built in 1588 is lined with tiny shops, most of which are tourist related, but this was originally the location for the Merchant of Venice to peddle his wares.

Burano, Murano, and Torcello

Explore these fascinating Venetian islands by boat. Visit the lace shops of Burano and tour the museum. Enjoy a glass-blowing display by skilled craftsmen in Murano. Torcello boasts some of the area's oldest churches.

Padova (Padua)

35 km west of Venice lies Padova, a thriving town distinguished by its ancient university and the remarkable Cappella degli Scrovegni, home of Giotto's groundbreaking frescoes. This delightful town inspired Shakespeare who used it as the setting for *The Taming of the Shrew*.

Gondola Ride

You can take a trip through the smaller canals on board a gondola. For many, this is the most romantic experience that Venice has to offer but it comes at a considerable cost. A gondola ride can cost $100. Singing and serenading is optional and will usually cost extra.

Walking Tours

Most tours are three hours long and the places visited depend on the tour taken. They can include the Bridge of Sighs, the Doge's Palace, and the largely unspoiled Cannaregio District. Tours usually depart from hotels or from St Mark's Square.

Milan

Tram Tour

Take the number 20 tram, which is identified by a large Ciao Milano sign painted on its side. It will give you a well-rounded tour of the city, commencing from the Piazza Castello, and there is an English commentary. Tours can last 45 minutes to an hour and are held daily at 11 a.m. and 1 p.m.

Milan Walking Tours
Daily walking tours are popular and take in many of the city's most interesting attractions. Lasting around two hours, the tours depart from the APT Information Office at Via Marconi 1 every Monday morning at 10 a.m.

Cathedral
This is the world's largest Gothic cathedral. It was begun in 1386 and it took 500 years to complete. The result is a majestic building which is almost Disney-like. Above the 135 spires and 3,500 statues, the small gilded copper statue of the Virgin stands 109 meters above the city.

Teatro alla Scala
This large opera house was built in 1776 by Giuseppe. In 1943, it was badly bombed and rebuilt three years later. Highlights include the Museo del Teatro (theater museum).

Galleria Vittorio Emanuele II
This is a large and elegant arcade, lined with shops, bookstores, cafés, and restaurants. It was designed to join the Piazza della Scala and Piazza del Duomo. It features a 47-meter-high glass dome, standing above the central octagonal area and also some beautiful mosaics on the floor.

Palazzo Borromeo
Situated in central Milan, this grand 15th-century palace was badly damaged by bombing in 1943 and much of it has since been rebuilt and restored. There are courtyards and many frescoes.

Palazzo Real
This was the seat of the commune administration in the 11th century. In 1598, it housed the first permanent theater in Milan and Mozart played here at a young age. It now contains the Civico Museo d'Arte Contemporanea.

Lake Como

This is one of my favorite places in Italy and you must get out on the water. Boats crisscross the lake offering views of small villages, hillside cultivation, and lovely gardens. There are some wonderful lakeside villas. Isola Comacina is the only island in Lake Como. There are ancient remains of homes dating from Roman times, late medieval fortifications, and early Christian churches.

Verona

Arena Di Verona

The Verona Arena is the largest Roman amphitheater in northern Italy. It was constructed early in the first century A.D. Nowadays, it is a wonderful venue for concerts and opera performances, and is the focal point of the city's famous opera festival every summer. It can hold 25,000 people.

Basilica San Zeno Maggiore

One of the finest examples of Romanesque architecture in Italy, San Zeno Maggiore, built in the 1120s and 30s, is the most attractive of Verona's churches. It has an imposing façade that completely dominates the large square in front of the building. Beside it stands an impressive bell tower

Casa Giulietta (Juliet's House)

This is one of Verona's biggest tourist attractions. It is very unlikely that Juliet ever lived in this building, and the balcony was actually put up in the 1920s to satisfy visitors. Still, the tourists keep coming, and at least there is a statue of Juliet in the courtyard.

Castelvecchio

The Castelvecchio (Old Castle) was built in 1354-56 and belonged to Verona's medieval rulers, the della Scala family. The building was converted from a military fortress in 1925, and today the castle houses a museum.

Giardino Di Palazzo Giusti

Undoubtedly, one of the most beautiful Renaissance gardens in Italy and well worth a visit. It is a spacious garden featuring flower beds, fountains, statues, a cypress-lined avenue, and one of Europe's oldest labyrinths. It dates from the late 16th century but has been redesigned since then.

Mountain biking in the Lake Garda region
With the hills and valleys around the lake littered with some of Europe's finest trails, there are many classic rides blending kilometers of grin-inducing single track and impressive views of both the pre-Alps and the expanse of Italy's largest lake. Companies offer pre-prepared rides if needed.

Skiing
The Dolomites offer spectacular mountain scenery and a number of skiing villages. Because of the height of some of the mountains, it's possible to ski nearly year-round in some places. The Dolomites are good for beginning to advanced skiers and offer other winter sports as well. Ortisei is a great place for cross-country skiing. Cortina d'Ampezzo and Val Gardena are two of the most well-known ski areas.

Turin and Aosta

Cathedral and the Holy Shroud
The 15th century Duomo contains the Capella della Sindone, built to house the Holy Shroud.

Mole Antonelliana
Built as a synagogue in the 19th century, this striking building now houses Italy's Museo Nazionale del Cinema (National Museum of Cinema) while the tower (reached by lift) has a viewing platform offering panoramic views of the city and the Alps.

Museo Egizio (Egyptian Museum)
This museum contains the finest collection of Egyptian artifacts outside Cairo, including items from the tomb of the architect Kha, and a reconstructed tomb from 2100 B.C.

Palazzo Reale (Royal Palace)
The most accessible of the former Savoy royal residences, this 17th century palace contains lavish furnishings and paintings and is set in grounds designed by Andre Le Notre, who also laid out Versailles.

Skiing

The Piedmont Region offers skiing and mountain sports in the villages that hosted the 2006 Winter Olympics. You can ski where the Olympic skiers competed and enjoy the great cultural and gastronomic traditions. Piedmont has 53 ski resorts and 1300 km of runs.

Near the Swiss ski resort of Zermatt, the village of Cervinia is at the base of the Matterhorn. Cervinia has a run over 20 km long, one of the longest in the world. Courmayeur is on the side of Mont Blanc and is a traditional alpine village in a fantastic location with great scenery.

Emilia – Romagna

Food experience

Visit a Parmigiano Reggiano factory, discover balsamic vinegar, and eat at a Wine Cantina on the Hill of Bologna. Regional delicacies include Parmesan cheese and Parma ham, balsamic vinegar, and truffles.

Ravenna

This is a center of art, culture, and famously 'the city of mosaics'. There are several Christian buildings from the fifth century which are worth seeing. Perhaps most notable are the Mausoleum of Galla Placidia and the Basilica of Sant' Apollinare in Classe with their striking mosaics. The Basilica of San Vitale was started by the bishop of Ravenna in the early sixth century.

Bologna

The largest city in Emilia Romagna is a fascinating town and is renowned for its excellent food. The porticos are probably the first thing people notice about the downtown. They dominate every street, and the wide walkways underneath are excellent for strolling. Piazza Maggiore the expansive piazza features a white and pink stone center.

On the south side is the giant Basilica di San Petronio, the 5th largest church in the world. Italy is full of churches, but rarely can you find seven (four remain), all attached to one another. Santo Stefeno church embodies centuries of history and art history.

Bologna nightlife

You can find many bars on Via Zamboni in the university district. They are mostly frequented by college students and have a raucous atmosphere. Via Pratello is another street that hosts a large number of nightspots, where there is more a mix of ages.

Modena

A superb and unspoiled medieval center is the chief reason for visiting Modena. The 12th century cathedral is one of the finest Romanesque structures anywhere. The ancient Via Emilia carves through the center of the city and runs right by the Piazza Grande.

The city is also well-known because the factories of the famous Italian sports car makers Ferrari, De Tomaso, Lamborghini, and Maserati are, or were, located here.

Ferrara

The town is still surrounded by nine kilometers of ancient walls. Castello Estense, sited in the very center of the town, is a brick building surrounded by a moat, with four massive bastions. It was built starting in 1385. The Palazzo di Lodovico Il Moro houses a museum with well-displayed exhibits set in a beautiful, ancient building. Al Brindisi is supposedly the oldest *osteria* in the world. This atmospheric wine bar was established in 1435.

Parma

This is an elegant, affluent city with its own opera house and, of course, its famous ham and cheese. The Romanesque Cathedral houses both 12th century sculpture and a 16th century fresco masterpiece. The adjacent Baptistery was begun in 1196.

13 WHERE TO STAY

Riviera.

Royal Hotel. ***** Corso Imperatrice 80, 18068 San Remo. http://www.royalhotelsanremo.com/eng/
This has an excellent position in the middle of the San Remo seafront and near to the casino. It is an old hotel still in the hands of the same family. There are spacious rooms, excellent service, and heated salt water pool.

Melia Genova. ***** Via Corsica, 4, 16128 Genoa. https://www.melia.com/en/hotels/italy/genoa/melia-genova/
It's in a very nice part of the city within walking distance of all the main attractions and there are plenty of shops and cafés around. The 99 rooms are nicely decorated and have all necessary refinements. The fitness area is good, with water and apples provided for guests and the pool, while small, is set in a relaxing environment. The complimentary breakfast is an impressive spread.

Best Western Plus City Hotel. **** Via San Sebastiano 6, 16123 Genoa. http://www.bwcityhotel-ge.it/en/home-page.aspx
The hotel is modern and located very close to the city center. Rooms are a good size and well appointed. The staff are very welcoming. A good buffet breakfast in a nice room is provided. The "Le Rune" restaurant has Ligurian cuisine served by personnel who will recommend local wines and olive oils.

Belmond Hotel Splendido. ***** Salita Baratta 16, 16034 Portofino. https://www.belmond.com/hotels/europe/italy/portofino/belmond-hotel-splendido/
The views are breathtaking. This hotel has an old-world charm that's quite rare. The hotel is tranquil and refined. The 30 basic rooms are perhaps small and simple for this class of hotel, but the 39 suites are larger and more luxurious. The La Terrazza Restaurant has fine Italian food with breakfast a particular delight. The service throughout the hotel is second to none. Facilities include a pool, terrace, gardens, tennis court, fitness center, and wellness center.

Hotel Villa Steno. *** Via Roma 109, 19016 Monterosso al Mare. http://www.villasteno.com/
The hotel is perched above the noise of the town so it is very quiet but is only a few minutes from the water. It offers friendly and personal service. There are 16 comfortable rooms with air-conditioning, telephone, TV, safe, refrigerator, balconies, and views of the surrounding mountains and ocean. It offers a good complimentary breakfast. Some parking is available.

Hotel Pasquale. *** Via Fegina 4, 19016 Monterosso al Mare. www.hotelpasquale.it/en/
This 15-room charming family run hotel is situated 300 meters from the beach in old Monterosso. There are stunning views from the hotel of the beach, harbor, Ligurian Sea, and the cultivated hillsides. The air-conditioned rooms have good facilities. Breakfast is good and there is a small bar. Some parking is available.

La Scogliera. *** Salita Castello 178, 19017 Riomaggiore. www.la-scogliera.it
Although it's a little tricky to find and has some amazing steps to climb, the two apartments and one room are large, clean and charming. All have amazing views. The apartments have a kitchen and can sleep 3-4. The room has a double bed. All have a bathroom, television, and refrigerator.

Hotel Villa Agnese. *** Via alla Fattoria Pallavicini, 1A, 16039 Sestri Levante. http://www.hotelvillaagnese.com/en
Excellent if you have a car. The hotel is located outside town, close to the autostrada and there is safe parking. The rooms are situated in two

separate small low-rise buildings which overlook the garden with its heated swimming pool. Rooms are clean and new. Some rooms have a small kitchen. San Marco 1957 restaurant has a nice view over the old fishing-port.

Best Western Hotel Metropoli. *** Piazza Fontane Marose, 16123 Genoa. http://www.hotelmetropoli.it/en/home-page.aspx
It has a perfect central location, extremely efficient and friendly staff, and clean, quiet rooms with **pastel colors, chestnut furniture, and parquet floors.** This is a value for money hotel. Most rooms face the Piazza Fontane Marose, which is one of the most elegant and ancient in town. The buffet breakfast is good and there is a bar and free Wi-Fi.

Olympic Hotel. ** Via XX Settembre 21, Genoa. http://www.olympiahotelgenova.com/
It's a quaint, very clean small hotel on an upper floor of a building, centrally located on the main street and just a few blocks from Piazza fe Ferrari. There are only 9 rooms and few facilities but there is excellent shopping and restaurants nearby. The staff are friendly and helpful.

Chopin Hotel. **. Via Andrea Doria 22r, 16126, Genoa. http://hotelchopingenova.it/en/
This small, family run hotel is a good budget choice if you want to stay near the Genoa train station. It has simply decorated basic rooms but they are clean and have the necessary amenities. The area is not great after dark but the hotel is safe and friendly. A small buffet breakfast is provided.

OStellin Genova – Hostel ** Vico Dei Parmigiani 1-3, Genoa. http://www.ostellingenova.it/en/
It's in the old town, near Garibaldi Street with its palazzis and only a 15-minute walk away from the Brignole station. It is clean and extremely friendly. There is a full kitchen, laundry, and good shared bathroom/showers. Don't be put off by the dark entrance or the climb up four flights of stairs.

Florence

Four Seasons Hotel Firenze. *****. Borgo Pinti 99, 50121 Florence. http://www.fourseasons.com/florence/

Although the hotel is quite large, it feels more like a boutique hotel. The restored building is elegant and attractive and the large garden quite lovely. The gym is large, the spa spectacular, and the restaurant exceptional. Guests continually comment on the standard of the staff.

Il Salviatino. ***** Via del Salviatino, 21, 50137 Florence. http://salviatino.com/
Set in an idyllic setting high in the hills, the views are stunning and the building itself impressive. The lack of a front desk, however, can make finding someone to help a challenge on occasions. There is a shuttle service to town on the hour for part of the day which takes about 20 minutes. The hotel restaurant outside on the terrace serves excellent food. My favorite location is the library with its leather lounges.

Portrait Firenze. ***** Lungarno Acciaiuoli, 4, Uffizi, 50123 Florence. http://www.lhw.com/hotel/Portrait-Firenze-Florence-Italy
With panoramic views of Florence and the Arno River, this hotel offers luxurious rooms with handcrafted furniture and amazing service from the excellent staff. It is 30 m from the famous bridge Ponte Vecchio. The 37 suites come with full entertainment systems including an iPad, iPod docking station, and flat-screen TV. Bathrobes, slippers, and free toiletries are provided. Guests can enjoy free access to the nearby White Iris Beauty Spa.

Palazzo Magnani Feroni. ***** Borgo San Frediano, 5, 50124 Florence. www.palazzomagnaniferoni.com
This hotel on the south side of the river only has 12 rooms and all are suites. The property has great charm and character. Rooms are oversized, very comfortable, and there is free Wi-Fi and friendly and effective service. The view from the roof top bar is spectacular. The excellent buffet breakfast is served in a sumptuous salon and there is a bar which opens in the evening. The billiard room is outstanding and the gym adequate. Espresso/coffee machines are available.

NH Collection Firenze Porta Rossa. **** Via Porta Rossa 19, 50123 Florence. https://www.nh-hotels.com/hotels/florence
This is in a building from the 1200's but it is modern and has staff that are most helpful and welcoming. The 72 rooms are a bit on the small side and some bathrooms are quite small, but we love the style and cleanliness, and the free internet. The location is excellent within

walking distance of everything. The buffet breakfast is adequate and the cocktail bar enjoyable. The hotel received a fifth star in 2018.

Hotel L'Orologio. **** Piazza Santa Maria Novella 24, 50123 Florence. www.hotelorologioflorence.com
It is in a recently renovated old Florentine Palazzo only 5 minutes from the train station and a short walk to the major attractions. Rooms are large and modern and the bathrooms are spacious. There is a lovely breakfast room on the top floor and a café on the ground floor. This is a man's hotel with leather, parchment paper, dark brass, and woods. There is a breakfast room, bar, sauna, and fitness center.

Hotel David. *** Viale Michelangiolo 1, 50125 Florence. www.davidhotel.com
The hotel is about 30 minutes' walk from the main center, however, the buses are quite frequent, and taxis are available. Housed in a completely renovated villa, the antique-filled hotel provides private free parking, and wireless Internet. The main salon is filled with books about Florence, and English and Italian newspapers and magazines. Every evening, it becomes the scene for a free wine and appetizer hour. The mini-bar is complimentary.

Hotel Davanzati. *** Via Porta Rossa no 5, 50123, Florence. http://www.hoteldavanzati.it/
This small family run hotel definitely has a prime location but note that the reception area is up a steep flight of stairs. The 17 rooms are comfortable and charming with modern conveniences, and most are very quiet. The breakfast is good with plenty of choice. It has a nice daily happy hour with free wine & appetizers - great to meet other tourists.

Hotel Alessandra. ** Borgo SS. Apostoli, 17, 50123 Florence. www.hotelalessandra.com
This is an old hotel but it is well maintained and clean and is decorated in the Florentine style. It gets marks for hospitality, location, and value. It is just around the corner from the Ponte Vecchio and within a five-minute walk of the Uffizi Gallery and other major sights. Dining options are plentiful nearby. The hotel staff are friendly and well trained. The downside is the 30 or so steps you need to climb before reaching the two-person elevator.

Tuscany

San Luca Palace Hotel. **** San Paolino 103, 55100 Lucca. www.sanlucapalace.com
This is a lovely, small hotel within the walled city. Rooms vary in size but are well furnished and very clean. The hotel has courteous staff, a great breakfast, nice public rooms with English-language newspapers, a small bar, and a small secure car park. It does not serve lunch or dinner. The hotel provides free bikes to guests.

Hotel Bologna. *** Via Mazzini, 57, 56125 Pisa. http://hotelbologna.pisa.it/en/
Hotel Bologna is in the historic center of Pisa, 5 minutes' walk from the train station and 10 minutes from the Leaning Tower. All 64 rooms have a minibar, flat-screen TV with satellite channels, and heating. Breakfast is a cold buffet with good choice. The bar offers free tastings of traditional Tuscan products every evening. The hotel operates a free shuttle to the airport.

Fortezza Medicea. **** Strada del Ceraiolo, 1, 53100 Siena. http://www.aiamattonata.it/en/
This is an old farmhouse which has been beautifully restored. There are only five rooms and a family suite. You need a car because it is about 4 km from the center of Siena. Rooms have private bath, air conditioning, satellite television, Wi-Fi, hair drier, and a safe. They are not luxurious but quite adequate.
The service is outstanding. On the ground floor there is a typical Tuscan kitchen and spacious sitting area with a fireplace. Outside is an infinity salt water swimming pool. There is a wellness center equipped with a Jacuzzi and Turkish bath. Mountain bikes are available.

Adler Thermae. ***** Via Bagno Vignoni 1, 53027 San Quirico d'Orcia. https://www.adler-thermae.com/en/
There are spacious, bright rooms, all with a terrace or balcony and fantastic panoramic views of the Orica Valley. Afternoon buffet with home-made cakes and fruit salad is provided while you can enjoy an a la carte gourmet dinner in the romantic atmosphere of the open-air restaurant. The spa has a great choice of treatments, the pool area outside is clean and relaxing. It is a 10-minute walk into the quaint little

village where there are a few shops and small bistro-type restaurants. You will enjoy the vineyards and towns perched on hill tops nearby.

L'Antico Pozzo. *** Via San Matteo 87, 53073 San Gimignano. http://www.anticopozzo.com/en/
This good value hotel is located in the heart of the ancient city. Rooms are average size, neat and clean, and bathrooms well kept. The reception staff are extremely friendly and helpful. The public areas are very nice - especially the beautiful courtyard for breakfast.

Vogue Hotel Arezzo. **** Guido Monaco 54, 52100 Arezzo. http://voguehotel.it/en/
The hotel is located in the heart of the city. It offers 26 exceptional rooms all different in design and layout and all with fabulous bathrooms. There is opulent decor in the reception area and reasonable service. Breakfast is simple but ample and the coffee is good. There is limited paid parking available in a parking garage.

Venice

Luna Hotel Baglioni. ***** San Marco 1243, 30124 Venice. https://www.baglionihotels.com/branches/baglioni-hotel-luna-venice/
This historic luxury Venetian hotel, a member of the Leading Hotels of the World and Fine Hotels & Resorts, is housed in a magnificent, aristocratic Venetian palace a stone's throw from Piazza San Marco. The hotel's luxury rooms are all very spacious, tastefully furnished, and fitted with all conveniences. The Canova restaurant provides an intimate, cozy atmosphere. The hotel is home to a fully-fledged art gallery.

Ruzzini Palace Hotel. **** Castello 5866, 30122 Venice. www.ruzzinipalace.com
The hotel has both an entrance from the street and the water which is good if you have a lot of luggage from the airport or train. The hotel is a five-minute walk to Saint Marks Square and the Rialto Bridge but it has a peaceful and calm atmosphere. The 28 rooms and suites are modern and comfortable. Staff are smart and efficient and speak excellent English. There is a small breakfast area and a small bar serving hot, cold and alcoholic drinks and a selection of snacks.

Hotel Moresco. ******** Dorsoduro 3499, Dorsoduro, 30123 Venice. http://www.hotelmorescovenice.com/
This is a small, boutique hotel situated close to the railway and bus stations. It has 19th-century Venetian styling and its elegant rooms are a luxurious mix of old and new. The staff are attentive, knowledgeable, and focused on you. Excellent restaurants are close by and there is a quiet section of the canal right outside the front door. Their morning buffet is lavish and their evening "happy hour" is plentiful with an outstanding variety of local dishes.

Ca Maria Adele. ******** Dorsoduro, 111 – 30123 Venice. http://camariaadele.hotelinvenice.com/
This charming hotel is located inside an historical Venetian Palazzo which has been recently renovated and offers all the modern amenities. A combination of exotic, romantic, and mystical makes this a rare find. It looks onto a picturesque view of a canal and the glorious church of Santa Maria della Salute. There are 14 rooms over 4 floors with some having the sexiest bedrooms imaginable. Children are not catered for.

Al Ponte Antico. ******** Calle dell'Aseo, Cannaregio 5768, 30131 Venice. www.alponteantico.com
The hotel is located in a palace from the 1500's. It is an island of tranquility away from the crowds, where you can view the Grand Canal in relative solitude. The hotel's balcony/patio overlooks the canal, with an expansive view extending to the Rialto Bridge. All rooms are equipped with a direct telephone line, private safe, satellite TV, radio, mini-bar, air conditioning, and free Internet connection. There is nice personalized service.

Hotel Antiche Figure. ******* Santa Croce, 687, 30135 Venice. www.hotelantichefigure.it
The hotel is on the Grand Canal opposite the main train station in an historic building from the 15th-century. Rooms have furnishings in traditional Venetian-style, with gold leaf, red carpeting, elegant Murano chandeliers, and silk tapestries. A buffet breakfast is available in the Breakfast Room. The Garden Caféteria, which overlooks the canal, is good for unwinding.

Hotel Al Ponte Mocenigo. ******* S. Croce 2063, 30135 Venice. www.alpontemocenigo.com

Its ten elegant rooms, combining traditional beauty and modern comfort, occupy two levels of a finely restored building in a tranquil, neighborhood. Rooms are furnished in 1700's Venice-style, with big beds, chandeliers in Murano glass, and varnished furniture. During the summer season, guests can have breakfast or sip on an evening drink in the courtyard.

Hotel Casa Petrarca. ** San Marco - Calle Schiavine 4386. http://www.casapetrarca.com/
This is very cozy and clean and it has a nice and quiet atmosphere. It is located in the heart of Venice very close to San Marco Square. You go up one floor for reception and the hotel has just 7 rooms. Only 5 of the rooms have en suite bathrooms. Continental breakfast is served in a cozy room overlooking the canal.

Around Venice

Villa Margherita Hotel. **** Via Nazionale 416, 30034 Mira. www.villa-margherita.com
The hotel is furnished like a stately home, and service is of an excellent standard. Rooms are well-sized and have modern conveniences and amenities and nice bathrooms. The downstairs sitting areas are charming and the breakfasts are good. There is an elegant restaurant and nice bar.

Hotel Villa Cipriani. **** Via Canova, 298, 31011 Asolo. http://www.villaciprianiasolo.com/en/
A small hotel in a charming ancient Italian building but with all the service and luxury you can expect. There is an outstanding garden for leisure and after dinner coffee. The 29 rooms overlook sweeping hills and vineyards. The hotel's restaurant and American Bar are open daily and offer an elegant setting for dinner and a refined atmosphere for lunch.

Savoia Excelsior Palace. **** Riva del Mandracchio 4, 34124 Trieste. https://www.starhotelscollezione.com/en/our-hotels/savoia-excelsior-palace-trieste/

This is just a few steps from the main piazza and there is plenty of parking nearby. The 106 rooms and 36 suites have luscious fabrics, sumptuous wood, and marble bathrooms. The lovely Savoy Restaurant serves à la carte food and has spectacular sea views. Le Rive bar enjoys equally wonderful views and features a majestic shell-shaped ceiling.

Victoria Hotel. *** Via Alfredo Oriani, 2, 34131 Trieste. http://www.hotelvictoriatrieste.com/en/
The hotel is centrally located in an historic building and is only a short walk to restaurants, shopping, and cafés. The 44 rooms are very clean and spacious. It provides good quality for the price. Breakfast is very good and service is courteous. The Wellness Center, located on the 5th floor, is well equipped. Secure paid-parking is available.

Milan

Park Hyatt Milan. ***** Via Tommaso Grossi 1, 20121 Milan. https://milan.park.hyatt.com/en/hotel/home.html
The hotel location is perfect, the entrance hall is sublime but there is no real lobby area. With only 117 rooms this is not a large chain hotel in the usual sense. The rooms are spotless, spacious, and have big bathrooms. Service is professional and formal, yet friendly. Food is excellent at VUN Andrea Aprea a two Michelin-starred restaurant, and La Cupola the all-day dining outlet. Mio Lab is the exclusive cocktail bar while Retreat to Dehors, is a stylish outdoor lounge. The fitness center is small but is equipped with the latest equipment.

Armani Hotel Milano. ***** Via Manzoni 31, Milan. http://milan.armanihotels.com/
This is in the same Griffini-designed, thirties building as the Armani Privé boutique and Armani/Nobu restaurant. There are 95 guest rooms and suites, all furnished with Armani Casa linens, fabrics, and custom furniture. Rooms are decorated in beige, grey, cream, brown, olive, and pearl. The furniture has dark wood accents. The seventh floor features a glass restaurant and the eighth floor houses an elaborate spa and gym.

Hotel Berna. **** Via Napo Torriani, 18, 20124, Milan. https://hotelberna.com/en/

It is known for its extremely nice and helpful staff and rooms which are very clean and comfortable. Room sizes vary so check before accepting. The location is close to the train station and to the Metro station, and there is a parking garage. There is the main hotel of 106 rooms and a small modern annex. This is a good value hotel with free Wi-Fi, non-alcoholic beverages, and some snacks.

Straf. **** Via San Raffaele 3, 20121 Milan. www.straf.it
The hotel is modern, chic, and stylish so it will not appeal to everyone. The staff are friendly and helpful. The location is close to the main tourist attractions, and the shopping district. The 64 rooms are comfortable in a modern and sparse kind of way, and the bathrooms are very special. Rooms contain a massage chair. The restaurant is used as a breakfast room and for lunch. The hotel bar is funky and very popular and offers an all-day bar and restaurant service with an à la carte menu.

Hotel NH Milano Palazzo Moscova. **** Viale Monte Grappa 12, 20124 Milan. https://www.nh-hotels.com/hotel/nh-milano-palazzo-moscova? This began in the 1840s as a railway station and the exterior shows this perfectly. Inside, it is a different world. The hotel features the innovative Truffle Restaurant and Cocktail Bar. The Spa and Wellness Area of the hotel is open to both hotel guests and external customers,

Lancaster Hotel. *** Via A. Sangiorgio, 16, 20145 Milan. http://lancasterhotel.it/en/
The hotel is in an Italian Art Nouveau style building in a residential district near the center of Milan. The 30 comfortable rooms are clean and well equipped. Breakfast is adequate and there are many restaurants close by. The Parco Sempione is a few blocks away. Staff are helpful, courteous, and very professional. This is good value for money.

22 Marzo Hotel. ** Piazza Santa Maria del Suffragio 3, Angolo Bonvesin de la Riva, Milan. http://www.hotel22marzo.com/
With excellent public transport links and a central location in a green area of Milan, Hotel 22 Marzo offers air-conditioned rooms with free Wi-Fi and a flat-screen TV. It has a safe, work desk, and a private bathroom with hairdryer. A buffet breakfast is served and drinks are available throughout the day from vending machines in the lobby.

Lake Como Region

Villa d'Este. ***** Via Regina 40, 22012 Cernobbio. www.villadeste.com
An opulent hotel overlooking glorious Lake Como, this famous resort has been widely praised for its beautiful gardens, exquisite cuisine, impeccable décor, and extraordinary hospitality. Dining options are available throughout the day and the evening. The Veranda Restaurant and the Grill both have outstanding views. Bar Canova is stunning. The design of the lower part of the gardens is from the Renaissance period.

Villa Arcadio. **** Via Palazzina 2, 25087 Salo Lake Garda. www.hotelvillaarcadio.it/
This is a revamped monastery on a wooded hillside overlooking the lake. It's a serene sanctuary, with just 18 simple yet stylish rooms, many with terracotta floor tiles, beamed ceilings, and 14th -century frescoes. The restaurant serves good regional food and in summer you can dine alfresco on the lantern-lit terrace. The snug bar area is suitable for winter cocktails.

Hotel La Darsena. *** Via Regina 3, 22019 Tremezzo. https://www.ladarsena.it/en/
There is a warm feeling throughout the hotel. It is on the lake and a 2-minute walk to the ferry stop. It is 5 minutes to the center of Tremezzo. The hotel is simple but all rooms have a bath, telephone, satellite TV, and air-conditioning, and some rooms have water views. The cuisine is regional, seasonal, and presented elegantly in the glass walled restaurant which looks out onto the lake.

Hotel du Lac. *** Via del Prestino 4, 22050 Varenna. www.albergodulac.com
The hotel is perched right on the lake and is very well designed for spectacular views and privacy. There are marble columns and wrought iron balustrades in this warm, gentle hotel. The terrace is immersed in flowers. It operates as a bed and breakfast.

Hotel Bellavista. ** Via Pare 87, 23868 Valmadrera. http://www.hbvl.it/en-gb/
This is a friendly family owned and run place and is the kind of hotel you want to go to if you travel with family and kids. The 18 rooms which

have nice views are very clean and spacious with all the necessities. There is free wi-fi and parking, and a small bar, restaurant, and TV room. The quiet but slightly remote location is best if you have a car.

Grand Hotel Des Iles Borromees. ***** Corso Umberto I 67, 28838 Stresa. http://www.borromees.com/en
The hotel's location overlooking Lake Maggiore is spectacular and the luxury of its furnishings overwhelming. The rooms are gorgeously over-the-top with inlay work in every door, richly wallpapered and gilding wherever possible. The indoor swimming pool/ sauna are surprisingly contemporary. The restaurant "Il Borromeo" and the Hemingway Bar are both elegant. The waterfront lush gardens are filled with hydrangea and oleander.

Verona and the Dolomites

Accademia Hotel. **** Via Scala 12, 37121 Verona. http://www.hotelaccademiaverona.it/en
This is not the biggest, most luxurious, or most splendid hotel in town but it is very well located. It is a traditional hotel: very comfortable, good spacious lounge areas, and excellent amenities. The staff are formal and professional. The 94 rooms are clean and well equipped and come in singles, doubles, and suites. There is an elegant room for breakfast and a fitness room, and free bicycles are available.

Hotel Milano. *** Vicolo Tre Marchetti 11, 37121 Verona. http://www.hotelmilano-vr.it/
The hotel is compact, and the rooms are not large, but they are clean, well furnished, and modern. Bathrooms have an unusual colorful light system. The location is excellent close to the Arena. Staff are courteous and friendly. You can enjoy a glass of champagne or have dinner in the spectacular Arena Sky Bar Lounge and Restaurant Terrace. The buffet breakfast is good. Parking is available.

Hotel Gardena Grodnerhof. ***** Vidalong Street, 3 Val Gardena, 39046 Ortisei. https://www.gardena.it/en/
This is a stunning five-star, family run hotel set in a narrow valley with the Dolomite mountains close by. The 54 suites are a blend of traditional and modern style with all necessary facilities. The service is

impeccable, and the food is excellent. There is a covered parking garage for cars. It is only a 5-minute walk to the center of town. There is a relaxing spa and pool.

Parkhotel Laurin. **** Laurin 4, 39100 Bolzano. www.laurin.it/en
This elegant hotel dates back to 1910 and is built in the Art Nouveau style. Each room features designer furniture and original artwork by contemporary artists. There is a mix of regional and Italian cuisine at the restaurant, which opens out into the garden during the summer. It is 200 meters from Bolzano Station and close to the main square and all the city's attractions.

Cristallo Hotel Spa & Golf. ***** Via Rinaldo Menardi 42, 32043 Cortina. https://www.marriott.com.au/hotels/travel/bzolc-cristallo-a-luxury-collection-resort-and-spa-cortina-dampezzo/
This is the first 5-star luxury hotel in the Dolomites. It offers great views, superb facilities, and a free, shuttle service to/from Cortina. All rooms feature a spa bath or shower, and free internet. There is a large wellness center, where you can enjoy beauty treatments, and an indoor heated pool. The Veranda del Cristallo is one of the most exclusive restaurants in the valley.

Turin and Aosta

Grand Hotel Sitea. ***** Via Carlo Alberto 35, 10123 Turin. http://grandhotelsitea.it/en/
This is a fine deluxe hotel. It is intimate and features wonderful old-world charm in the public areas. The 114 rooms are elegantly furnished in a classical style. The "Carignano" restaurant is elegant and refined. The Bistrot "Carlo and Camillo" combines charm and informality for lunch or dinner. The bar is quite impressive in a classical way and very inviting. There's a lovely courtyard for a drink or breakfast.

Il Gioiellino. *** Corso Vittorio Emanuele II 100, Porta Susa Station, 10121 Turin. http://www.gioiellino.com/en/
This charming B&B with a smart but informal atmosphere is in a 19th century building in Turin's center, next to the Vinzaglio Metro stop. It has classic rooms with city-view balconies. Each room has air conditioning, a minibar, and flat-screen TV. The private bathroom includes a shower and hairdryer. Breakfast is provided every morning.

Residence Sacchi. *** Via Sacchi 34, 10128 Turin.
http://www.residencesacchi.it/en/
There are 40 apartments and suites in this aristocratic ancient palace from the 19th century. The decor and furnishings are modern, comfortable, and very clean. All units have elegant bathrooms. The kitchenette in the smaller units is small but efficient with everything you need. You can always order food in your room. The nearby tram/bus/or train will take you anywhere you want to go in minutes. Fresh flowers and free internet are welcome touches.

Hotel Milleluci. **** Località Porossan Roppoz 15, 11100 Aosta.
http://www.hotelmilleluci.com/homepage.asp?l=1
Nestled on the hills overlooking Aosta, this family-run hotel offers panoramic views, an outdoor pool, and a wellness center. Guests can relax in the sauna, hot tub, and Turkish bath. The outdoor pool is open throughout the summer. The historic town center is 1 km away.

Etoile Du Nord. ***. Frazione Arensod 43, 11010 Aosta.
http://www.etoiledunord.it/en/
Set in the center of the Aosta Valley, 5 km outside Aosta town, Etoile du Nord offers extensive gardens, a partially covered 30°C heated pool, and panoramic mountain views. The 60 rooms come with air-conditioning, a TV, minibar, and a private bathroom. The large restaurant is open at breakfast and dinner. The hotel offers free secure parking.

Emilia-Romagna

Hotel Residence La Reunion. **** Via Corrado Ricci, 29, 48100 Ravenna. www.lareunion.it
This self-catering hotel in Ravenna's heart is in front of Dante Alighieri's tomb. The 44 rooms are air conditioned and have two TVs and a fully equipped kitchenette. A breakfast buffet is served in the hotel's breakfast hall. There are parking facilities and free use of bicycles.

Hotel Annunziata. **** Piazza Repubblica 5, 44100 Ferrara.
www.annunziata.it/en
The hotel is located right by the Palazzo Ducale and the Cathedral. The shops, bars, and restaurants are only a few steps away in a lovely pedestrianized area. The 21 rooms in the main hotel and the 6 rooms in

the 14th century residence are spotless with fresh and clean linens, comfortable beds, and roomy bathrooms. The breakfast buffet is very impressive and delicious. Staff are extremely friendly and helpful

Grand Hotel Majestic gia' Baglioni. ***** Via Indipendenza 8 Bologna. http://grandhotelmajestic.duetorrihotels.com/en/
This is the oldest and most prestigious hotel in the heart of the city. The 109 rooms have a mix of antique furniture with modern amenities. The hotel is famous for its I Carracci restaurant with its frescoes and authentic Italian masterpieces. Café Marinetti serves snacks, drinks, and desserts, while Enoteca Morandi is the historical cellar.

Il Convento dei Fiori di Seta. **** Via Orfeo 34/4, 40124 Bologna. www.ilconventodeifioridiseta.com
It doesn't look much from the outside but this 10 room hotel is a real find. It was once a convent and still has some of the original frescoes. The rooms are small in size but made extremely comfortable through interesting decor. The staff are welcoming, friendly, and extremely helpful. The hotel is in the old part of town and is a pleasant 10-minute walk to the center. Continental breakfast is provided and there is a small private spa area, a tiny bar, but no restaurant.

Aemilia Hotel. **** Via Giovanna Zaccherini Alvisi 16, 40138 Bologna. http://www.aemiliahotel.it/en
The location, just outside the walled city, is close enough to be within walking distance to all the shops, sights, and great food. This location is ideal if you are driving and need secure parking. There is a bus from the station and central city which stops nearby. The 124 rooms are spacious, modern, comfortable, and clean, with large bathrooms. There are excellent friendly staff. The sixth-floor solarium terrace is pleasant.

I-Suite. ***** Viale Regina Elena, 28 Rimini. https://www.i-suite.it/en/
This is very elegant, quiet, and stylish and is just across the road from the beach. The rooms are cute, comfortable, elegant, and cozy but the technology can be a bit difficult to use to begin with. The spa is top quality with great sea-views. There is a good breakfast buffet and excellent food at lunch and dinner at reasonable prices. It has very helpful staff.

If you have enjoyed this book, please give us a brief review on the Amazon web site https://www.amazon.com/dp/1792035128 so that others will be encouraged to also enjoy it.

This was the third book in the **Experience** series. There are now an additional eight.

We hope you also enjoy the other books in the series:

Experience   Thailand   e-book;
https://www.amazon.com/dp/B07L9KYGCK

Experience   Thailand   paperback;
https://www.amazon.com/dp/1796256722

Experience   Norway   e-book;
https://www.amazon.com/dp/B07L4CMGS4

Experience   Norway   paperback;
https://www.amazon.com/dp/1790786223

Experience   Northern   Italy   e-book;
https://www.amazon.com/dp/B07L8T3V4G

Experience   Northern   Italy   paperback;
https://www.amazon.com/dp/1792035128

Experience Ireland e-book; https://www.amazon.com/dp/B07L8PX6SF

Experience   Ireland   paperback;
https://www.amazon.com/dp/1791958281

Experience   Myanmar   (Burma)   e-book;
https://www.amazon.com/dp/B07LC6L5G7

Experience Myanmar (Burma) paperback; https://www.amazon.com/dp/1793041067

Experience Istanbul e-book; https://www.amazon.com/dp/B07LD3JT2S

Experience Istanbul paperback; https://www.amazon.com/dp/1793826404

Experience Singapore e-book; https://www.amazon.com/dp/B07LCG6TDV

Experience Singapore paperback; https://www.amazon.com/dp/1792175698

Experience India's Golden Triangle e-book; https://www.amazon.com/dp/B07L89H3VW

Experience India's Golden Triangle paperback; https://www.amazon.com/dp/1791842984

Experience Melbourne ebook; https://www.amazon.com/dp/B07LBDHQD2

Experience Melbourne paperback; https://www.amazon.com/dp/1794022120

We welcome comments from readers. Please send them by email to len_rutledge@bigpond.com

Index

ABOUT THE AUTHOR

Len Rutledge has been travel writing for more than 40 years. During that time, he has written thousands of newspaper articles, numerous magazine pieces, more than a thousand web reviews and around 45 travel guide books. He has worked with Pelican Publishing, Viking Penguin, Berlitz, the Rough Guide, and the Nile Guide amongst others.

Along the way he has started a newspaper, a travel magazine, a Visitor and TV guide, and completed a PhD in tourism. His travels have taken him to more than 120 countries and his writings have collected a PATA award, an ASEAN award, an IgoUgo Hall of Fame award, and other recognition. He has around twenty thousand social media followers.

You can follow him on Google+ at https://plus.google.com/u/0/+LenRutledge, Facebook as **Len.Rutledge,** and as **experience_guides,** and **len.rutledge** on Instagram. You can read more about the author on his web site www.LenRutledge.com

About the Photographer

Phensri Rutledge was born in Thailand but has lived in Australia for many years. For 30 years her photographs have appeared in a range of guidebooks and in newspapers and magazines in Europe, North America, Asia and Australia. Her travels have taken her to all continents except Antarctica through over 80 countries.

She contributes to several travel web sites and has a number of popular social media sites including a Google+ site with over 5 million views and thousands of followers. See http://google.com/+PhensriRutledge

You can follow her Facebook page as **World Travel Photography** and as **pensri_focus** on Instagram.

Made in the USA
Lexington, KY
16 March 2019